Customer.Community

Drew Banks
Kim Daus
Foreword by Scott Cook
Afterword by Michael Lowenstein

Customer.
Community

Unleashing the Power
of Your Customer Base

JOSSEY-BASS
A Wiley Imprint
www.josseybass.com

Published by Jossey-Bass
A Wiley Imprint
One Montgomery Street, Suite 1000, San Francisco, CA 94104-4594   www.josseybass.com

Jossey-Bass books and products are available through most bookstores. To contact Jossey-
Bass directly, call (888) 378-2537, fax to (800) 605-2665, or visit our website at
www.josseybass.com.

Substantial discounts on bulk quantities of Jossey-Bass books are available to corporations,
professional associations, and other organizations. For details and discount information,
contact the special sales department at Jossey-Bass.

We at Jossey-Bass strive to use the most environmentally sensitive paper stocks available to
us. Our publications are printed on acid-free recycled stock whenever possible, and our paper
always meets or exceeds minimum GPO and EPA requirements.

Library of Congress Cataloging-in-Publication Data

Banks, Drew, 1961-
    Customer.Community : unleashing the power of your customer base
/ by Drew Banks and Kim Daus ; foreword by Scott Cook.
        p. cm—(The Jossey-Bass business & management series)
    Includes bibliographical references and index.
    ISBN 978-0-7879-5621-9
    1. Customer relations.   2. Market segmentation.   3. Electronic
commerce.   I. Title: Customer base.   II. Daus, Kim.   III. Title.
IV. Series.
HF5415.5 .B363 2002
658.8'12—dc21   2001008161

FIRST EDITION
HB Printing   10 9 8 7 6 5 4 3 2

The Jossey-Bass

Business & Management Series

Contents

Foreword: The Right Thing to Do

It all starts with customers. If your business is not producing better and better things for customers, what are you doing? The role of companies is to create products customers can use. The future belongs to companies that intimately understand what customers need and innovate to better meet their needs.

Delivering what customers need is not just a solid business idea; it's also the right thing to do. In fact, the prime reason to do it is almost religious—it's more about your attitude to life and making a difference. Is your attitude toward meaning in life to just provide more of the same, more "me too"? I don't think that's why we're here.

Drew and Kim's concept of customer-community presents a way to tap into the passion and depth of customers and to understand what they really need and want. Every company's passionate customers constitute a reservoir of energy and expertise that until now has had no output. Even dull products have passionate customers. Have you ever seen customers work hard to use bad products? There is no rational explanation for this. They do it because they are passionate about the product. Those who tap into this power of customer-community can recognize both business and customer benefit.

I've learned a lot about customer behavior over the years. In my early career at Procter & Gamble, I was transformed by witnessing firsthand the company's dedication to excellence, innovation, and customers. I've never lost that fire. It's also been the bedrock of Intuit for eighteen years. If you want people to pick your product, they should want to do so primarily because it's better for them—*in their opinion* it's better for them. To achieve that, you have to understand their opinion early in the process, and you need to hear them talking about your product after they have it. The whole secret lies in figuring out what people want and then providing it. And if you can improve their lives, you have a huge advantage. This book presents some innovative ways to do just that.

Looking at commerce and customer-communities on the Web, we can learn from the heroes—companies that brought their customers into community and enabled commerce to happen. You simply have to notice Amazon.com and eBay: customer-community powers each company.

Amazon.com explicitly uses customer-community to add value and aid commerce in many ways. One way is the simple concept of user reviews. With user reviews, Amazon.com has turned its customers into content experts who create valuable information used by other customers. I can remember when CEO Jeff Bezos mentioned the idea of including customer reviews on the site—at first I thought he was crazy. Why would I listen to people I don't know, who may or may not have any knowledge of the subject matter, who may have different tastes than I do, who are going to write about some viewpoint that may mean nothing to me? What's amazing is that I now rely much more on user reviews than I do on canned reviews from official sources! In fact, for books, toys, and DVDs, I ordinarily skip the official reviews and go right to the ratings from the community reviewers. Amazon.com really has something extraordinary. With no cost to the business, Amazon.com has engaged its customers to provide rich and valuable information that then helps other customers make commercial decisions. It's part of what makes Amazon's site better than any one else's—and it's free.

Amazon.com also uses collective behavior to aid commerce. Customers need not take any special action, but by analyzing the behavior of the many customers who have bought a given item, Amazon.com can instantly show each customer other items that customers with similar interests have purchased. You can immediately see what other books or movies might interest you. Again, at no cost to Amazon.com, collective customer-community behavior provides value for customers without the community doing any additional work. Their behavior as a community creates value and contributes to the community. It's like glancing into a bar or restaurant, seeing that it's crowded, and concluding that the food must be good. No one did anything special or differently, but you obtained valuable information.

eBay wouldn't exist without community—it's the essence of the company. The entire business is created by the community and customers rating each other's behavior as sellers and buyers. The community's Feedback Ratings are essential; without them, eBay would not exist as we know it.

If you're thinking that the idea of customer-community is only for relatively new companies or solely for Web-based companies, think again. The idea of customer-community also plays at Intuit. We are helping TurboTax customers, for example, get advice and service from a tax expert in their local community. The expert can answer questions by phone or e-mail or can show a business owner how to use a feature. We're actually connecting two parts of our community—the professional accountants, tax preparers, and computer installers and the customers who need the services of those people. In the past, we've had contacts with both groups of people but didn't do anything to put them together. Now we are finding ways to bridge the gap—to help our customers find service providers to provide service and answer questions. And we're adding feedback ratings and community accountability to this.

Intuit is now beginning to connect customers to the company and to each other as a way to get feedback and to improve products. We've always been big proponents of calling customers for feedback—and we still are. It's exceptionally useful to hear directly from customers how they use tools and services. But now we are also using the Internet to do the same sort of thing, but with an additional dimension of allowing customers to talk to each other and improve on or answer each other's suggestions.

These are all ways to engage your customer-community. They are also ways to create and strengthen ongoing customer relationships. What's great is that you can help customers build on each other's ideas and ultimately produce a better product or service. So far, though, I've only mentioned how community can help commerce. Drew and Kim also discuss how commerce can help community. The Web enables customers who have a specific interest to find others who share that interest, regardless of where they are on the planet.

Pierre Omidyear, eBay's founder, has done this amazingly at eBay by allowing people with very specific passions to connect with others who share the same passion. What starts as a commercial transaction often turns into a friendship or mentorship. It's like a recursive system.

I've bought some World War II movies for my kids from Amazon.com. There are many such movies out there, and I didn't know which are better than others. I would ask my neighbors, but they don't know either. But at Amazon.com, some of the reviews are written by people who are passionate students of World War II and movies about it. They discuss how realistic and factual the movies are. They talk about whether the movie has authentic staging or moralistic messages. This information is far richer than I can get from my neighbor. In a sense, special-purpose communities are flourishing with far greater depth than with neighbors. This is a great example that shows how the technology can connect those with common interests and how rich communities can flourish around common commercial interests.

What's the biggest source of your new customers? We've studied that for years at Intuit, and the answer has always been the same: word of mouth. The biggest percentage of our new customers come to us because of recommendations by peers or by influencers. Your customers likely buy thanks to word of mouth. Isn't that community? The opportunity for word of mouth on the Internet is huge, and tapping that power to help your business is what this book is about.

Drew and Kim don't just talk about the power of connecting people; they also make the business case. Customer-communities not only get more needle-focused data for customers, but they also help the business. When information flow and accuracy are higher, confidence is higher, and loss for the business is less. Talking with and listening to customers is a great way to build confidence. Customers will not always say that things are perfect—they wouldn't be speaking the truth if they did. When you can hear personal experiences, warts and all—that breeds confidence.

Having customers talk about problems, losing control—these things can shoot fear in the minds of marketing managers and executives. That fear is real. The best way to work with that fear is to get them to see the benefit. Point to the psychology of customers and of service delivery. On eBay, participants *know* that people will be writing about them and rating them publicly. As a result, you see people hustling to make sure that service is good and that customers are happy. The very existence of public ratings in commerce creates an energy—a discipline on behalf of the person serving—that results in happier customers. I think companies that expose themselves to public discourse by their customers will see mostly positive comments (if not, they have bigger problems). And I also think that employees will hustle more when they know that customers are freely talking. When employees are performing directly for the customer, not just the boss, isn't that the best accountability of all?

We are talking about a dramatic shift in how you think about customers. I don't think you can convert a nonbeliever through argument, analysis, or cold facts. Deep change is experiential. You have to experience it for yourself—to see the value you're getting. Get your people to experience the power. One way is to use the person-to-person trading system at eBay to buy and sell.

Customers will do much more for you when they are personally invested. Community is a powerful way to get them personally invested. Personalize what's important to them. Establish a group of people who rely on ratings. Invest time. And you will soon see the benefits of a customer-community.

Remember too that we're placed on this earth to improve the lives of those we touch. In business, we're here to improve the lives

of our customers, employees, and neighbors. When you delight customers, they will tell their friends. With a customer-community,
you can give those customers a broader outlet.

There's no reason for our thinking to stop at the boundaries of
business or the borders of one country. I wonder if the concepts in
this book could play even broader at the level of the global economy and social causes throughout the worldwide customer-community. I'd like to invite you to think about that.

January 2002   Scott Cook
                            Cofounder, Intuit Corporation
                            Board member, eBay and Amazon.com

Preface

The best way to introduce our thesis is to tell you how *Customer.Community* came to be. We were responsible for "community" at ThirdAge Media when Jossey-Bass approached us to write this book. Oddly enough, we ran into our editor, Kathe Sweeney, while we were standing in line at Chatz, a popular San Francisco dot-com coffee "hut" in the South of Market neighborhood. We chatted about our first book, *Beyond Spin*,[1] and then about our current job at ThirdAge and our ideas for building radical new virtual communities. We told Kathe that we were trying to create a more expanded, integrated online community model. ThirdAge.com was our petri dish, and we were—like all the dot-coms in the neighborhood at that time—heavily financed by venture funds. Plus the company had a healthy relationship with CBS that included a substantial dose of advertising media. A week or so later, Kathe called and asked if we would consider writing a book on the "new virtual community." We said yes, and at that time we dubbed the book *Dot-Community*.

Of course, shortly afterward, all hell broke loose in dot-com land. In a few months, virtual communities—the previous darlings of venture capitalists—came to be viewed as investment pariahs. As we struggled with profitability at ThirdAge, we examined the underlying foundations and motivations of online communities. We scrutinized the most financially successful community sites, those like eBay and Monster. We discovered that financially viable community sites were centered on commerce and had straightforward business models that didn't require much more than customers and a way to connect them. Throughout our first draft, we kept pointing out the strategies that these marketplace sites incorporated to "monetize" community more effectively.

One day while lunching at Zuni Café in San Francisco, we marveled at the rich community interaction that Zuni catalyzes with its unique combination of simultaneously intimate and open spaces. As we were drawing virtual community parallels, one of us noted that it was easier for a restaurant to build community because the central purpose was a commercial one. The community is drawn to it with a mindset to spend money. The restaurants or food services that try to feed people just because they are collected in one place are transitory and opportunistic. This is no way to build sustainable communities or business models. At that moment, we flipped our central thesis from "monetizing" community to "communitizing" commerce. We felt the switch mandated a new moniker. There you have the birth of *Customer.Community*.

Most companies have customers who patronize the business for commerce-centric reasons. Many have developed e-commerce sites and serve Internet-connected e-customers. These e-customers are connected to each other, yet often companies treat them as a set of disparate individuals. Why not proactively create opportunities for them to interact with one another?

In *Customer.Community*, we examine the business benefits that can be achieved through igniting the collective potential of your customer base. We draw from the lessons of the past three decades of virtual community exploration to create a provocative argument for building, leveraging, and sustaining a customer-community. *Customer.Community* showcases the social nature of the customer and how the Internet has unleashed this power. Chances are that in serving your customers, you are currently focusing solely on customer service to *individuals*. Chances are that you are not giving your customers a voice in your business operations, nor are you fully conscious of how much your success depends on customer-to-customer advocacy. If you ignore the customer-community's social characteristics and continue to treat customers as isolated individuals, you will entirely miss an enormous power of the Web.

Customer.Community is structured in three parts. The first part sets up our argument that the Internet economy has eliminated the virtual borders between people and that businesses must now engage with their customers, not only as individuals, but also as a collective or customer-community.

Chapter One explains the basic characteristics of a customer-community. Chapter Two examines Albert Maslow's hierarchy of human needs, demonstrating how these needs drive behavior on the Internet. Through highlighting examples at each level of the psychological framework, it becomes clear why and how a business can address the individual, social, and soulful needs of its customer base online.

Part Two examines the foundation, growth, and sustainability of customer-communities. Chapter Three details the twelve foundational principles of community building. You will see how the elevation of customer-centric business practices, community-building principles, and the Internet has created the possibility for broad-scale customer-community. Chapter Four moves from conceptual to actual. Ten virtual community categories showcase thirty-five important examples in the evolution of the customer-community. Neither the category segmentation nor the examples listed are comprehensive, but they collectively shed light on possibilities for specific customer-community implementations. Chapters Five and Six analyze the two longtime barriers to successful large-scale community building—growing and sustaining a community. These two chapters showcase how the Internet has, in general, enabled virtual customer-communities to scale larger than in the nonvirtual realm.

Part Three turns to considerations for implementation and tackles the business model head on. How do companies make financial sense of the customer-community concept? Chapter Seven is devoted to making money and creating value; it outlines how the two are inextricably linked with the customer-community concept.

Chapter Eight offers several recommendations for cost-effectively organizing for and managing your customer-community. Considerations are presented for organizational structure, interdepartmental efficiencies, required infrastructure, and an intra-customer-community leadership structure. In our final chapter, we present a few questions to help jump-start a customer-community program in an effort to guide you to the appropriate next step for your business.

January 2002   Drew Banks
                                               San Francisco, California

                                               Kim Daus
                                               Sausalito, California

Acknowledgments

The two of us partner in such beautiful ways—we've worked in business at several companies together, now written two books together, planted gardens together, spoken at conferences as a team, traveled, and grown through life together as best friends. We often say that in our case, one plus one equals far more than two. We are blessed with a precious gift. We are grateful for each other, and we are jointly grateful to many people who helped make this book more than an idea.

We would like to thank our editor, Kathe Sweeney, and the fantastic Jossey-Bass team who cajoled and prodded us along the way. And there are three people whose assistance was invaluable: Corey Cleek, Kevin Morgan, and Cynthia Typaldos.

Customer.Community was conceived during our time at ThirdAge Media, where many people helped us craft our community strategy: Kate Antheil, Jim Barnett, Chas Brown, Shireen Burns, Scott Butler, Mary Furlong, Anupam Garg, Jennifer Glos, Eric Hallquist, Henry Kwan, Alysoun Mahooney, George McDonald, Dave MacFarland, Judge Muscat, John Ogden, Corby Ong, Anastasia Poland, Olivia Smith, Marla Stollar, Joe Szuecs, Darryl Toney, and Judy Walket. Joe Katz and Paul Kaufman were also valuable partners with us.

Finally many people graciously offered to be interviewed for this book: Jeff Arcuri, Gaia China, Scott Cook, Anthony Christopher, Charles Decker, John Duhring, Dale Hagemeyer, Beliunda Hankins, Julius James, Candice Kwok, Brett Lauter, Glen Van Lehn, Jennifer Lind, Michael Lowenstein, Mary Luciano, Dennis Madsen, Terry Marasco, Chris Michel, Raymond Mulvey, Craig

Newmark, Ellen Pack, Mike Pugliese, Heath Row, Beerud Sheth, Jeff Siegle, Megan Smith, Margaret Spencer, Jeff Tidwell, Joel Truher, Natalie Wallace, Wes Weber, and Natasha Zaslove.

D.B. and K.D.

I would like to thank my family and friends who supported me and this project through the intense times of this last year, specifically, Mom, Dad, Ken and Charlene (and Brandon, Braxton, and Matthew), Ron and Ginger (and Zachary), Marisa Arrona, Karren Baker, John Barnhill and Pierre Barral, Peter Birch, Akiko Bristol, Dan Bunker and Alan Pellman, YaYa Cantu, Wendy Chin and Leigh Sata (and Reid and Kai), Deb and Dan Dagit (and Alina, Marina, and Van), Judy Lewenthal Daniel and Brent Daniel, Mavis Dewees and Carole Hines and Danielle Laurent, Durval Dias, Carlos Dornelas, John Dye, Jerre Dye and Adam McLaughlin, John Ebner and George Limperis, Mauricio Flores, Kirk Froggatt and Marco Gazzetta, Clare Giesen, Phillip Goerl and Roger Spring, Gary Higgins and Mark Siurek, Tarek Ibrahim, Derek Jentzsch, Leslie Katz, Matt Leum and Edward Tipton, Dana LeVan, Michael Lindsay, Jorge A. Lopez Colunga, Franck Marchis, Fernando Martin Del Campo, Greg Matsunami, Darin Medeiros and Glenn Cortu, Kenny Monnens and Jim Uyeda, Sean Murphy, David Ottenhouse and Andy Shipps, Kile Ozier, Devan Pailet and Steve Turnbull, Bill Perrault, Thibaud Paquin, Diane Perro, Douglas Plummer and Tim Frantz, Andre Portasio, Luis Prada and Jeff Hansen, Mike Reilly, Sergio Repka, Nick Rubashkin, Teresa Ruelas, Mary Beth Sammons, Carol Sanford and Dave Ely, Chris Seabolt, Kristin Spence, Joycelyn Sperling, Wes Stander, Leslie Stern, Bob Sundstrom, Darryl Toney (and Ma Toney and Kai), Sheila Von Driska and Dorothy Dotcom, Tim Warmath and Ned Walley, Mark and Cami Weaver, Claudia Welss and Tom Halbach, Shawn Wilson and Mylène Najoan, and Ken Wingard. Below Kim honors our mutual friend Cam Clarke, who died during this project. I would also like to honor another friend, Mark Bingham, and an acquaintance, Tom Burnett, who on September 11, 2001, were two of the people who courageously thwarted the fourth hijacked plane from reaching its target.

D.B.

I would like to thank an amazing family—a group of people who support each other strongly even from afar. Mom and Phil, Dad, Jeff, Amy, Erik, George, Sarah, Cathy, David, and Kelly—no one would be holding this book if it weren't for you. Corey Cleek gets special thanks because he actually reviewed a really ugly draft and offered support and ideas to make this manuscript better. And so many people prayed and talked with me through the project—thank you, Jan, Lou, Taylor, Ty, and Spencer Beck, Charlotte Albright, Glenn Bonci, Tamara Cotten, Rhonda Davis, Dave Day, Becky Dickinson, Gail Doering, Kevin Edwards, Beth Fraker, Lisa Harvey, Richard Harvey, Maggie and Ed Hays, the Heindels, Joel Henderson, Suzzanne Ippel, Chris James, Melissa Jones, Christine Kelly, the Kiernans, Wes Kimmey, Joe Knopinski, Keefer Lanham, Lynda Larsen, Christen Latham, Curt Longacre, Kate and Doug Loub, Ernesto Mayans, Mike Messinger, Richard Park, Ed, Terrie, Rachel and Joel Pinkusoff, Evelyn Pinney, Tony Petrotta, Craig Ramsay, Theresa Robison, Mary Sage, Justin Sherman, Gena and Mary Stripling, Olivia Smith, Greg Stipa, GradyJimHuie Tripp, Libby Vincent (forever, pal!), Vinh Vu-Gia, Jane and Jim Ware, Sherry Whiteley, Karen Wilson, Owen Winstead, and Karilee Wirthlin. And since we share many friends as well, from Drew's list I would also like to thank Akiko, Judy, Durval, Jerre and Adam, Kirk, Kristin and Colin, Gary, Leslie, Matt and Ned, Fernando and John, David, Diane, Douglas, Teresa, Wendy, Sheila, Claudia, and Shawn. Two of my friends passed away during this book project, and they both supported me dearly—Cam Clarke and Elaine Kozak. God be with them both. And as always, I acknowledge that nothing I do is possible without God, who blesses me so abundantly.

K.D.

Customer.Community

The Customer-Community

In a *BusinessWeek* interview with Steve Case, chairman of AOL Time Warner, when asked, "What is AOL's contribution to the world of e-biz?" Case replied, "Instead of viewing the PC as a productivity machine that runs productivity software, we are turning it into a communicating device. We recognized that it's not just about software or content, but building a sense of community and engaging people."[1] Because AOL is an Internet Service Provider (ISP) subscription service, AOL's community members are, by definition, AOL customers. AOL's business model is one way to create a customer-community. Arguably, AOL has indeed transformed the computer into an easy-to-use environment for its customers.

A customer-community is simply a group of customers interacting with one another. Why should you care if your customers are interconnected as a community? Loyalty, advocacy, better target marketing, and even more reasons that we will explore throughout this book. Possibly the most compelling reason is that it's inevitable. If your customers use the Internet, they will eventually build a customer-community themselves. They will search each other out and talk about you and your products. Their collective voice will reverberate. They may say good things; they may say bad things. Don't you want to listen?

A Customer-Community Tale

There's a classic black-and-white movie that many people can identify with just two clues: Jimmy Stewart and Bedford Falls. It's an all-time favorite flick, a film of redemption where good conquers evil; it's a story that magically shows commerce and community intertwined. The plotline is simple: Stewart, who plays good guy George Bailey, takes over his family's banking business, which has served the community for decades. In extremely difficult times, when Bailey Building and Loan is on the brink of foreclosure, George becomes filled with despair. He finds salvation in his customer-community. In the closing scene of *It's a Wonderful Life*, George and his family are supportively flanked by members of the local community. In the Bailey living room, they all bring companionship, cheer, and even money to help with George's big problem. It's a lavish feel-good scene.

There's no secret why this community comes to the rescue. For years, George Bailey has served this little town, treating customers with dignity, trust, and authentic concern. This respect engendered reciprocity from a customer-community that cared enough to stand by him when he was in trouble. Strong communities are tightly bound, loyal, and supportive of their members; customer-communities are no different.

Why This Book?

Customer.Community helps cultivate the mindset to leverage the collective power of your customer base. This book is about understanding what your customer-community is and can become. It's about the growing scope of what your customers can do for you—from lower cost of customer acquisition to demand generation to peer-to-peer customer service. We will offer some strategies and review some case examples, but the focus will be on getting you to think actively about your own customer-community and the potential it holds for your business.

Customer.Community is applicable to any Internet-enabled business. It is for managers who believe in top-notch customer service and sustainable customer loyalty. *Customer.Community* is for customer service leaders and Internet strategists who want to cost-effectively increase and retain their local and virtual customer base. It is for e-commerce companies and traditional consumer and affiliate organizations that have a Web-connected clientele. It is especially relevant for complex or high-cost product or service providers like business-to-business vendors who have customers that need to share a large quantity of information to feel comfortable with their decision-making, implementation, and maintenance processes. *Customer.Community* explores how to nurture the bond of the customer-community that Jimmy Stewart had in Bedford Falls and how to create it on the Internet.

An Interconnected (and Internet-Connected) Customer Base

"*It's a Wonderful Life* is a nice little fairy tale about small-town camaraderie," you say, "but how does that relate to my business? How does it affect my global customers, who are a disparate collection of people I never see and who never see me?" Most people don't even know their neighbors' names these days, much less the names of customers to whom they are related only because they purchase products from the same vendor. In fact, you might even wonder whether "community" has become much less important to business in the digital age now that customers are spread out all over the globe and have absolutely no interaction with each other.

Think again. The Internet, while it has expanded the customer reach far beyond local boundaries and has lessened the need for businesses and customers to interact with each other on the "real" plane, has also eliminated the digital boundaries between customers. What's actually happening on the Internet is that customer service and community building are growing closer and closer to each other. Many e-commerce sites have capabilities where customers can easily meet other customers, discuss different products or services, and even rank or rate products. This "community-generated feedback," which can be challenging to catalyze or aggregate in nonvirtual space, is as intrinsic as breathing in the virtual world. Conversely, almost all "community" sites have shopping areas and special discounts for community members.

On the Web, everything and everybody is interconnected. For business, one of the implications of this gestalt is that the customer operates differently . . . and the same. Customers, as always, want their purchase experience to be as informed, efficient, and pleasant as possible. It's just that in the digital realm, "informed, efficient, and pleasant" have much wider ranges of possibility due to massive information availability; distribution efficiencies; better access to competitive offerings; lower barriers to communication; and many more effective tools for group communication. Most of these differences empower customers to connect and interact with each other as individuals *and* as one large customer-community. A customer base of individuals is built one customer at a time, but the collective becomes more powerful with each customer added. If connected into a community, the power of this collective grows exponentially.

If the benefits are so obvious, why haven't all Web-enabled companies adopted a customer-community approach? There are many reasons. Let's start by exploring the history of online communities.

Misperceptions of Online Community

The early turbulent years of the Internet have created many false perceptions. Among these is one in particular that we are trying to debunk—the perception that there are two completely different types of people who interact within e-commerce and e-community spheres. In this misperception, there are the isolationists who want personalized, efficient purchasing transactions and don't care about interacting with one another. And then there are the anticommerce community types who just want to meet new, similar, anti-establishment minds, hang out with each other, and bash the profit-driven motives of the business world. Many factors have influenced this separatist perception. We will examine a few, some of which are beginning to fade in the face of virtual community evolution.

Limited Definition of Community

On the Internet, the word *community* is most often used for a shared-interest club or discussion that you must join. Most other noncommunity aspects of the Web are designed for the independent individual. This separation is not so distinct in real life. We are simultaneously both individuals and social creatures. When we dine out, we may choose a restaurant occupied by other patrons, even if it's just to see and be seen, hear other glasses clinking, or return a smile or two. We visit vacation spots that are isolated yet have some level of social interaction. Do we really want to sip our umbrella drinks alone? Community on the Web, as in real life, is not just about clubs, forums, and chat rooms but also about the duality of individual and social needs. We believe that this compartmentalized perception of virtual community will shift to honor the inherent nature of the human species with our need to be both independent and part of a group. Online communities will merge the best of both worlds.

Early-Adoption Dynamics

Regardless of how quickly the Internet has been adopted, it is embryonic and is just beginning its technology and usage life cycles. The baby may be big for its age, but it's still a baby. Early life cycle industry dynamics are not necessarily predictive of future usage patterns. It is not uncommon for the early adopters of a new technology to use that technology in a limited manner. In the infant years of the telephone, most people restricted calls to close family and friends. Likewise, early personal computer owners used their new toys primarily for word processing. There are a variety of reasons for this myopia—a tentative "testing the new waters" psychology to collectively expand usage dynamics, too few users (well below critical mass), fledgling technology constraints, and early-release, nonintegrated, proprietary software among them. Whatever the reasons, technology usage is usually fragmented and narrowly bound during the early stages of its life cycle. So it is not surprising that neophyte Internet users were typecast into separate camps of e-communities and e-consumers. As we have moved beyond this early-adopter stage, attitudes and usage have begun to normalize. Consequently, the Internet culture is beginning to broaden and embrace collective commercial e-business.

The Dot-Com Survivor Game

Just as the birth of the Internet was overhyped, so was its death. Early 2001 reports of the Internet's death were greatly exaggerated. In fact, according to Forrester Research, "by 2004 total annual e-commerce spending in the U.S. will hit $3.2 trillion, up from $488.7 billion in 2000."[2] Dying industries don't grow by $2.7 trillion in just a few years. Perceptions can be misleading. The simplistic reasons cited as the cause of the Internet's untimely demise further solidified many misperceptions. It wasn't the Internet that died but rather its hyperbole that bit the dust. What seemed to rise from the flames was a transformed e-audience. Now Internet users tend to prefer integrated functionality rather than "siloed" or specialized sites. This shift is almost identical to the evolution of personal computer software preferences from best-of-breed applications like WordPerfect and Lotus to more integrated product suites like Microsoft Office.

The Community "Chicken" and the Commerce "Egg"

In the past, the virtual community commerce mantra was "If you build a community, they will shop." This is the converse of another: "If they shop, they will form a community." With the latter—the customer-community—commerce, not community, is top of mind.

Profit models are much easier to construct if business- or product-specific commerce is the common interest that links a community together. Also with the latter, you don't need to *build* a community. If your customers already access the Internet, you already have a customer-community. You simply need to catalyze and leverage. What is their common interest? You and your products. Why would your customers want to interact? Because they are human, and commingling is part of their nature.

Consider the social interaction of shopping malls. People who shop at the same place have common interests—"I want a good product," "I want a good deal," "I like the status that comes from buying here." Communal dynamics can increase the frequency with which people shop. How many times have you struck up a conversation with another shopper while standing in the checkout line? Maybe this is not what many people think of as a community, but it is a social interaction that can create an affiliation. As you read this, you might think, "I don't do malls; I cringe when I see long checkout lines or full parking lots." Yes, but would you shop at a deserted store? Even as consumers, most us want some level of interaction with others. In Chapter Two, we dig deeper into the human need to mix socially with one another.

Artificial Boundaries

Although the Web has obliterated boundaries between customers, most Internet technologies and site designers reintroduced them within their respective architectures. Community members are isolated from transacting individuals; perusers are separated from purchasers; chatters are split from dialoguers. Certainly there is some precedent for this—urban zoning, retail clustering, technological best-of-breed purism—but the Internet is more about integration than separatism; its hyperlinked underpinnings play to the unbounded, nonlinear nature of the human brain. Although it is easier to design and implement separate Internet activities, it is counterintuitive to the social nature and the full-integration promise of the

Web. It's not enough to put Web links between community and commercial assets. This is like advertising for a yard sale on a church bulletin board. There must be a more seamless interweaving and collaborative architecture. The next generation of Internet sites will be far more integrated, like a self-sufficient neighborhood, where you glide fluidly from individual to community, from interaction to transaction, from perusing to consuming.

Access Speed

The in-context hyperlink introduced the ultimate in nonlinear access that allows Internet surfers to jump from here to there in the blink of an eye. Well, theoretically. In reality, it is a very slow blink. Jumping from one Internet space to another can be tedious. The hyperquick, nonlinear, tangential nature of the human brain allows it to switch from self-dialogue to planning a family outing in a fraction of a second. The Internet has promised us the same nonlinearity, but the speed just isn't there. Many people don't want to waste loading cycle time switching from one Internet page to the next. E-shoppers aren't going to read the product review if the pages take too long to load. As Internet access speeds continue to decrease and approach brain access speeds, we'll see more and more nonlinear activity where customers jump from here to there and back again. Future surfing will be nearly as instantaneous and tangential as our thought patterns.

Hyperfocus on Market Efficiency

The Internet's no-barrier-to-entry, immediately available alternatives and distributed technological backbone create a more efficient marketplace than brick-and-mortar commerce. And the elimination of switching barriers was the sole driver of most e-commerce businesses. Market efficiency usually translates to "the lowest price wins." Lowest price often means lowest margin, which means lower per-sale profit, which, without adequate volume means *Hasta la vista*. As many early e-tailers discovered, sustainable volume is challenging in the fickle Web marketplace. Even early Internet darling Amazon.com was plagued by its lowest-price business model. But e-shoppers, just like brick-and-mortar shoppers, will pay for—and potentially be more loyal to—convenience, customer service, distribution efficiency, and possibly a positive social dynamic. Many e-commerce companies have shifted toward value-added models. There will always be a few price-competitive volume players, but there is much more room for robust offerings that include merchandising and service differentiation.

Repercussions of Simplistic Valuation Metrics

Early dot-com valuation metrics greatly rewarded membership acquisition and eyeballs-per-ad impressions. How much your dot-company was worth depended on how many people visited or were members of your site. It didn't matter why the visitors came or how the members signed up. It didn't even matter if they were the right audience. You could acquire another site and accrue its members or strong-arm visitors into membership by offering some sweepstakes that required all entrants to become "members." Sites with more members and visitors were blessed with a higher valuation because for most of these sites, membership meant community and a large membership meant a vibrant community. Ick. This is like saying a densely populated area is a healthy community. If this were true, some of the world's largest cities wouldn't be so economically challenged and plagued with social ills. Is it any wonder these "vibrant" Web communities didn't produce expected revenues? On the Internet, as in most living systems, there is healthy focused growth and unhealthy unchecked growth. We will explore virtual community growth and sustainability in Chapters Five and Six.

As valuation metrics migrated from membership to profitability, Internet strategies adopted more traditional business models.

Sustainable growth goals are now oriented toward customer acquisition (as opposed to membership acquisition) and loyalty. A vibrant customer-community helps with both.

Industrial Era Legacy of Control

In business, many residues from the industrial age still exist; one is the mistaken belief that vendors can control their customers. This industrial mindset tricks you into believing that you can control customer perception through marketing, customer satisfaction through quality and service, and customer loyalty through incentive programs. The concept of the vendor as catalyst instead of conductor is a fairly new psychology. The very nature of a customer-community requires a slight power transfer from vendor to customer, and power shifts always cause anxiety. There is a fear that customers talking with each other could spread uncontrollable perceptions, could drive new customers away, and could even open the door to legal liability. But customers have always talked to each other, and e-customers do so even more due to the simplicity and relative anonymity of electronic communication. Control is no longer an option. But catalyzing and leveraging the resulting community is.

———————

With all that baggage, it is not surprising that early e-businesses focused on the individual customer rather than the collective. But if you are exclusively focusing on the individual customer, you are missing an opportunity. We are not promoting a virtual community business model or even necessarily the "building" of a customer collective; we are simply recommending that you acknowledge and leverage the communal dynamic that exists within your current customer base. Embedded firmly at the crux of our argument lies a simple fact: customers are humans, members of a communal species with social needs. We have a need for each other, and once we interact, we often stick together. This communal bond benefits both customer and vendor alike.

Industrial Economy to Internet Economy

Broad-scale customer-community has been enabled not just by the Internet itself but also by the Internet mindset that has embraced integration concepts throughout business. This is a shift in thinking from the industrial era's fragmented approach. The industrial age deconstructed the fundamentals of business strategy into individual widgets, each to be separately evaluated and maximized. Throughout the twentieth century, this mechanical approach was applied to employee productivity, but in the early 1980s, business strategists turned their widgetized eyes toward the customer. The individual customer was segmented, analyzed, and deemed "always right." Businesses reacted with customer loyalty and reward programs, market-research-driven marketing, call management centers, customer-driven merchandising, and other customer-centric programs. In the 1990s, the Internet emerged as a new commerce and distribution system, and businesses quickly tried to replicate these traditional customer service practices in the e-business landscape. The Internet and its ability to capture transactional data led customer service down the path of efficiency but away from "human touch."

Yet during this nascent period, the inherent connectivity of the Internet allowed virtual community activists to experiment with integration and interactivity. As we set off into the twenty-first century, the industrial era is truly coming to a close. We have learned much from the individual-widget and highly mechanized and controlled systems; we must now embrace the collective system.

There are many Internet community sites that enable millions of like-minded people to interact. There are also commerce and customer service sites that meet the needs of those transacting on the Web. Obviously, some of the same people communing on the Web are also consuming on the Web. To meet the dual needs of these folks, there are sites that try to do both community and commerce. Yet most still keep virtual barriers between the two. Even business-to-business sites that try to meet their various customers' information and service needs often don't effectively facilitate connecting these various customers so that they can serve each other's needs. Few truly realize the inevitability and the benefits that result from an interconnected customer base. Few businesses align online community management and customer service. This book is not about the fundamentals of community building—virtual or real; many good books on this topic already exist. *Customer.Community* is about building on these foundations to form a community that supports a business. It's about creating a customer-community.

Small-town and neighborhood businesses have long understood the power of community building. Customer-community concepts now apply, not only to a local community but also to a global interconnected customer base. Merging an individualized customer approach with collective customer-community will be a hallmark of all successful next-generation businesses—not just e-commerce sites, but any Web-enabled business. With a loyal customer-community, you just might find your customers flocked around your virtual living room enlisting help to solve your problems and helping your business grow to the next level. It could be *A Wonderful Virtual Life*.

Part One

Why Customer-Community?

Chapter One

The Business Case

The first decade of Web-enabled business has focused on the efficient integration of critical relationships. *Business-to-customer* (B2C), *business-to-business* (B2B), and *peer-to-peer* (P2P) have become buzz adjectives behind which are entire industries. In *Customer.Community*, we highlight a subset of the P2P landscape—one that directly intersects with your B2C strategy. Depending on your service orientation toward employees, developers, and partners, lessons can be drawn and applied to your B2B operations. This subset is called *customer-to-customer* (C2C).

Figure 1.1 is a simplistic depiction of basic commerce-oriented communities with which most companies interact in order to achieve their business goals. In this book, we will focus primarily on the B2C relationship between the business and collective customer-community (or C2C) relationship between the customers themselves.

Fortunately for the customer, the Internet revolution has overlapped with the era of customer centricity. "At the beginning of the 20th century, Neiman-Marcus, one of the great retailers of all time, changed the doctrine of 'let the buyer beware' to 'let the buyer decide if he is satisfied.'"[1] In 1901, John W. Nordstrom used his stake from the Alaska gold rush to open a small shoe store in Seattle. For Nordstrom, customer service was as important as product selection and quality.[2] But then came the industrial revolution, which back-burnered customer service in lieu of efficiency. Around the birth of the Internet, customer service once again entered the limelight. Nordstrom's phenomenal growth and unique centering

Figure 1.1 Communities of Commerce

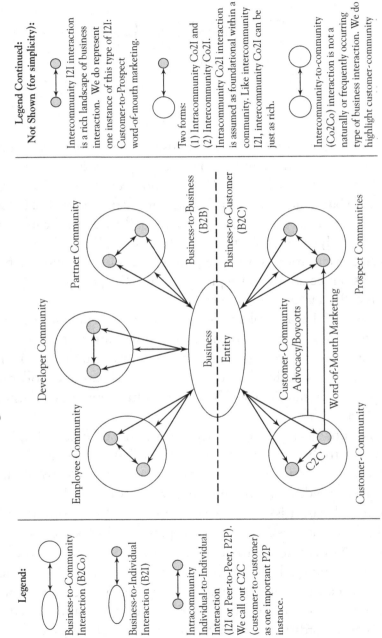

Legend Continued: Not Shown (for simplicity):

Intercommunity I2I interaction is a rich landscape of business interaction. We do represent one instance of this type of I2I: Customer-to-Prospect word-of-mouth marketing.

Two forms:
(1) Intracommunity Co2I and
(2) Intercommunity Co2I.
Intracommunity Co2I interaction is assumed as foundational within a community. Like intercommunity I2I, intercommunity Co2I can be just as rich.

Intercommunity-to-community (Co2Co) interaction is not a naturally or frequently occurring type of business interaction. We do highlight customer-community

Legend:

Business-to-Community Interaction (B2Co)

Business-to-Individual Interaction (B2I)

Intracommunity Individual-to-Individual Interaction (I2I or Peer-to-Peer, P2P). We call out C2C (customer-to-customer) as one important P2P instance.

of service attracted many an observing eye. Business gurus began preaching for more intense relationships with the customers. A quick look at the evolution of customer service buzzwords and management book titles (see Figure 1.2) will illuminate this fiery customer courtship. From "customer acquisition" to "customer winback," we have come far from our first date, explored intimacy and commitment, and are now even learning to make up after a fight.

For the most part, this customer courtship has been a personal one between the vendor and the individual customer. In *Customer. Community*, we are recommending a parallel path to customer loyalty.

Imagine your customers interacting. Imagine them getting to know each other or even befriending each other. They talk on a regular basis—they discuss you, your products, and your customer service. They compare you against your competitors. They recruit other friends into this community, and they promote the benefits of your products and services. They sometimes disagree with you and tell you so—en masse. But they stand behind you when you need

Figure 1.2 The Evolution of Customer Service Through Buzzwords and Books

Buzzword	Book Title (Year of Publication)
Customer acquisition	
Customer service	*Total Customer Service* (1989)
Customer satisfaction	*World-Class Customer Satisfaction* (1994)
Customer loyalty	*Building Customer Loyalty* (1994)
Customer retention	*Customer Retention* (1995)
Customer bonding	*Customer Bonding* (1995)
Customer intimacy	*Customer Intimacy* (1996)
Customer relationships	*Relationship Marketing* (2000)
Customer winback	*Customer Winback* (2001)

help. They are linked together as an aggregate force: a customer-community. For years, business experts have explored how to lever-age a collective employee base. They have realized the value of aligning a workforce. Some of the same benefits result from lever-aging a unified customer base: loyalty, evangelism, product feed-back. And with a customer-community, there's an extra potential benefit of direct revenue growth.

In the Introduction, we outlined many false perceptions of vir-tual community. Online community has such a narrow, anticom-merce reputation that it is no wonder businesses are skeptical of applying community-building concepts to their most valued asset—their customers. In *Customer.Community*, we will attempt to dispel these misperceptions and clearly demonstrate the undeniable busi-ness case for proactively interconnecting and empowering your col-lective customer base.

A Broader Look at Virtual Community

In his book *The Virtual Community*, Howard Rheingold defines vir-tual communities as "social aggregations that emerge from the Net when enough people carry on those public discussions long enough, with sufficient human feeling, to form webs of personal relation-ships in cyberspace."[3] This definition is very limiting; it requires "enough people," "discussions long enough," "sufficient human feeling," and "personal relationships." The early years of virtual community experimentation further narrowed this definition to a specific psychological profile that is usually at odds with commerce. In the nonvirtual realm, the definition of *community* is much broader. We say that a neighborhood has a strong community if its members work toward the betterment of the neighborhood, even if they never talk with one another. We say that a store or restau-rant has a community feeling if there is an amicable or social atmosphere where people interact freely, even if they don't know each other. We notice a strong minority collective presence and assume that the "likeness" of a minority status forms a community, even though many of its members will never interact or have any type of relationship with one another.

In *Customer.Community*, we are not as interested in building textbook communities as we are in the continuum of communal bonding that can lead to customer loyalty. A community bond can result from many different types of interactions. It is simply a psychological affinity based on the benefit derived from a peer or group of peers. (This choice of words does not imply that communities do not have varying levels of status. They often do, especially large communities with a defined leadership structure. We use "peer" merely to imply common status or interest, as opposed to a hierarchical relationship as exists between, say, teacher and student or master and apprentice.)

Before exploring why you should consider your *community* of customers, we'd like to broaden the definition of online community. We define online community as *a continuum of online interactivity spanning individual transaction to group interaction*. This continuum has many stops along the way. Stops like reading things written by other people. When you read a newspaper, you are engaging in a community. Stops like paying attention to others' viewpoints. When you reject an empty restaurant, you are responding to a nonverbal community recommendation. Stops like giving feedback to a vendor. Usually, feedback given to a service provider will not only benefit the individual but will also benefit other community members who use that service. Using this broader lens, a customer-community is a continuum of online interactivity spanning individual customer transaction to customer group interaction. Figure 1.3 depicts the customer-community continuum, showcasing sample customer-community activities.

Note that many of the customer interactions we have pinpointed on the continuum are not usually considered "community" activities because individuals aren't meeting other community members and commingling with them. Some people may feel that this definition is too broad, opening the community concept up too widely. We believe that it is not only the proactive desire to be in

Figure 1.3 The Customer-Community Continuum

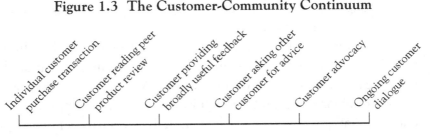

a group that builds community but often the reactive bond formed through individuals interacting with one another. The difference is causal, and since it the primary reason that a customer-community can be so powerful, let's unpack it a bit further.

Most virtual community advocates have explored how electronic communication has assisted people of similar interests in searching, finding, forming, and building e-communities. There is an assumption that these e-community types are consciously looking to find and join a community. While obviously this is true of many of the notable online communities, we also believe that there can be an unconscious community formed around a broad spectrum of similarities. Basically, either the chicken or the egg can come first. For the customer-community, this means that shoppers of like products, customers of the same vendor, or people simultaneously milling around the same store are connected by a subtle customer-community thread. If you are thinking of buying a certain computer, you may find another person who has that same computer and ask what he or she thinks of it. And when you are installing that computer, you may skip the instruction manual and call a technically savvy friend to ask for help. Have you ever felt a slight affinity for someone who drives the same car you have—even though you've never met the person?

What is this subtle thread interlinking your customer base? It is you—your company or your products. Commerce with you is the unifying interest. This commonality is crucial to our discussion because it sets customer-communities apart from most virtual communities. "Monetizing community" has been plagued with difficulty because most e-communities aggregate around some noncommercial shared interest. For a traditional business model to profit from these communities, non-commerce-focused community members must be enticed to spend money. This is not a hurdle for customer-communities that are already commerce-centric.

The more important, expensive, or long-term the customer's decision is, the less subtle this connective thread becomes. If you are purchasing a multimillion-dollar financial database for your company, you will definitely want to talk with peers at similar companies to discuss why they chose the software they did and how they implemented and maintained it. Why is MacWorld Expo so popular with Apple customers? Is this megaconference just to peruse the new products or to meet other similarly interested Apple customers? Why is "Community" the second major category (the first is "Products") on www.oracle.com, linking to various customer-communities that encourage intercustomer dialogue? These customers didn't "join" a community; they became a community after purchasing or when deciding to purchase similar products.

If a customer-community is an unconscious bond, should you pay attention? Yes, for two reasons. First, some of the most powerful communities begin reactively. Look at neighborhood communities. When you move into a new neighborhood, you may not consciously join a community of your neighbors. Yet you probably share a bond around the shared interests of safety or beautification. This nonplanned shared interest resulting from simple proximity can grow very fast and very strong. Second, unconscious motivators can be far more powerful than conscious ones. Take branding. Branding experts did not invent the concept of brand allegiance. Some time ago, someone noticed that certain customers were more loyal to certain brands. Often this loyalty was unconscious, illogical, and possibly even unwarranted. This insight spawned the birth of an entirely new marketing approach, an approach on which businesses spend significant time, effort, and money.

The branding corollary to community goes much deeper than the fact that they both can be somewhat subconscious. Brand awareness and customer-community are both bonds to a specific vendor by affiliation. We will explore affiliation in more depth with a brief exploration of customer loyalty later in this chapter and also as we examine community sustainability in Chapter Six. Many branding campaigns even attempt to link brand identity directly to demographic communities, especially ethnocultural, gender, and generational communities. This underscores the overlap of these two affiliative concepts.

Jonathan Spira, chief analyst at the New York–based research firm Basex, explores the power of the unconscious commercial community when he talks about "communities of reliance": "Communities of reliance use the best aspects of community in an e-commerce setting, without specifying a community in the first place," he says. "They are predicated on the fact that you do not have to join anything." Well-built communities of reliance have the potential to breathe new life into e-commerce sites. He dubs these groups "stealth communities" (identified by five characteristics: they are *voluntary*— there is no official membership or organization; they are *ad hoc*—the community forms for each transaction separately; they are *nondenominational*—participants can be members of many such communities; they are *transaction-oriented*—the community lasts only as long as the transaction taking place at the moment; and they are *ephemeral*—the community disappears after the transaction is completed) and proclaims that they can affect e-commerce transactions nearly 100 percent of the time.[4]

Spira's reliance dynamic is a significant element of customer-communities but only one dimension of it—the isolated transaction piece and the community that forms around it. In *Customer.Community*, we'll explore other dimensions as well that lead to a more lasting bond.

The History of Customer-Community

The idea of interacting with your customers as a community is not new. Before transportation and information technologies expanded distribution networks beyond local boundaries, customer service and community were inseparable. Most prerailroad businesses were geographically centric and therefore had a vested interest in serving their neighboring communities. A local business's interest in the community is a dual one. First, the success of the business is completely dependent on the customer-community. Second, the business owner and employees have a personal stake because they are members of the same community they are serving. Local businesses hone their products and services to meet community needs by listening to customer-community feedback. The customer-community rewards the business owner through patronage but also through word-of-mouth support for the business. The business owner then often gives directly back into the community both financially and otherwise—business-sponsored Little League teams, community bulletin boards in store entrances, donations to local causes, and other community programs. Sometimes these businesses even become a gathering place for the community or various subcommunities. Many small-town commercial squares are the primary social catalyst for the community.

Though you could argue that the small-town-square concept is waning in America, other businesses are waxing as community gathering places (malls, neighborhood cafes). In fact, this local dynamic is still alive and well within neighborhood commerce. Why do you choose a particular coffee shop? Hair salon? Movie theater? Does the social atmosphere ever affect your decision for one venue over another? Do your personal interactions with your service providers or other customers ever influence your patronage? Do you appreciate vendors who make an effort to give back to the community in which you live? Customer-community interrelation may not be a primary reason for your vendor selection, but it can have some affect on your choice and possibly an even greater impact on your sustained loyalty.

In today's global marketplace, commerce is no longer confined to localities. In fact, for two hundred years leading up to the Internet revolution, business advancements had the effect of decreasing the need for customer-community building. In the 1800s, when the railroads expanded distribution reach, a positive community perception was not as critical because a merchandiser's customers became a disparate collection of individuals who no longer identified with one particular community. In the 1900s, as the industrial era began deconstructing systems and microanalyzing specifics, the collective became even less important. Finally, the global adoption of capitalism moved businesses even further toward isolated consumerism. The individual customer became all-important; the customer-community had faded.

If today's customers aren't necessarily part of the same local community, why do they need to interact? Branding departments heighten customer perceptions; customer relationship management (CRM) systems monitor customer interactions, coupling findings with industry data to determine product strategies; customer service databases aggregate customer feedback to expose customer satisfaction issues and determine service level requirements; membership departments create loyalty incentive programs. The aggregate is under control; therefore, all energy is focused on the individual customer.

What has changed? The Internet, while further disintegrating the geographical boundaries and isolating the customer, has interconnected all aspects of business. Previously unrelated customers are once again part of the same customer-community. Customer interaction has never been so easy: a simple e-mail, an anonymous posting to a forum, reviewing a product, rating a vendor. You can interact with other customers at the drop of a hat, and you don't even need to make eye contact. But here's the question: Except for the occasional personal recommendation, do we, as customers, want to interact with one another? Do we as vendors and service providers care about this customer-to-customer interaction?

Business Benefits of Customer-Community

Why do we care if our customers interact with one another? There are many answers to this question that we will explore throughout *Customer.Community*: deeper customer loyalty, additional revenue streams, powerful collective voice, broader market research, focused product input, partnership development, peer-to-peer customer service, lower operational costs, and low risk to terminate.

Deeper Customer Loyalty

Loyalty is probably the most prized benefit of engaging your customer-community. Customer loyalty is a complex multifaceted business challenge. There are multiple reasons why a customer will remain loyal to a vendor—superior product selection, personalized customer service, and convenience are a few. Some loyalty factors are discrete and quantifiable; others are more vague and amorphous. The affiliative bond is more difficult to pin down—it's not always easy to know why people who feel a part of something are more loyal to it. But affiliation is a psychological bond that can be as cohesive as bonds derived from hard-edged factors like price competitiveness or product line breadth. Psychological consumer bonds, once ignored, have come a long way in the past few decades—probably because branding analysis has revealed the strength of psychological bonds and has also proved the possibility of actively targeting and measuring such bonds. In Chapter Six, we explore in more detail various affiliative bonds like proximity, habit, and culture.

Affiliation is a communal psychology that can be at least as strong as individual psychology. Richard Cross and Janet Smith in *Customer Bonding* say, "Customers or supporters who form a communal bond around your brand, product, service, candidate, cause, or organization are usually *extremely* loyal. Your competitors will be hard-pressed to shake their allegiance."[5] As an example, consider advocacy.

If you recommend a product to someone else, you are likely to be more loyal to that vendor. Murray and Neil Raphel, in *Up the Loyalty Ladder*, discuss how to turn occasional customers into full-time advocates for your business. They argue that "the overriding factor of brand leadership is not quality, not advertising, but customer advocacy."[6] And Cross and Smith point out, "Constituents with whom you have developed the advocacy bond are almost universally dedicated to your brand or your organization."[7] In the early 1990s, MCI realized the power of community advocacy with its "Friends and Family" discount calling program. Cari Sanborn, former "Friends and Family" marketing director, notes, "Friends and Family customers are good quality customers. They stay with us longer, spend more, and save more than if they were just straight MCI customers."[8]

The Apple computer customer-community may be one of the most loyal large customer-communities in existence. There are many reasons for this loyalty. Apple elevated the personal computer from a technology to a creative platform and then all the way to a lifestyle accessory. In the 1980s and early 1990s, Apple targeted primary educational and creative customer-communities and was obsessive about meeting those communities' needs. This focus created extreme loyalty within these customer segments. In the mid-1990s, when it looked as if Apple's proprietary business strategy was caving under the weight of IBM and Dell, many Apple customers illogically clung to their beloved Apples. Jeff Arcuri, former vice president of marketing for MacWorld Expos, indicates:

> Expos have been able to enjoy the benefits usually limited to professional association events. Attendees [Apple technology consumers] feel and act like they are members of an industry community for which the event is created. As long as the event continues to create this environment of "like community," the Expo is almost guaranteed to provide a strong buying audience to the exhibitors on the floor. Even when Apple lost a great deal of its market share and the exhibit floor shrank significantly, attendees showed up in larger

numbers each year. They came to show support to the brand. I can only dream to have that kind of loyalty for the industry events I manage now.[9]

Ongoing interaction with other Apple groupies continued to fuel this loyalty even through the toughest of times.

Additional Revenue Streams

A customer-community provides opportunities to directly augment revenue. If you use a subscription model, you could charge to access to your customer-community. Match.com, "the Web's largest online dating community," is a fee-based service that is able to charge premium subscription rates only because of the breadth and depth of its customer-community. There are many indirect revenue opportunities as well. Subcommunities can allow you to target customers of interest-specific products more directly. If www.gap.com created a dialoguing microcommunity within its GapMaternity channel, it could have an intensely interested audience for targeting not only maternity clothes but BabyGap products as well.

Cocreated revenue is a distinct possibility for some e-commerce sites. Affiliate programs, where customers direct referral traffic from their own personal Web sites, are probably the most common cocreation revenue strategy. Customer-to-customer commerce and incubation are two more extremely engaging ways to cocreate revenue opportunities with your customers.

Peer-to-peer Internet marketplaces are ripe. eBay has paved the way. Other companies, especially business-to-business marketplaces like VerticalNet and Bizland.com, have quickly followed suit. Even traditional e-businesses can, if adventurous, play in this realm. A tradition-rich e-tailer like Disney can engage its customer-community in the commerce. Or a vertical-product company—say, a plant nursery—could allow its customers to promote complementary product offerings or services like gardening or landscaping. For example, www.nationalgardening.com has a seed-swap program whereby community members can barter seeds.

Revenue possibilities may come from the most unexpected customer-community corner. Incubating a customer's business idea is an extreme cocreation possibility, one with rich profit-sharing possibilities but one that, due to resource intensity and contractual liability, must be well thought out. Some customer-communities are so tightly interwoven that there is revenue to be had from live events, conferences, or training seminars. Aveda.com has a rich network of salon and store franchises. These offer live classes and seminars that not only help the store owner (and Aveda) sell more products and services but also generate additional revenue. As any business does when searching for additional income potential, you should evaluate your customer-community for all possible revenue streams—looking under every customer stone and in every community corner.

Harnessing the Collective Voice of Your Customers

Even before the Internet augmented global communication, a collective customer-community voice would sometimes affect a business. Widespread community boycotts—like the early-1990s U.S. boycott of tuna caught in nets that trap and drown dolphins—can force companies to alter practices. Customer-community support can also powerfully bolster a company, as in the 1996 Odwalla *E. coli* scare. Odwalla, like Ben and Jerry's before it, created a loyal customer following through its commitment to socially aware business practices. When an outbreak of *E. coli* bacteria was linked to Odwalla juice, the company's loyal customer-community supported the company both vocally and financially—through continued loyalty and outspoken testimonies—for the way the company handled the crisis. Odwalla was honest, accepted responsibility, and showed that it would go above and beyond to avoid any risk to its customers.[10]

As information technologies have connected customers, the voice of the community has grown louder and more powerful. The collective now has a much more efficient and more effective broadcast media, and it's one the customers can control. The power here is just beginning to be realized. Virtual communities now have a much easier time approaching a business with a unified voice. They also have a much easier time lending a helping hand . . . and becoming a much more loyal customer base in the process.

In the mid 1990s, as soon as use of the Web hit a critical mass in the United States, there was an immediate awareness that the Internet was a place where collective options could easily be aggregated to help guide consumer choices. Take, for example, Epinions.com, where customers can easily rate vendors' products that they like or don't like, or badbusinessbureau.com, a nationwide consumer reporting Web site, to enter complaints about companies and individuals who are "ripping people off." Gómez.com, the e-commerce experience measurement firm for both consumers and e-businesses, presents an aggregate consumer voice through its trademarked "scorecards" that rank e-commerce and e-service Internet sites according to a set of 120 customer satisfaction criteria.[11] An aggregate voice has never been so easy to cull. You may choose to ignore the unified voice of your customers, but you can be sure that other potential customers won't, and neither will the media.

Broader Market Reach Through Customer Advocacy

Customer advocacy can market your company and potentially lower the cost of customer acquisition—a double bonus. As we mentioned earlier in this chapter, advocacy can also lead to loyalty—a triple bonus. People love to share personal stories; what better way is there than to have them sharing stories about your product? Customer recommendations can be far less expensive and much more compelling than traditional marketing techniques—a company telling you about its product has a built-in agenda; two customers swapping experiences is more convincing.

Looking to purchase a multimillion-dollar financial database? A billboard or magazine ad is not going to convince you. You want to talk with someone in similar shoes who has made a similar decision and managed a successful implementation. In the high end of the B2B world, marketing reach is driven primarily by market penetration statistics and word of mouth. Vendors cherish positive customer testimonials so that they can match potential new clients with like-minded, satisfied peer-level customers.

Focused Product Input

Focused, pertinent customer input can potentially lower the cost of product development. Customers can participate in competitive research, test products, give feedback, and even play a collaborative role in product development. For years, management gurus have evangelized the concept of tying the customer into the product development cycle. The argument is that customers are in the best position to know what they need, and therefore guidance from the customer would lead to more timely and appropriate products and services. But this theory is difficult to translate into reality. Why? First, do customers really know what they want? Sometimes not. It's often difficult for the customer to envision next-generation possibilities without understanding the product development process or the inherent capabilities of the technologies or materials involved. But mostly, it is difficult to aggregate qualitative individual customer input at any useful level. Surveys work for quantitative feedback, but how do you really engage customers in a future product brainstorming session? How do you aggregate what people are saying and deliver a product before they change their minds or preferences? The customer-community helps solve these conundrums.

In the 1980s, SGI, a computer manufacturer of high-performance servers and workstations, created a community of "lighthouse customers." These customers were SGI's obsessive early adopters, who often understood the technology at a much deeper level than SGI's other customers and who also pushed SGI to develop faster and more powerful systems. SGI engineering teams brainstormed with this customer-community to determine the next generation of SGI's products. This collaboration not only advanced product development but also engendered loyalty in the process. Due to their solidified loyalty, the lighthouse customers were featured in SGI videos, ads, and testimonials. Since so many of these companies, such as Jet Propulsion Laboratories (JPL) and Industrial Light and Magic (ILM), were innovation leaders, SGI quickly built enormous word-of-mouth buzz as the preferred cutting-edge solution provider to these industries.

Benefits from this kind of customer collaboration are not limited to technology companies. Consider Holiday Inn's Priority Club.[12] "Twice a year since 1989, the Atlanta based mega-hotel chain has enticed five hundred to one thousand of its most frequent guests to bring themselves and their families out to a resort property for a weekend of hobnobbing, recreation, and roundtable discussion with hotel management." Ken Pierce, Holiday Inn's vice president of frequency marketing, claims that this program deepened customer loyalty. He adds that many people who attend these conferences stayed in touch with him and each other afterward, calling or writing with ideas and competitive information. "They're helping us do our job."

With the Internet, this type of customer-community culling does not have to be so logistically intensive as an offsite retreat. You can easily coordinate a live product development chat session or an ongoing product feedback forum. Obviously, this type of customer collaboration would not replace product development expertise and ingenuity, but it certainly would augment the effort and build customer loyalty in the process.

Partnership Development

Future customer-communities will continue down the path of virtual collaboration following in the footsteps of Usenet, the grandfather of virtual communities. This interchange will be most significant in the B2B developer and partner communities, where the open development advocates like UNIX and Linux developers have paved the way. Parent B2B businesses will be delighted. Microsoft and PeopleSoft have showed the power of collaboratively connecting their developer environments. In the 1990s, PeopleSoft catapulted to the head of the human resource database solution pack. One primary reason for PeopleSoft's success is the quality and breadth of their application partners. Look at www. peoplesoft.com and www.microsoft.com to discover the effort these companies expend to deepen and broaden their developer and partner communities.

An immense integrated suite of compatible products, sales outlets, and support partners can be an enormous differentiator for many different types of companies, especially in the B2B space. Consider how manufacturers in the automobile industry compete via a wide partner network of sales dealerships and maintenance shops. Could a partner strategy be even more effective by engaging these partners as a partner community? Could partners share best practices and help get new partners up and running? The likely answer is yes, unless the partnership strategy is one in which partners compete head to head. Even then, microcommunities could be formed that included specific noncompeting partners. Developing and enabling partnership communities to evangelize, collaborate, and go forth and multiply could mean getting a larger network faster. Igniting faster B2B partnership expansion almost assuredly translates into competitive advantage.

Peer-to-Peer Customer Service

Peer-to-peer customer service is an especially attractive benefit for companies with complex and customizable product lines. Computer hardware or software vendors' products can often be manipulated into a myriad of configurations. It is impossible for customer service representatives to be prepared for all of the different permutations in which customers use these products. Often other customers who use the products similarly are in a much better position to help with a specific customer issue. If a company connects similar customers together so that they can help each other, everyone wins.

Hewlett-Packard has gone so far as to provide its IT customers with an eBay-like rating system so that customers can rate how well they help solve each other's problems. A customer can easily peruse other customer-community members profiles and ratings to see if that might be an appropriate member to ask a specific question.

Intuit has created a service called Intuit Advisor, which is a network of expert customers—accountants and tax specialists—who advise other Intuit customers on tax issues and how to use Intuit products. Intuit Advisor members get product discounts and also get a kickback if they sell Intuit products to their customers. The individual specialists also benefit from the upsell potential for their services. Customer-to-customer assistance need not be limited to the computer industry. Any company with customers who are willing to help each other can benefit.

Obviously, if you formally support customers serving other customers, you need to communicate appropriate disclaimers regarding accuracy and quality of service provided. As with most customer-community implementations, the marketing and legal departments should be involved to avoid liability and ensure brand protection.

Some companies may reap so much value from peer-to-peer customer service that they are able to realize expense savings through decreased call volumes. Or they may even decide to cut operational costs further by formalizing a virtual customer-community customer service staff. Customer-community employees can, like an effective college intern program, even decrease overall cost per employee due to many factors such as geographically variant pay scales, home offices, and lower benefits costs, since many customer-community members may have their own benefits coverage.

Lower Operational Costs

Cost-effective customer advocacy, efficient product input channels, and peer-to-peer customer service are not the only customer-community benefits that result in operational savings. There are many possibilities for recruiting your customer-communities to help with your business operations. Two specific areas that are additional targets for expense reduction through customer-community assistance are content creation and community leadership. With customer-generated content, not only can expenses be reduced, but you can reap other cocreation benefits as your customers help you build out your site. Cocreation is a sticky proposition—sticky in that it leads to intense loyalty and also because it can be logistically challenging. The concept is simple: people embrace what they help create.

Member-generated content and affiliation programs are both incarnations of cocreation. Bolt.com, a demographic portal targeting fifteen- to twenty-four-year-olds, was one of the first Web sites to understand the stickiness of member-generated content. Bolt almost completely handed over the content creation reins to their community. Even expert or authoritarian content sites like WebMD.com have discovered that members want to hear from each other. In response, WebMD publishes live member chats as feature articles in the most popular content areas. Sites embracing member content realize the triple win of customer loyalty, membership generation, and lower cost of content creation. It is for this reason that e-tailers often allow customers to post product reviews. This type of promotional customer-generated content can lead directly to additional revenue. Many sites have affiliation programs that enable customer-community members to link their modified Web sites into the parent company's Web site index. These affiliate members get paid for every customer click-through. In a way, affiliates help cocreate the broader site. Affiliates have two bonds—the psychological cocreation one as well as a personal financial incentive.

A few companies have ambled all the way down the cocreation path and have extended job offers to members within their customer-community. Community leaders on some Web sites get paid for content or for running portions of the public Web site. AOL has a comprehensive leadership structure to manage the behemoth AOL community. About.com pioneered and even patented a business model that hinged on recruiting customer-community members as paid topical "guides" who help the company create original content and search and categorize Internet links for their respective topics. The e-customer turned e-employee can solidify loyalty even further as well as decrease the cost per hire.

As with peer-to-peer customer service, when formalizing a relationship with your customers whereby they are doing actual work for you or helping you lower operational expense, it is wise to get advice from legal counsel. AOL has experienced the legalistic brunt of being a pioneer in recruiting "volunteers" and virtual employees from within its community. Legal precedents have now been set clarifying the lines between an informal and formal customer relationship; the role distinctions between a customer-volunteer and a customer-employee are therefore clearer to develop and communicate.

Easy Start-Up, Low Risk to Terminate

It is relatively easy and low risk to enable your e-customers to talk with one another. If there is even a chance that customer-to-customer dialogue will result in something positive, why not try it? A business can easily inch its way toward customer-community. To start, simply leverage connections that already exist. Determine if customers are currently talking with one another, and facilitate or elevate that dialogue to a newsletter or discussion forum. Neither requires a heavy investment in technology. You can even, instead of implementing your own infrastructure, outsource the operation and support of your community tools.

If your customer-community trial doesn't work, closing the door may not be terribly difficult. Whereas eliminating customer functionality like personalization or membership programs can cause customers to lose accrued benefits, discontinuing support of your customer-community will affect only your customers' ability to communicate with one another. You may make a few customers angry by thwarting their conversations, but with proper communication, you can terminate a trial or shift directions without alienating your customer base.

Control Issues

Although the customer-community benefits we have enumerated are clearly attainable and getting started can be relatively easy, many companies are afraid that connecting their customer base will cause a power shift from company to customer. They fear losing control. Charles Mann, writing in *MIT Technology Review*, attempts to refute three Internet myths: that the Internet is too international to be controlled, that it is too interconnected to be controlled, and that it is too filled with hackers to control.[13]

The loss of control associated with the Internet obviously scares business leaders. This fear is illogical. Customers are already connected; the power has already shifted. Not convinced? A *Fast Company* article, "We Won't Take a Backseat," reveals that American Airlines (AA) frequent flyers are more connected—and more powerful—than ever. The article details how AA faced a Web-enabled customer revolt because of the way the company handled some frequent flyers' miles. In fall 2000, AA published a frequent flyer program that limited eligibility to people in certain cities. The change to this program was quickly picked up by members of FlyerTalk.com, "a community Web site where anal-retentive mileage hoarders swap notes on strategy."[14] According to the article, "The hue and outcry" from ineligible frequent flyers "was immediate and fierce." The members of AA's customer service department was caught off guard because this new program had not been clearly communicated to them. FlyerTalkers who were initially told they were ineligible managed to get unaware AA customer service reps to sign them up anyway, and they then posted information to FlyerTalk.com telling others whom to call. AA eventually gave into the mayhem and expanded eligibility. Control is more elusive now than it has ever been.

Loss of control does not mean losing control. Chaotic mayhem is different from organized activism. The former rarely yields positive results, while the latter exemplifies the potential for the multi-faceted benefits of a collective. Yet the line between the two is subtle. An orderly crowd can turn into an unruly mob in the blink of an eye. A lot depends on structure and leadership. The same goes for the virtual realm. There are strategies for letting go in a controlled manner. Appropriate membership agreements and guidelines should be thought through, clearly posted, and stringently enforced. There should be some sort of leadership structure, even if it is a single customer service representative monitoring the customer-community interaction. If discussion boards are used, it is wise to consider moderated discussions so that tangential conversations don't spin out of control.

As your customer-community grows and segments into various microcommunities, you will want to consider a more robust leadership that may or may not include customer-community members themselves leading areas within the community. The leadership should be empowered, with varying authority, to enforce the customer-community contract or agreement. Enforcement is the key to retaining control. In the American Airlines example, Richard G. Barlow, chairman and CEO of Cincinnati-based Frequency Marketing, Inc., which develops loyalty programs for companies like American Express, GE Capital, and Microsoft, says it was a mistake for AA to have backed down. "There is nothing in your frequent-flyer agreement that says you will get every offer every time."[15] Catalyzing a collective voice doesn't imply you don't talk back to it at times.

"The customer is always right" doesn't truly mean that the customer is *always* right. There are guidelines for physical customers. Shoplifting and violence are usually not acceptable. Customers are reprimanded for such activities, and other customers are appreciative because they understand that these guidelines benefit both the vendor and the vast majority of customers. Virtual community is the same, though some of the issues are different. For instance, do you let customer-community members be anonymous? What level of registration do you require? What is the membership agreement? What are the behavioral guidelines? Be as comprehensive as possible. Don't shy away from the touchy stuff like harassment. If you don't allow customers to yell at each other in your store, don't allow it within your virtual customer-community. As Terry Marasco, West Coast director of customer service for Terra Lycos, says, "Don't be afraid to 'fire customers' who are overtaxing your business or abusive with your customer service team."[16]

Terry also raises another control issue: partner control. "You may not care what your customers are saying, but your partners may." This issue could be especially tricky for retailers of high-profile brands who care deeply about customer perception. If you have an exclusive relationship with a significant partner who doesn't want you sponsoring customer dialogue, you have a control impediment to overcome. Eventually even control issues like this will dissipate because of the inevitability of customers voicing their opinions, on your site or another. But in the short term, partner control can be a big customer-community obstacle.

Finally, and we will reiterate this many times throughout this book, as you start down the customer-community path, consult legal counsel every step of the way. What opens you to liability? What is your remuneration strategy regarding member-generated content? When does member "volunteerism" become indentured servitude? Where is the virtual line between harassment and freedom of speech? There is now a lot of virtual community legal precedent out there; you are wise to learn from it.

Summary

The Internet has given new life to the customer-community, and it has necessitated a new definition of online community. While the basic fundamental community-building tenets have remained unchanged, the new virtual media landscape has drastically altered how these principles affect customer-community evolution. Some attributes of virtual customer-communities are seemingly identical to their local counterparts, and some are very different.

There are many reasons to care why your customers are interacting: deeper customer loyalty; broader market reach; a powerful collective voice that can promote and support your business; valuable, focused product input; partnership development; effective peer-to-peer customer service; and lower operational costs are a few. Some of the same benefits corporations have reaped by aligning internal employee communities shed light on potential bottom-line benefits of catalyzing customer-communities. Learn from the work that has been done so far. The collective psychology of the employee base has been analyzed to determine win-win strategies to increase employee productivity and loyalty. Customers, like employees, are human, with both individual and social needs. Customer productivity may not translate directly, but customer loyalty certainly does.

Chapter Two

The Customer Case

Most customers want both individual efficiency and some level of social interaction with one another. We are humans, and regardless of our personalities—from gregarious extrovert to reclusive introvert—we are a species with both individual and social needs. It is next to impossible to separate the two. The social constructs that attempt extreme individualism (for example, libertarianism) or extreme community (such as communism) highlight the challenges when either piece is not addressed adequately. While consumerism often skews to our individual needs, it doesn't mean that our social nature should be ignored. Consider the analogy of commuting to work—is this an individual or a social need?

A colleague of ours, Meg, takes a one-hour train every day from Rockridge, New York, into New York City to work. Since there are only a few options, the riders are usually the same people, day after day. Although most of the commuters work during the ride, Meg describes a familiarity that has developed over time—a recognition that is acknowledged with a glance or a nod. She also tells of the Irish ticket collector who has become very familiar to all of the riders—not too personal but very friendly. Every year, on St. Patrick's Day, this ticket collector decorates the train in green streamers and balloons. He serves green beer to all passengers on both the morning and afternoon trains. Meg says that this loosely congenial group of people becomes the most intimate community imaginable, laughing and sharing stories. The Irish ticket collector is transformed into a convivial entertainer who tells scandalous commuter stories, dances through the cars, and "comps" many of the passengers. He becomes the life of the party—his party—and he brings the community into unity. Certainly the camaraderie and appreciation of his riders also fuel his ego. This is a small example of how individual interests can serve both the individual and the collective.

Communities almost always bridge both individual and communal needs. Tenants who live in an apartment building and have the same landlord may form a community where each tenant can voice and gain support for the specific maintenance issues of his or her apartment. Each resident will also join the rest of the tenant community in supporting the maintenance of common areas. Customers who regularly shop at the nearest grocery store begin to develop loyalty toward that store. The grocery store meets each neighbor's individual shopping needs, but it also addresses the neighborhood community's needs by providing a catalyst for neighborhood socialization and possibly even increasing property values.

Humans have repeatedly invented technologies to enhance both individual and communal activities. Oddly enough, some of the same technologies that promote community also enable independence— look at the telephone, the automobile, the Internet. On the one hand, these technologies help connect us to other people, and on the other hand, they let us live in our own little worlds without having to interact with anyone. The point is that any technology can be designed and used to connect or to isolate.

No matter what communication technology you plunk in front of us, we are ultimately wired to use it for individual efficiency and to interact with others. Just as technology doesn't make us who we are as individuals, it also doesn't dictate why and with whom we form our various communities. But unfortunately, when asked what makes a successful online community, people will jump right to talking about the tools and technologies that enable a community— e-mail, discussion boards, chat. Tools do not a community make. It doesn't work that way in real life, and it doesn't work that way online.

The global embrace of the Internet has caused a worldwide technology adoption curve. As is common, during the rollout period of new technologies, the overwhelming focus in initial stages is on the technology itself, rather than on what it enables. For virtual communities, the result has been a bunch of incredibly technically sound or even advanced virtual communities that have been mostly focused on the logistics of virtual communication. Still today, in most virtual communities, there is a heavy concentration on the technology and only nominal focus on other social characteristics required to sustain a solid community. As we climb this adoption curve, people will eventually forget about the technology and focus on the totality of social dynamics at play. You never think of telephone conversations as virtual communities; you just naturally call your friends and family. The same will eventually be the case for Internet-enabled virtual communities. Maybe a few years from now, the adjective *virtual* or *online* will be dropped and communities will simply be communities regardless of the technologies or methods used to form and sustain interaction.

In fact, this line of reasoning is just one step away from the next: what lies beneath successful human face-to-face connections is also the foundation of successful online communities. Designing communities—online or in real life—that don't address the needs of human beings will fail. Humans are social creatures; we need to interact with each other; we need community.

The Individual and Social Customer

Why do we as customers want to interact with other customers? Because customers are human. Coalescing community and customer becomes very apparent when there is some commercial benefit to the customers' interaction—as in bars or coffee shops where profit is directly derived from the customers' need to commune with one another. This interdependence is most obvious for extremely social businesses like dance clubs or when an essential community service or an esteemed institution is threatened. Consider, for example, how a community can come together when a long-established neighborhood store is forced out of business. On such occasions, a loosely connected neighborhood customer base can turn into a unified voice of defense overnight.

We cannot be fulfilled unless both our individual and social needs are met. Abraham Maslow, one of the giants of sociology, is known for his theories about our constantly seeking to meet a series of instinctual needs. He postulated that humans strive to climb a ladder of needs, advancing upward one rung at a time. As you fulfill the needs of the lower rungs, you reach upward toward the next-higher rung. For example, you don't worry about your aesthetic surroundings until you are certain that you are safe and secure. In Figure 2.1, we have annotated Maslow's Hierarchy of Needs to showcase that our needs are both individual and social. We have also included examples to show how this duality plays out online.

Of course, this doesn't mean that every activity needs to fulfill both individual and social needs. You may believe that bathing is an individual need and never have any desire to take a Japanese-style communal bath. Or you may feel that commerce is solely about individual efficiency and never want to interact with another customer. Certainly that is what many e-commerce strategists would have us believe. Individual efficiency. Customized service. MyPage. MyWishList. Me. Me. Me. If there is no "we," then why do customers commune at shopping malls? How has the Emporio Armani been able to capitalize on an in-store café? What about the power of flea markets, sporting events, or movie theaters? Why are business-to-business user groups and exchanges so popular?

You may think that a desire to commingle commerce and community in the physical realm is not predictive of that same need in the virtual realm. Then why do Amazon.com customer write reviews? Why do eBay collectors rate sellers or attend eBay university gatherings? What explains the success of the Motley Fool investment forums? There is definitely some precedent for the virtual customer-community, but that is not to say that virtual customer-communities operate in the same manner as nonvirtual ones.

We are not denouncing the need to serve the individual e-customer. There will always be customers who want customized

Figure 2.1 Maslow's Hierarchy of Needs—Online

Need	Definition	Type	Online Examples
8. Transcendence	Helping others find self-fulfillment	Social	E-giving, virtual mentoring, online spirituality
7. Self-Actualization	Maximizing one's potential	Individual	Experiential design, holistic e-learning
6. Aesthetic	Symmetry, order, and beauty	Individual/Social	Site design and architecture, multimedia integration
5. Cognitive	Knowing, understanding, and exploring	Individual/Social	Search functionality, site indexing, online learning
4. Esteem	Recognition, prestige, power	Social	Personal Web sites, peer visibility, status, and leadership
3. Social	Interaction with others, acceptance	Social	E-mail, message boards, chat rooms, instant messaging, e-communities
2. Safety	Freedom from accidents, crime, and disease	Individual	Secure data and transactions, freedom from harassment and viruses
1. Physical	Shelter, food, clothing, income	Individual	Available access, intuitive interface

efficiency and personalized customer service. Don't we all? Some of us will never want to interact with other customers; we just want to transact in virtual isolation and be done with it. There are also those community-loving types who never really want to buy anything or help out in any way; they just want to jabber. But most of us, at our core, want both. That is why we like to shop where our friends shop or where interesting people are. And why we seek recommendations or product advice from those we trust. Most of us want both individual efficiency and service *and* some level of customer-community interaction.

Notice in Figure 2.1 that our needs seem to be split pretty evenly between individual and social. In examining this hierarchy more closely, we see that Maslow's ladder ascends from animal instinct to the psychological traits that many people consider the primary differentiators that set humans apart from the rest of the animal kingdom. We present Maslow's hierarchy again in Figure 2.2, adding a further layer of granularity, from instinctual to spiritual. You will notice in our discussion in this chapter that as we move from survival to the social layer, the customer-community is driven primarily by basic human needs. But as we progress from social to soul concerns, customer behavior becomes more and more influenced by aspirational needs.

Instinctual Level

Rungs 1 and 2: Physical and Safety Needs. Survival is the strongest instinct in any animal species, including humans. In survival mode, we think of nothing but acquiring the fundamental physical and safety requirements necessary for us to live. In the early days of the World Wide Web, we started here at the bottom of Maslow's hierarchy. People needed access and assurance that they would be safe and "survive" in this new environment. Each of these needs has several online layers. What's my access quality? Is there an Internet café in my vicinity? Can I connect from home? How fast is the modem? Do I need DSL? Which browser is best?

Figure 2.2 Maslow's Hierarchy from Instinctual to Spiritual Concerns

	Need	Definition	Type
Spiritual	8. Transcendence	Helping others find self-fulfillment	Social
Soul	7. Self-Actualization	Maximizing one's potential	Individual
	6. Aesthetic	Symmetry, order, and beauty	Individual/Social
	5. Cognitive	Knowing, understanding, and exploring	Individual/Social
	4. Esteem	Recognition, prestige, power	Social
Social	3. Social	Interaction with others, acceptance	Social
Survival	2. Safety	Freedom from accidents, crime, and disease	Individual
Instinctual	1. Physical	Shelter, food, clothing, income	Individual

What other software do I need to use the Internet effectively? Which sites are down frequently, and which are more reliable?

In the wired sections of the world, as users became comfortable with their level of access, they quickly climbed to Maslow's second rung, safety or security. Can I enter my credit card number safely? Does my boss track my Internet usage while I'm on the job? Will anyone know that I went to this site? Will this site sell my personal information? Does my company have an impermeable firewall to protect my intellectual property? Newbie surfers psychologically lingered at the safety level as Hollywood and the media overplayed extreme scenarios involving identity-snatching hackers, computer-destroying viruses, and easily orchestrated conspiracies. Technologists focused on securing data and transactions on the Web. Billions of dollars were spent on firewall technologies, secure network applications, and much more to make sure we feel secure in cyberspace.

Statistically speaking, Maslow's physical and safety needs have been met on the Web. Access in the North America is near pervasive— different sources claim that 100 million to 400 million Americans are online.[1] Internet service providers (ISPs) are in fierce competition for good connections at reasonable rates. In corporate America, we have migrated from twisted-pair phone lines to Ethernet cable to fiber optics. Individually, we have moved from sluggish modems to ISDN to DSL. Access will be more pervasive in remote places in the world, and access speeds will continue to approach "real time." In general, companies and people are also feeling more secure. Firewall technologies are tried and tested. They are funded, implemented, and maintained by information service (IS) departments as a matter of course. Edge Research reports that "in 2001, 77 percent of the online population will use the Web to buy or gather information on products and services," up from less than 15 percent in 1992.[2] IS departments and individual users are more aware of and able to disarm potentially damaging viruses. Hackers who produce these viruses are prosecuted more severely.

Of course, our collective psychology does occasionally backslide. In the real world, a natural disaster or a war can cause a shift in focus from community actualization back to safety. In the Internet environment, advancements in access technologies, the rising cost of usage, or a severely damaging or pervasive virus can also cause a temporary collective psychological shift back to access and security issues. But in general, the majority of Internet users spend more of their time on the higher rungs of Maslow's ladder.

Social Level

Rung 3: Social Needs. As people became comfortable with the fact that they could surf and transact around the Internet with only a small chance of being watched or having their information stolen, we pushed upward toward Maslow's third rung, the need to interact with others and feel accepted. Communication and interaction technologies were introduced right and left. We were e-mailing, chatting, posting to forums, "IM-ing," "Egrouping," "Eviting," "outlooking" . . . We were augmenting old or creating new social networks. Usenet connected UNIX engineers. CompuServe introduced its forums. The Well was dug. AOL became more than an ISP. The community site was born.

In the beginning, the "community site focused purely on the social level, ignoring all the work that had been done on the physical and safety levels. Those who could figure out how to access these communities could meet and interact. Yet virtual communities like Usenet and The Well could be a bit intimidating to newcomers, and there was no certainty that virtual social interactions were secure from voyeurs. Only the most socially passionate, intellectual, needy, or curious jumped in. It was an early adopter community who forged uncharted territory and carved the initial path necessary for expansion into this new realm.

During this nascent phase, general perceptions of "virtual community" were being formed that linger still today. The media portrayed the "online community" as an aggregate of these early experiments. The composite e-community was anarchistic like Usenet, socialistic like The Well, technically unsophisticated like AOL, full of chatterboxes like those on CompuServe, and obsessed with cyberporn. This oddly conflicting and myopic view of virtual community still exists today, even though it is based on a number of outdated circumstances:

- There was little infrastructure supporting community interaction.
- The number of e-community venues was limited.
- Community members were an early-adopter crowd (early adopters are rarely representative of the eventual user base).
- Basic community principles and norms had not yet been translated online (for example, etiquette is something that we take for granted in physical interactions; the emergence of netiquette marked the beginning of the translation of these norms into the virtual realm).

As we indicated in the Introduction, virtual community has moved far beyond these early years. Embedded perceptions change much more slowly.

During the late 1990s and early 2000s, as access became easier and social interactions more secure, more and more people began interacting virtually. By 1999, the Internet was rife with community sites. Some were very broad, like CompuServe and AOL; some were less broad, like Women.com, MyPrimeTime, and Zing. Community sites were developed for even the narrowest niche communities. Some sites simply supported a specific type of communal interaction, like Egroups and Evite. Some sites, like NetNoir and Women.com, homed in on a demographic segment, and others, like Beliefnet and Ancestry.com, focused on a specific shared interest. Sites like Match.com were centered on meeting new people, while sites like MyFamily.com helped people stay in touch with their existing offline communities. Virtual life was becoming more and more social.

Content and Community . . . It was during this era that a more sophisticated convergence of content and community emerged.

People of similar interests not only wanted to talk about their common interests but also wanted content aggregated around those interests. For nonvirtual communities, media industries like magazines, newspapers, and television fulfilled this content role. How was it to be fulfilled for virtual communities? Many community sites simply copied what worked in the offline world. The virtual community portal became more complex. Portals rearchitected their sites into e-zines, believing that the demographically targeted magazine was the ideal blueprint. They created expensive live media events and forged liaisons with ABC, CBS, and NBC trying to replicate or augment television programming. It was like the early days of TV, when the programmers of the new medium copied what they knew—radio. Instead of leveraging the inherent differences of television, most TV shows were aired as static radio-like broadcasts.

Many community sites did explore new Internet-specific ways to create the content and community partnership. MyFamily.com built its following by focusing not on published content but on user-created content. MyFamily realized that the communal glue for families was content—like family photographs and family histories generated by different family members. In response, MyFamily provided its members with an easy way to build their own family Web pages where member-generated content could easily be added.

PlanetOut.com, a gay and lesbian (G&L) portal, acquired content through a media aggregation strategy that included merging with other G&L media and Web companies to become PlanetOut Partners, Inc., and aligning with major media entities like AOL, MSN, and Yahoo! In fact, PlanetOut Partners' goal is not to unify one G&L Internet community but to create the largest G&L-focused interactive community, services, and media company through a network of branded virtual G&L communities and related sites and products.

. . . *and Commerce.* As it became painfully clear that online advertising was not going to meet the revenue requirements of most virtual community sites, portals began trying to integrate the third C of the Internet Holy Grail: commerce. As clumsy as community sites were about integrating content, they were even clumsier with commerce. First of all, there weren't many role models. The shopping channel was as close as it came, and that's what most sites tried to emulate. Click over here to this separate channel that we call "shopping." You can't read content while you shop, and you can't talk with anyone else. You just shop. You can go back to reading and talking after you finish.

Some sites also tried to hide the fact that they were attempting to make money by selling things. Because community sites had been trying to portray themselves as almost altruistic, the commerce juxtaposition seemed oddly conflicting. The marketers of these sites knew this, but instead of hitting the "we need to make money to survive" nail on the head, they tried to sneak commerce in the back door. Click here and "Surprise!" We'll try to sell you something. And then they tricked you even further by confusing you when you wanted to get back to content or community areas. It was sort of like a Las Vegas casino where you can't quite find your way from one end to the other and you don't really know what time it is so what the heck, why not just play another slot machine? What do you mean you want to try to navigate back to content or a dialogue? Just click here and add it to your shopping cart. We may even send you off into a partner company's commerce area to buy more product and muddy the waters even further.

No wonder there is a perception that virtual community and commerce are incompatible. If a city all of a sudden plopped a department store down in the middle of a residential neighborhood, there would be uproarious complaints even from the most avid of shoppers. Even more so if the new neighborhood shoppers were tricked into going into the store and then couldn't find their way out and back home again.

The community e-commerce challenge wasn't exactly the same across the board. Some demographic portals were able to form alliances with consumer product companies that segmented their customers into similar demographic slices. This customer-commerce alignment is probably the reason that so much venture capital was directed toward women's portals. Military.com microanalyzed its community and defined five different community profiles, the "joiners," the "movers," the "just leaving," the "GI Bill-ers" in school, and the people responsible for procuring military equipment, each of which had different specific commerce needs.[3] PlanetOut discovered that the G&L community has a significantly higher frequency of traveling together and thus invested in this revenue opportunity. But in general, since these communities were not commerce-centric, profitability was—and still is—a constant challenge.

It wasn't just community sites socializing. Barnes & Noble offered instant messaging access from its front page. Boo.com began hosting the Boo Party. Internet surfers across the Net were interacting with each other and as they were doing so, they were building their own individual identities among their virtual peers. We ventured further up Maslow's ladder of needs to the fourth rung, esteem.

Rung 4: Esteem Needs. People need a way to feel validated. Positive interactions in a virtual community can build esteem, but interactions are transient. How do virtual community members build a solid status or reputation? So much of status in the nonvirtual world is visual. Your clothing, your home, and your personal belongings can immediately give clues to your status in a community. Even your body language during interactions can give status clues. Dogs show beta status (second place) to an alpha dog (first place) by rolling over on their backs and exposing their bellies. How do you expose your belly online?

The Well explored the concept of status by delineating moderated and unmoderated dialogues. Status emerged naturally and unfettered in an unmoderated dialogue, whereas in a moderated discussion, an assigned moderator led the discussion. AOL designed a leadership structure that clearly identified and rewarded community leaders. Online marketplace eBay and the bandwidth hog, avatar-thick Worlds Away, both pioneered virtual status in a different way. eBay allowed the community to rank or vote on business practices or style of individual sellers and buyers. Worlds Away's avatars were associatively more complex, based on how much time you spent online. Bolt.com elevated user-generated content, enabling members to showcase their personalities and ideas in the limelight of primary Bolt.com real estate. These practices have all been adopted by other sites. Most online forums have moderated and unmoderated discussion threads, and some have defined leadership structures. Many sites now have eBay-like democratic status flags, and Amazon.com has taken associate status to a whole new level.

Intracommunity esteem is most often generated and solidified through interactions among community members. Community members observe each other and build varying degrees of respect. Of course, in e-communities, as in all groupings of people, there is titular esteem as well. Recognizing leadership is important. Before Wine.com was purchased by eVineyard, it had a robust customer-community that recruited its leaders with the following pitch: "Do you consider yourself an expert on wine and/or food? Would you like to share your knowledge of wine with others online? If so, we're looking for people to help lead our online community. . . ." Esteem and leadership often go hand in hand, both online and off.

As eBay has demonstrated, esteem can be more important when sellers are competing to make a sale. Any business-to-customer (B2C) site with an affiliate program will underscore the competitive characteristics of the customer-vendor. This incarnation of esteem is more apparent in B2B portals like bCentral (www.bcentral.com) and Bizland.com (www.bizland.com), whose central purpose is to showcase wares of often competing businesses and who by their very nature elevate this characteristic to greater heights.

Exclusivity can promote both individual and group esteem. Membership benefits play as much to the psychological importance of esteem as they do to tangible benefits. That is why the names of ascending membership levels often directly convey status. Consider

American Express's Gold and Platinum cards or United Airlines' Premier frequent flyer program. Is flying first class simply about better service?

Collective esteem can be far more powerful than individual esteem. Many organizations have used collective empowerment to help strengthen disenfranchised communities like ethnocultural minorities, the elderly, and the disabled. Since its founding in 1958, AARP has lifted the nationwide esteem of the U.S. elderly ("Age isn't just a number—it's about how you live your life"), and that group esteem has been translated into one of the most powerful lobbying voices in Washington, D.C. Yanous! (www.yanous.com) is a five-language portal dedicated to disabled people and disabilities. It's name "Y'a nous!—There we are!—We do exist!" is in itself an assertion of group esteem. In an essay titled "Why Is the Americans with Disabilities Act Good for Our Country?" Dr. John B. Joyner writes, "ADA is more than practical solutions to physical and mental discrimination. It showcases an intuitive power available for change when branches of government collaborate with the private sector on issues of self-esteem and belonging."[4]

Rung 5: Cognitive Needs. Next in Maslow's hierarchy is cognitive need. We need to research, learn, and validate. The Web is the world's largest library and is ideal for individual exploration. Even the most unsophisticated e-consumer understands this. But collective cognitive awareness—though still ideally suited for the Web—is a bit different. Groups learn differently than individuals. They trust and learn from each other. They look to members with specific skills and expertise. For the e-customer-community, this means relying on the product recommendations of others, reading testimonials, and asking other members for tips. The need to learn and validate is often the way customers initially connect with one another. Wine and book clubs, customer reviews, online universities, peer references, and e-mail to a friend are all examples of this. And as we mentioned in Chapter One, someone who proffers advice is putting himself or herself in an advocacy role.

This translates into loyalty. And the person who has received the advice has possibly begun a communal bond. This also translates into loyalty. It's a dual win for the e-tailer.

According to market researcher IDC, the online learning industry is expected to grow from $6.3 billion in 2001 to more than $23 billion in 2204.[5] These statistics show that many people are using the Internet as a way to educate themselves. So why not help your customers educate themselves? Many sites facilitate customer-to-customer knowledge sharing. In a way, most customer dialogue is about cognitive exchange. But some sites can benefit from more formal learning programs. We are not necessarily advocating the Internet for formal customer training (but if you do have formal customer training, we would definitely recommend analyzing your curriculum and considering including some Internet-based training). Rather, we are advocating linking your customers together so that they can train each other. Often learning is not from formal teacher to formal student but rather from student-teacher to teacher-student. With the Web's dissolution of boundaries and variety of communication technologies, it is easy for everybody to become both a student and a teacher.

Possibly the most crucial component of B2B exchanges is the learning that passes from attendee to attendee. What does this mean for one's customer-community? Create customer-community exchanges. Have you ever wondered what really happens at those annual picnics where Saturn car owners convene and commune? Does it matter as long as connections are being made and product loyalty is secured? It is interesting to note that the first module that Real Communities (a fully integrated community infrastructure company now owned by Mongoose Technologies) completed was not chat software or discussion boards but rather a mentoring module that enables community mentors to link up with mentees.

At eBay University gatherings, power sellers educate other eBay community members. Hewlett-Packard has created an icon-annotated message board system that clearly identifies which messages are "magic answers" to previously posed customer queries. We believe that e-tailers have bottom-line incentives to link customers together in an educator-learner dynamic as often as possible.

Spiritual Level

Let's now move from online socialization to online soul and explore the highest levels of Malsow's needs—aesthetic, self-actualization, and transcendence—as they manifest within a customer-community.

Soulful Internet. Oxymoron? Diametrically opposed? Many people believe that the Internet is an utterly soulless medium. Some even believe it is the cultural bane of today's society, distracting people from truly soulful, real-world interactions or worse, drawing us into a hedonistic web of e-mail spam and cyberporn.

Obviously, the Internet is not inherently good or bad, but it can be used for either end. Many technologies get labeled as antispiritual, especially communication technologies. For years, television was the scapegoat technology most often blamed for the growing global spiritual void. The Internet has taken its spotlight. In its relative infancy, the Internet has almost equaled the global access reach of the television. Furthermore, the broad spectrum of Internet technologies not only enables broadcast communication but peer-to-peer interaction as well. It's this functionality that in the eyes of many people makes the Internet much more powerful, much more dangerous, and much more soulless.

Yet it is precisely group-based communication that some people feel enables more soulful connection. Think about what happens when the human spirit is ignited within a group. Think of the magic of a sports team, a musical group, or an ensemble cast performing together in a way that achieves far more than the sum of its parts. Have you ever experienced a powerful team dynamic? Your customer-community can possess this same energy.

Shopping is an experience often enhanced by the presence of other customers. Why does an empty store have a difficult time luring in shoppers? Why does a busy sale sometimes have a magnetic draw? There is a quality to an auction—offline or on—that engages us beyond social interaction, competition, and the possibility of getting a bargain. With a good auctioneer and a responsive crowd, the collective fervency of an auction pushes a unique button within our human psychology. It is this element—not the products being bought and sold—that was the fuel behind the instant success of eBay. A similar psychological button is pushed in a spiritual revival, a parade, organized group activism, or any other collective experience where a group of people come together as one.

This button scares business folk because it is unpredictable and uncontrollable. It is associated with a mob mentality and product boycotts. But it is also behind the one-day-only sales frenzy and brand loyalty. It is what drove George Bailey's *It's a Wonderful Life* customer-community to help him out of a seemingly insurmountable business catastrophe. Can you imagine if, at a time when you are facing a business challenge—a shortage of cash, an executive crisis, a business reorganization, a surprise competitive blow—not only your employees but also your customers pulled together to help you in a way that tapped this collective strength?

Rung 6: Aesthetic Needs. Symmetry and order. How many times have you gone to the store and been frustrated by the shopping experience? Finding a parking place? Searching through illogical layouts of products to find what you need? In what department will you find condensed milk in a grocery store: dairy, baking, or canned goods? Do you like waiting in the checkout line, especially if *People* magazine is sold out?

Have you ever chosen to shop at a store because of aesthetics? Anne, a friend of ours, tells us that she relieves her Christmastime shopping anxiety in downtown San Francisco by simply walking into the cool, quiet, ordered beauty of the Tiffany's store. It is not surprising that at www.tiffany.com, you can experience the same comforting aesthetic. It is a calming break from the sensory overload of the Web.

There is a definite experiential difference of e-commerce sites that understand the importance of brand aesthetics. Look at Williams Sonoma (www.williams-sonoma.com), Dean & Deluca (www.deananddeluca.com), Abercrombie & Fitch (www.abercrombie.com), Godiva (www.godiva.com), Louis Vuitton (www.vuitton.com), and Red Envelope (www.redenvelope.com). Not only do these sites reflect many visual aesthetic elements of their respective brands, but they enrich the aesthetic with personality and history as well. For example, Tiffany's, Godiva, and Louis Vuitton include histories of their companies or crafts. Tiffany's even includes archive services and biographies of its founders. It's the *Architectural Digest* or Martha Stewart type of aesthetic where beautiful design reflects rich tradition and personal attentiveness.

Ken Wingard gets even more intimate by telling a personal story of why he founded Wingard Inc. (www.wingardinc.com). Ken's story is conversational in tone and as accessible as if you were talking to a friend. It includes a casual picture of Ken, his signature at the end of the letter, and even a reference to his mom's Lazy-Boy chair. After reading this letter, you feel that you have made a personal connection.

Obviously not all sites choose a soothing tradition-rich design. The Abercrombie and Fitch site has created a more media-rich "MTV-esque" look that includes A&F TV, A&F Music, A&F Lifestyle, and even an A&F e-mail service in a blatant attempt to define and solidify a youthful customer-community.

Other sites steer toward order as the prime aesthetic. Major retailers like Macy's (www.macys.com) and JC Penney (www.jcpenney.com) have spent much more time ordering their sites into categorical representations of their stores. The challenge with order is that like beauty, what is orderly to some is chaos to others. Two good examples of this are Louis Vuitton (www.vuitton.com) and Herman Miller (www.hermanmiller.com). The Vuitton site was obviously created by an "artist" who wants the customer to organically explore the site, while the Miller site, like Herman Miller Furniture, was seemingly created by an architect who believes that information should be categorized in columns and matrices. Different approaches, resonating with some, alienating others. This is a design challenge.

Yahoo!'s "My Yahoo!" concept has enabled customers to personally reorder the various elements of Yahoo! in the manner that best suits them. The Net-wide adoption of this type of personalization is an unmistakable sign that e-tailers will continue to push this envelope. On effective e-commerce sites, customers will be able to create their own shopping experience aesthetically ordered in the exact way that they like to shop.

E-tailers choose to address Internet site design in various ways—splashy multimedia, brand reinforcement, and highly structured architecture—but generally speaking, there is a broad understanding of the aesthetic need of the e-consumer. This unfortunately does not hold true with traditional "community" elements of many Web sites. Since dialogue infrastructure (chats and message boards) is often isolated within its own separate area and usually outsourced, the experience can often seem jarring and not integrated with the rest of the site. This can reinforce the perception that the individuals engaged in dialogue are not an integral part of the customer base. It can feel as if you are shopping and a salesclerk tells you, "If you two are going to talk, could you please go outside." Many sites that didn't originally develop an integrated design for content, community, and commerce are now dealing with segregation issues caused by this ghettoization. Sites like eBay, Amazon.com, and The Motley Fool that built their own communication infrastructure have avoided this pitfall. Unfortunately, this type of vertical integration is neither feasible nor desirable for smaller e-tailers. Eventually, B2B community communication infrastructure companies will provide more aesthetically integratable technology so that this core piece of a customer's experience doesn't stand in opposition to the customer's ability to consume.

Rung 7: Self-Actualization Needs. When we reach this rung, we self-analyze and strive to be the best that we can be. As a consumer, how do you self-actualize? How do you better yourself; how do you become enlightened? There are obviously self-help books and meditation music that you can buy off or online. Online you can take courses. You can go to a worship service. Get therapy. Learn. There are also sites like www.beliefnet.com, www.essentia.com, www.soul fulliving.com, and www.improvingme.com where you can relax, meditate, and explore spirituality—as well as purchase associated products. But these are very specific to a small niche of e-commerce. Does self-actualization play out more broadly for e-consuming?

Self-actualization is the most complex of Maslow's needs to broadly enable online. It is one thing to offer peer-to-peer learning that meets your customers' cognitive needs; it is altogether different to develop holistic experiences that elevate your customers to a higher plane. Yet some companies have begun to play here. In its "Art of Travelling" section, www.vuitton.com presents virtual versions of the Louis Vuitton Travel Notebooks, "available only in exclusive Louis Vuitton shops." The description of the notebooks is as follows:

Louis Vuitton invites you to discover London, New York, Paris, Sydney and Tokyo while leafing through four travel notebooks. Illustrated by different artists, each notebook offers its own style while revealing a personal and colourful vision of monuments, unusual places and scenes of everyday life. Designed to accompany you in the most important cities in the world, these notebooks also provide blank pages for your own thoughts or drawings.

Louis Vuitton realizes that customers who can afford its luxury product line have most likely ascended Maslow's hierarchy of needs beyond survival and safety and that they might be more comfortable thinking about self-actualization or creativity.

Many retailers have learned from the burgeoning self-help industry and have picked up on the self-reflective elements of their brands and product lines. Colors, photos, imagery, sounds, layout, and page densities are chosen to create an inspiring ambiance. Aspirational verbiage is chosen, as in www.tiffany.com "Blue Is the

Color of Dreams" video clip. Product categories like "LifeStyle" or "Reflections" are chosen. Lotions, soaps, and massage oils are added as point-of-purchase items.

How can you use the Internet to further tap into this psychology? Imagery can get you only so far. Everything about the www.tiffany.com is symbolic of questing for enlightenment. Not just the site's outward appearance—the architecture of the site, the motion used, the video clips shown. This site is a masterfully produced experience that makes you feel that buying a Tiffany's product elevates you to a higher level. Martha Stewart built her empire through her higher-order "back to the basics" approach that directly targets the psychological nexus of our aesthetic and self-actualizing needs. Her magazines and television series showed us how to use our own hands to mold a simple yet enriched life. People clipped, filed, and discussed her monthly "good things" articles that offered handy little insights or shortcuts for weaving a beautiful wreath or repairing that old torn shirt. On www.marthastewart.com, she has provided an archive of these lessons complete with "Martha by Mail" links so that you can purchase all of the elements needed to create your own "good things."

You don't have to be Martha Stewart or Tiffany's to achieve an aspirational response from your customers. If you want to trigger this psychological lever, start with your site design. Choose colors, wording, and a clean, uncluttered layout to backdrop your customers' experience so that they feel that a visit to your site is a refreshing retreat from the manic overload of their day.

Rung 8: Transcendence Needs. Transcendence is "to rise above and go beyond the limits of material existence." It is the need of transcendence—the need to see beyond oneself and help others—that many philosophers associate with the human soul. Does this need translate to commerce? Without a doubt. Whether the transcendent needs stem directly from the corporate leaders themselves or are sparked by pressure from customers or employees, successful business enterprises often have a giveback element.

Neighborhood businesses regularly donate to the community by sponsoring community programs like Little League sports teams or leading fund drives. Corporations usually have a community relations department or foundation, many times reporting directly to the CEO, with a percentage of overall profit earmarked for charitable donations.

E-businesses have the same expectations. For example, as of April 2001, "the eBay Foundation had made grants totaling over $2,500,000.00 to over 75 non-profit organizations."[6] It is not just B2Cs. B2B associations often build networking events involving charitable giving. Even a relatively young association like the Association for Interactive Media (AIM) has an annual charity dinner at New York's Russian Tea Room and links its charitable program directly from the front page of its Web site (www.interactivehq.org).

Giving back is expected. It seems to pay off in dividends as well. Fully 76 percent of consumers polled in 1998 said that— assuming no difference in price or quality—they would switch brands to align themselves with a good cause.[7] Both Ben and Jerry's and Odwalla have built loyal customer-communities partly because of their respective corporate commitments to making a social impact.

Charitable giving was a part of Internet culture from the get-go. In an article called "The Business of Philanthropy," Bernadette Burke writes that "the emergence of the charity portal personifies what has also become known as 'social entrepreneurism.' The aim of these sites is to build an online community around people's desire to support a worthy cause."[8] But Internet giving was not relegated to nonprofit portals. E-tailers jumped on the giveback bandwagon in droves, for three reasons:

- Underlying database-driven e-commerce engines make the logistics of carving out a percentage of revenues easy.
- The fact that an e-commerce site is also a blatantly visible marketing program secures broad visibility of one's charitable giving.

- In the market-efficient space of the Internet, e-tailers need all the switching barriers they can create.

TheHungerSite pioneered the "donation per click" strategy. The word-of-mouth (or e-mail-of-hand?) growth of TheHunger-Site in 1999 and 2000 was unprecedented. E-tailing sites followed. Many e-commerce sites let their customers choose personal charities. They believed that customers would be more loyal and possibly even spend more if they knew a piece of their money helped their own selected cause.

The most demonstrative moment of e-giving in the Internet's brief history occurred after the September 11, 2001, World Trade Center and Pentagon terrorist attacks. Within hours after the disaster, most major Web sites had transformed their front pages to enable their customer-communities to donate to the American Red Cross and other major relief charities. The outpouring was so overwhelming that President Bush, in his many speeches during that time, repeatedly referred to Web sites where people could contribute and lauded the U.S. populace for its compassion.

E-commerce transcendence isn't always about money. Sometimes customers just want to help each other out. That is what Cynthia Typaldos, founder of RealCommunities and current president and CEO of Typaldos & Associates, believed when she created the mentoring module of her RealCommunities integrated community infrastructure. Not only did she believe that community members wanted to formally sign up as mentors for other community members, but she also believed that if there were payment associated with this mentoring service, many mentors would choose to have this payment in the form of donations to their favorite charity. Typaldos believed this so strongly that her team spent a lot of extra effort building the technology and relationships with charitable organizations to create this ability. In late 2000, when we both started working for ThirdAge Media, founder Mary Furlong publicly said that she wanted the primary differentiator of the site to be its charitable component—its aspirational and transcendent ambiance.

Furlong believes strongly that as people age, they have a longing to give back.

What about the spiritual side of transcendence online? However you define it, 89 percent of Americans call themselves "spiritual."[9] In a book called *God Talk in America*, Phyllis Tickle describes what might happen when cyberspace meets the spiritual world. At first, she merely compares the mystical and the Internet, trying to draw similarities: "Virtual space is mysterious because it is essentially imaginary."[10] She makes some interesting parallels, but the real provocative element in the book is when she talks about how pervasive online religion is. According to the Barna Research Group, by 2010, somewhere between 10 and 20 percent of all adult Americans will be having their total spiritual experience on the Internet, including not only their worship but also their spiritual instruction.[11] Will this affect customer-communities at all? Almost certainly.

When Blockbuster video was led by H. Wayne Huizenga, it attracted a Christian customer base due to its practice of infusing Christian and family-oriented principles throughout the company, from internal policies to video selection and promotion. In the integrated realm of the Internet, there is a much grander possibility for the integration of spirituality into e-business practices.

Customer-communities, like most communities, will transcend. They will help each other and expect you to give back as well. They will be more loyal to you because of your actions. If empowered, your customers can, like the Bedford Falls community in *It's a Wonderful Life*, pull together to help each other and the service provider who has faithfully and soulfully met their needs.

Maslow Consumers

Let's consider the Maslow's need levels 3, 4, and 5—social, esteem, and cognitive—and map these to a consumer experience. Basically, this means that as consumers, we want to be social—flirt, meet, and bond; we want esteem—to strut, compete, and lead; and we want to know—explore, learn, and validate. Think about it. San Francisco offers an extreme example of this social consumerism dynamic that was highlighted in Armistead Maupin's book *Tales of the City*. The venue is known as the "Social Safeway." People go to this particular grocery store on a particular night to socialize and be seen while buying groceries. Shoppers strut down the aisles; they flirt over canned goods; they share knowledge about seasonings; they exchange recipes. It is a conscious incarnation of a dynamic that is often unconscious or, at least, more subtle. But then again, San Francisco is not a very subtle city.

How does this translate online? Social: flirting, meeting, and bonding. Online attempts at social interaction are very blatant. Come join a chat room. Build a Web page to show others. "Hey, look at this photo of me." In the real world (excluding the "bar scene" way of meeting), some initial stages of social interaction can seem less obvious. This dynamic is even more oblique with regard to a customer-community where social interaction is likely not the primary goal but rather the secondary or tertiary goal. How can you replicate online the subtleties of scanning the crowd of shoppers in a store? What about nonverbal flirting or exchanges? What is the virtual equivalent of "Sorry, I didn't mean to bump into you?"

Nonverbal communication is difficult to replicate on the Web, though there have been attempts. Before it was purchased by eVineyard, Wine.com tried to leverage the social nature of wine consumption. Wine.com was one of the few e-tailers that actually fostered customer connections and leveraged this social behavior into revenue. Customers could join wine clubs to learn about and experience a specific category of wines. By joining a wine club, a customer signed up for periodic purchases of a certain category of wine. For example, the "Wines of France" included monthly wine selections for you to "Taste your way through the vineyards of France while learning about French wine regions and culture." The amount of effort Wine.com spent trying to replicate the social atmosphere of a wine-tasting club is unique. Upon first signing up for a club, a customer received an "introductory package, including a tasting-notes outline, glossary, food and wine pairing information, and an elegant folder or binder for storing your information." The tactile nature of an elegant folder connected the virtual experience back to reality. Each month, the wine was delivered with education materials about the selected wines that could be filed in the club binder. The members of the Wine Club also had the option to create a club discussion group where they could meet each other and discuss their opinions of that month's wine. Note that the joining of the discussion group was not tied in to the entire consuming experience. You didn't have to join a group simply to talk to others who share a common interest. It was merely one optional element. This lowered the intimidation threshold and allowed customers to meet each other without the expectations that are usually heaped on virtual dialogue.

Barnes & Noble offers a few other socially catalyzing tricks. In an attempt to compete with Amazon.com and explore the social dimensions of book buying, Barnes & Noble "has built an online community reflective of the casual reading-room atmosphere its real stores are known for—sans coffee bar and overstuffed chairs."[12] Barnes & Noble does an excellent job tying its virtual activities with its brick-and-mortar storefronts. It has also introduced Barnes & Noble University, offering courses like "Understanding Poetry," where there is the possibility not only to learn about poetry but also to meet other poetry newbies. Of course, this increases the likelihood that Barnes & Noble will sell some poetry books.

Another atmospheric feature is B&N Radio. A customer opens B&N Radio and listens to one of 140 music stations. Music has long been associated with social consumption, which is why so many stores have piped music to enhance the shopping experience. With B&N Radio, a customer can hear a song he or she likes, quickly click over to the CD sales page, peruse what other customers have said about it, and buy it with one click—all while still listening to the song. We can imagine B&N augmenting B&N Radio further to add a live discussion function whereby a listener could hear a song and jump into a discussion about it with others listening to the same B&N Radio station. This is another way Barnes & Noble could provide a social catalyst for connecting its customer-community.

Balancing Customer-Community and Individual Efficiency

How do hard goods and service providers address our individualistic yet social duality? Obviously, we aren't communal consumers all the time; we aren't always looking for a social or soulful interaction when we go shopping. We buy things because we are self-determined. We want our product and service providers to support our individual purchasing choices. We want personalized customization and service. And we want purchasing efficiency so that we don't waste time.

Retailers and service organizations that offer a range of consumer opportunities, from individually customized and efficient to communally interactive and supportive, will appeal to broader spectrums of customers. If those organizations go further to understand and catalyze the synergies between the individual and collective, they will empower the customer-community and engender deeper customer loyalty and support. Boutiques often lodge themselves on a neighborhood street or in a shopping mall to take advantage of associative shopping behavior. But secondarily, their positioning balances the boutique's more intimate or personal shopping experience with the larger group or neighborhood behavioral patterns. Many e-tailers are opening up physical storefronts to create a more localized group consuming experience, and likewise many brick-and-mortar companies have expanded into e-commerce space in an attempt not only to cut real estate and sales costs but also to offer more individualized and efficient consumer experiences.

Imagine a retailer that offered you the ideal combination of individualized service and social interactivity. You would be greeted upon entering the store—but only if you wanted to be greeted. The greeter would know as much or as little about you as you wanted to reveal. He would assist you or not, depending on your mood at the time. If your mood changed in the middle of the shopping experience, he would know, but only if you wanted him to know. If you wanted, this assistant would know from your purchase history items in the store that may interest you. He would collect and showcase these items for your purview only. You could interact with the other shoppers with whom you choose to mingle. You might simply chat with them, or you could ask them for their recommendations. If the retailer didn't have what you wanted, the assistant would recommend other retailers who carried the item. You would get discounts and additional services based on your previous buying pattern and your reputation as a valued customer. This reputation would take into account online activity, storefront activity, and any activity with partner product or service providers.

"Activity" would include not only purchases but also referrals to other customers and feedback that helped improve the customer experience. You could influence future service or merchandising simply by giving feedback. You would be rewarded for giving such feedback. Logistics for purchasing and shipping your items would be minimal. If you wanted, your assistant would unobtrusively contact you if an item that you liked went on sale or a new item came in that he thought you would like. Each time you returned, your assistant would know you better—to the extent you wanted him to—and you would trust him more. You could visit your assistant in an actual storefront, call your assistant on the telephone, or have your assistant guide you online. You could, once again, mingle with other familiar customers and meet other new customers. You and other frequent customers could become friends; you would trust their recommendations more and possibly pursue the friendship apart from the joint consumer experience. The purchase logistics would get easier and easier with each return visit. You would feel a sense of comfort and possibly community each time your entered the consumer space. And if all you wanted to do was get in, get what you wanted, and get out—you could do that too.

For most of us, the ideal consumer experience is a blend of customized service and social interaction. The more customized the service, the richer the social interaction, the better the consumer experience, the more loyal the customer. Obviously your customer-community will evolve over time.

The Evolving Needs of Virtual Communities

The first Web browser, Mosaic, was introduced in late 1993. The Web may be the fastest technological transformation in history. Computer-networked virtual communities, a bit older, date back to the early 1970s. Even the oldest Internet virtual community is thirty-something; most are not even ten years old. That is relatively young as communities go. Have you ever been in a community over a period of time and been a part of the changing needs and the community enrichment that comes with longevity and shared context? In most parts of the world, there are communities that have been around for centuries—cities, religions, extended families. These communities have grown, matured, backslid, and transformed over their many years of existence. The faces and players may change, but they share a rich community tapestry steeped in history. Contrast this with relatively new communities, and it becomes clear that the driving factor behind communal needs and the ability to meet these needs does not simply lie in the breadth and infrastructure of the community. As today's young virtual communities mature, their history and shared context will come as much into play as abilities enabled by the site on which they commune.

Stay aware of your customer-community's changing needs. Continue to morph with them over time. Build in history and tradition to reflect the community's heritage. The richness of your customer-community culture will grow over time, as will the strength of the community bond and the resulting customer loyalty.

Summary

As you look at this short evolution of Web sites and the infrastructure that we've designed, it's as if the capabilities of Web sites have grown over the years to aid us in meeting each level of our needs. As Web sites have become more complex and more valuable, they have naturally met some of the basic needs we have as customers. We needed access, speed, and a high level of comfort that our transactions and comments were secure. We have been able to meet, socialize, contribute, and be recognized as valued contributors. We have access to a vast virtual library. Internet architects have implemented varying gradations of order and aestheticism. We have e-questioned and e-learned. We post reviews, help newcomers, and patronize charitable sites. We have climbed Maslow's virtual ladder. As this eight-rung hierarchy has given us a framework to explore the fulfillment of human needs online, so does the rich history of real-life communities provide us with a guidebook for virtual community development. (Your e-presence can inspire and catalyze community or not. If it does, we do not mean to imply that you will need to satisfy all eight of Maslow's levels of your customer-community's needs. You may choose to focus on the bottom three, most basic requirements: physical, safety, and social. Or you may skip a rung offering a transcendent giveback element without a robust self-actualization component of your site. This is okay. Your customer-community will find various paths to achieve the totality of their needs. It is simply important that you understand these ascending needs and how each helps further strengthen the community bond.) In the next chapter, we will detail twelve underlying principles of community building and examine how they affect various customer-community approaches.

Part Two

Customer-Community Basics

Chapter Three

Twelve Principles
for Building Community

What makes a community? Do communities form naturally and organically, or does an organizer need to catalyze and influence? Or both? Community building has been studied since the beginning of sociological and theological analysis. Many experts have researched and deconstructed the communities that have emerged as human societies evolved. We have already shown the inherent social components underscoring Maslow's hierarchy of needs. Community fundamentals are also intrinsic to various other recent business trends.

For years, Margaret Wheatley and Myron Kellner-Rogers have urged corporations to consider the science behind human dynamics and the effect of systems theory on organizational behavior. The relatively new corporate adoption of system dynamics has led to an understanding of communities of practice and various leadership styles that build on concepts of community empowerment and service. The servant leadership model popularized by Robert K. Greenleaf, former AT&T executive, is one good example. What Greenleaf calls legitimate power and greatness in business or any large collective stems from a leadership behavior that serves others. The power of institutions, he says, is more powerful if it also has the ability to catalyze small communities within them.[1] All these experts agree on some basic building blocks for a successful community. They may differ on some principles or their relative importance, but most speak the same core language with respect to elements like communication, trust, and governance—the classic community basics.

The evolution of communication media through the decades has interwoven the dynamics of sociology and community. How did the telephone augment community bonding? What about radio—did it connect individuals with similar interests? Were geographically isolated communities better able to understand and participate more fully in the national community? Did television isolate the individual and replace social interactions essential to a healthy community? Communication technologies have had important sociological effects, but it wasn't until the early 1970s that intercomputer communication gave birth to the concept of the virtual community. Network technologies have created a connective tissue yielding potential benefits far greater than individual efficiency. The result is an exponential network effect that we will explore in depth in Chapter Five.

As these new electronic communities formed, many adventurers explored and noted the similarities and differences between the virtual and nonvirtual realms. Usenet and The Well were rich environments for experimentation. In 1993, Howard Rheingold wrote *The Virtual Community*, presenting his observations and learning during these formative years. Since the widespread adoption of the Internet and the financial community's early interest in virtual communities, the amount of analysis dedicated to the subject has been dramatic. Most analysts have discovered that the sociological and theological underpinnings of community remain unchanged, virtual or not. Certain limitations and new capabilities in the virtual realm have sparked e-community nuances—including the anonymous lurker and the antiestablishment technolibertarian—which have been analyzed ad nauseam. But the key here is that the underlying principles remain the same.

The Twelve Principles

Since it is important to have a cursory understanding of the building blocks of community, we will take a detailed look at twelve underlying principles of community building championed by Cynthia Typaldos, founder and former CEO of RealCommunities (www.realcommunities.com), an integrated Web community infrastructure provided by Mongoose Technologies. These principles are purpose, identity, reputation, governance, communication, groups, environment, boundaries, trust, exchange, expression, and history.[2]

Purpose: Raison d'Être, Communal Bonding, Cocreation

"Community performs a necessary and useful function for members."[3]

A shared purpose is the *raison d'être* of a community. Some communities, like families and neighborhoods, have an implied purpose from situational relationships. Others need to be more explicit about defining their common interests.

Customer-communities by their very nature have an implicit shared interest relating to commerce with a particular business. "Commerce" as an overarching shared purpose may be too general to achieve the bonding necessary for sustained customer loyalty. The more granular the purpose, the stronger the *communal bond*. Are customers interested in peer-to-peer product support or in trading best practices? Do they want to meet like-minded shoppers or simply discover the best deals? A great way to find out is to engage them in defining this purpose.

Community *cocreation* of a central purpose is a very powerful bonding agent. As Cynthia Typaldos, states, "The collaborative purpose is one of the Web's major strengths as a means of building community. Implementing purpose together drives stickiness and generates increasing network effects."[4]

Identity: Dynamic Profiling, Personalization, Membership

"Members can identify each other and build relationships."

Each of us wants to be recognizable as a unique individual. We want to identify others as well. Most commerce-oriented institutions have long understood the importance of the individual customer and already have a customer-tracking or customer relationship management system (CRMS) in place. The next step is to build a *dynamic profiling* functionality where data are constantly being captured on each customer who interacts with the site. *Personalization* goes even one step beyond and extends the profiling capability directly into the customer's hands. Since GeoCities and "My Yahoo!" brought to light the power of personalization, Web sites have invested much effort in ensuring that customers can mold an experience to meet their needs. E-individuals want e-individuality—partly because of personal efficiency and partly because of personal identity. Both the customer and the marketing department benefit.

For years, the airline and credit card industries have employed commerce-centric *membership*. The Internet has facilitated registration and tracking so that far more organizations can implement membership programs. But simply because the logistics are easier, don't underestimate the complexity of a membership strategy that creates true loyalty and is a win-win situation for both the company and the customer.

Reputation: Ego, Status, Individual and Collective Esteem

"Members have reputations based on their activity and the expressed opinions of others."

Individuals require *status* as a means to demarcate themselves from each other and as a way to build *esteem*. If a community member earns a positive status from her peers, she feeds her own *ego* while advancing a positive community reputation. This public reputation not only benefits the individual community member but all other community members wishing to interact with her. eBay has demonstrated the importance of reputation for peer-to-peer online commerce.

In most communities, there is also the element of *collective esteem*. Some people join communities specifically because of the esteem that comes from being part of a group. This can be a powerful bonding agent. In customer-communities, the concept of collective esteem does not have the potential strength that it does in traditional communities, but it can still be powerful. Some companies can achieve intense loyalty if their products are associated with a collective pride or association. Consider the international market share Levi's has sustained from its reputation as *the* American clothing company.

Governance: Bylaws, Leadership, "Chaordic" Balance

"The facilitators and members of the community assign management duties to each other, allowing the community to grow. Members agree that their behavior can be regulated according to shared or stated values."

Every community has some governing structure, stated or unstated. Otherwise it is doomed to being ineffectual at best and destructive at worst. The governance may be imposed or self-determined; it may be hierarchical or egalitarian; it may be permanent or fluid. Even if the community is extremely organic, some structure will emerge to enable the community to function. *Bylaws* should be established by which community members are encouraged or forced to abide. This structure may be as simple as netiquette rules of interaction or as rigid as restrictions on discussions or activities. Various virtual community experts espouse varying degrees of ideal governance structure. Though we believe that in most cases, the purpose and makeup of the membership should dictate the governance structure, the most sustainable communities achieve a *"chaordic" balance*—a kind of order within chaos—that promotes just enough order to enable unfettered but healthy organic growth.

The *leadership* of the community may be preestablished and maintained by the parent company, or there may be leadership opportunities for customer-community members. Whatever the strategy, the codification and enforcement of this structure is critical to sustaining a functioning community.

Communication: Synchronous and Asynchronous Communication Tools, Proximity and Offline Activities, Advocacy

"Members must be able to interact with each other, to share information and ideas."

Pioneering sociologist Robert Morrison MacIver noted in 1937, "Without communication there can be no community, and the life of the community revolves around the points where communication is most intense."[5] The early years of virtual community experimentation focused on communication. Many early "community sites" believed all that was needed to build community was the critical triad of *communication tools*—discussion boards, e-mail, and chat. This trio has indeed provided an interactive foundation for virtual communities. But the myopic attention toward communication technologies has overshadowed a broader understanding of the communication requirements of any community.

Community members need to communicate with each other and as a collective. They need to communicate in real time (*synchronously*), and they need to leave messages for later response (*asynchronously*). They need to communicate one to one and in small groups. They also need to broadcast messages to the entire community easily. Understanding the various permutations of required communication for groups is important. You must map communication strategies to those requirements. Since communication technologies are far from replicating the complex breadth and depth of communication that occurs in a real-life setting, customer-communities should consider integrating *offline activities* and communication opportunities. *Geographically proximate* local customer-communities still have an advantage here.

The same communication technologies that have powered intracommunity dialogue have also given virtual communities an extremely powerful collective voice. *Advocacy*, positive or negative, is one of the most significant and visible strengths of a unified customer-community. Honoring and leveraging positive advocacy and thwarting negative advocacy could be the sole argument for a company's investing in its customer-community program.

Groups: Segmentation, Microcommunities, Hierarchy, Threaded Dialogue

"Community members can segment themselves according to specific interests or tasks. Members can relate to each other in small numbers."

As any living system grows, it needs to subdivide. A growing embryo's cells divide; cities add subdivisions; growing organizations departmentalize. One of the major challenges for growing communities has always been sustaining a *hierarchy* of *microcommunities* under a broader connective umbrella. For example, consider political activism: How is a neighborhood organization tied to city legislation tied to the state tied to the federal government? Groups within groups within groups.

Customer-communities are no different. Communities interested in women's apparel are usually different from those interested in men's apparel. Mountain climbers don't care to understand the latest advancements in fishing attire. Luckily, there has been much experimentation with virtual community *segmentation*. In fact, the ease of subgrouping and *threaded dialogue* (an electronic way to chronicle multiperson conversations that take place over a span of time) differentiates virtual communities from nonvirtual ones. The ability to subdivide quickly while remaining threaded to the overarching community allows virtual communities to scale much faster and more cohesively than their offline counterparts. But large layered virtual communities can be overwhelming, disjointed, and difficult to navigate. Like an urban planner, a virtual community architect should anticipate potential growth and subdivision and design an appropriately accommodating environment.

Environment: Architecture, Navigation, Infrastructure, Seamless Integration

"A synergistic environment helps members achieve their purpose."

Community members need to understand how to navigate easily through their environmental backdrop to accomplish their purpose. If the environment is too complex, confusing, or disjointed, the community will suffer. If microcommunities aren't clearly linked to the parent community, people may lose interest. For example, the clearer the understanding of how local neighborhood activism influences city legislation, the easier it is for neighborhood communities to recruit people who will become actively involved. If you know that your effort can effect change, you are more likely to join a neighborhood association.

It's the same in virtual communities. The clearer and easier it is to accomplish a virtual community goal, the easier it is to attract and retain members. For a virtual customer-community, this means a *seamless integration* of e-commerce, customer service, and intra-community areas of a company's Internet presence. It means complete integration of all communication technologies. It means an intuitive architecture that guides the customer and reflects every step of the customer experience so that all options are clear and accessible.

Far too often, e-commerce and e-community sites create distinct boundaries between commerce and community. Commerce is one place; community, another. This would be like a department store that created distinct areas for socializing but forced customers apart while they were shopping. Separating environments will reinforce separate behaviors—minglers won't shop; shoppers won't mingle.

Creating an integrated environment is an *architectural, navigational,* and *infrastructural* challenge. Without an integrated technology foundation, this challenge can be daunting. It would be like the days before Microsoft Office when we tried to get a WordPerfect document to integrate with a Lotus spreadsheet or a Persuasion presentation. The hyperlinking nature of the Internet facilitates integration so that even if you choose separate technologies, an intuitive environment is not impossible. But simple links back and forth aren't enough; this interweaving must be more intrinsic and intuitive.

Boundaries: Clarity, Permeability, Exclusivity

"The community knows why it exists and who is outside and inside."

Seamless does not mean boundaryless. Resolute and *permeable boundaries* should be *clearly represented*. Membership programs often have many participation levels, from general to exclusive. *Exclusivity* is not exclusive if the boundaries are not distinct and enforced. Also, microcommunities need to feel comfortable that they have their own "space." Subcommunity activities should be clearly delineated from the broader community.

Instead of letting technology dictate the walls of the community boundaries, customer-community architects should, like housing architects, create necessary boundaries for space distribution and flow that achieve the appropriate combination of intimacy and openness.

Trust: Security, Privacy, Accountability

"Members must be able to build trust over time with other members and the community facilitators. Members know with whom they are dealing and that it is safe to do so."

If trust doesn't exist within a community, it will quickly stagnate, die, or even rebel against the parent company. There are two critical trust relationships—trust between the customer-community and the parent company and trust between community members themselves. Because there is a hierarchical relationship between company and customer, this trust is more difficult to achieve and more fragile to sustain. Companies, like governments, must continually prove their trustworthiness. Any slip can be fatal. Deceive or manipulate one customer, and you risk alienating an entire customer-community.

Sell your customers' personal data without their consent, and you'll never regain their trust.

Another word of caution here—don't pretend that the vendor-customer relationship is egalitarian. It isn't, and the customer knows it. But the customer has the power to walk away at any moment. Company representatives must do everything in their power to respect this relationship. *Security* must always remain a top priority. When possible, communication should be personal and attributed. Companies should hold themselves *accountable* to all customer-communications and to whatever customer contract they have crafted.

The customer-community must also have a way to build trust among its members. In general, this trust will build naturally over time, but you should consider the appropriate environment to engender such trust. Community rules, regulations, and *privacy policies* should be posted and enforced. Companies need to determine when to allow anonymity and when to require identification as well as which elements of a customer's profile are public and which are private.

Exchange: Peer-to-Peer Commerce, Advice and Support, Affiliation, Incubation

"The community recognizes an exchange of value, from knowledge and ideas to goods and services. Members can easily indicate their preferences and opinions."

Exchange is central in a community, especially in a customer-community that forms for the primary purpose of commerce. Customer-community members want value from their membership. In a social community, value may be in the form of friendship or intellectual camaraderie, but in a customer-community, value is more hard-edged, consisting of such things as advice, insight, or financial incentives.

Exchangeable value will vary between customer-communities. In the eBay community, exchange is clearly *peer-to-peer commerce.*

For Fool.com, it is financial *advice*. For the HP Information Technology customer-community, value primarily takes the form of product *support*. Some sites have incorporated *affiliate programs*; some sites have *incubated customer businesses*. Most sites have a variety of exchange opportunities. It is important for the customer-community to understand what is valuable to its customers and build exchange opportunities around these "currencies."

Expression: Personality, Design, Voice, Activity

"The community has a recognizable character and community; members are aware of what other community members are doing."

Why do we join a community? We may share a common goal or interest with a specific community but choose not to join it. We may resonate with specific community members but choose individual relationships rather than community involvement. We may even go to one community meeting and decide that it is not right for us. What influences that decision?

It is the *personality* and vibrancy of the community that attracts community members. For an Internet community, there are many elements that determine this personality. The *design* of the site, the balance of activities, and the tone of the content are three important ones. A community should be developed in such a way that it reflects its essence, its soul. Colors and images should be carefully chosen. Any published statements or documents should reflect the community *voice*. The *activity* within the site should be easily discernable so that members can sense the "energy" of the community. A potential member surfing a virtual community site should be able to immediately determine personal attraction for a community by the expression of the community's character inherent in all elements of the site design.

The customer's perception of a company has a key influence on the company's success. This is why many companies invest so much in crafting—or transforming—a particular image. When companies attempt to change their image, they may redefine their product line, redesign store layouts, and rework any element that is important to reflect the new image. Community expression is the same. Customers will be attracted and join a customer-community if they perceive an active, like-minded group of people with whom they can interact or exchange value.

History: Shared Context, Culture, Tradition

"The community remembers what has happened and reacts and changes in response."

Shared context, culture, and tradition are the bases for many real-life communities. Consider families, lifelong friendships, and ethnic and religious affinities. A tapestry of relationship woven over time creates a bonding force simply by the nature and richness of its history.

For some customer-communities, history is not a very important element, though it can sometimes come into play. Companies that sell cultural or religious products can leverage the tradition affinity among their customer base. Some companies present their longevity ("Faithfully serving our customers since 1947") as a way to entice those wooed by historical precedent. Others detail the history of their product offering ("Our recipes date back to 1890"). Finally some companies have retained the same customer-community long enough for them to regale in shared history. Because of the pace of technological change, some technology companies can achieve historically based bonding faster than those in slower-paced industries. For example, members of Apple Computer's customer-community can and do bond over their shared experiences using Apple's relatively short evolution of personal computers, from the Lisa to the iMac.

The Internet facilitates historical documentation and archiving. New community members can trace threaded dialogues back to their inception. Longtime community members segment themselves into an "old-timer" or veteran microcommunity. Community managers can easily present historical timelines with details that provoke nostalgia. History may not be important for all customer-communities, but for those in which it is, Internet technologies make archiving much easier than storing and accessing clunky, unmarked boxes in a closet.

Mapping Community-Building Principles to Virtual Communities

Since ARPAnet connected the first two e-mailers, these community principles have lit the way. The Usenet community quickly developed an ability to communicate via threaded dialogue and allowed users to establish their identities with representative and quirky usernames. They built reputations based on the frequency and tone of their postings. The Well was masterful at exploring the intricacies of self-governance and experimented with cocreating the rules of engagement. The Well's members were constantly queried about what dictated appropriate virtual communal behavior.

As specialty community sites began to emerge, the social concept of an "overarching purpose" came into question. Did The Well have a strong enough purpose? Was AOL's primary purpose as an ISP strong enough to sustain a community? If a large community's microcommunities were specific, did it matter? AOL had a gay and lesbian community area, so was there a need for a PlanetOut with an overarching purpose to serve this community? Was Yahoo!'s purpose as the Net's premier search portal strong enough to sustain its community membership? Did forum-enabled microcommunities have a strong enough say in the direction of the overall site? Or did microcommunity members completely separate from the parent community, forming their own site or joining another community with an overarching purpose more in line with their needs? Could a demographic community site like ThirdAge.com sustain a community if its overarching purpose (as a site for baby boomers) didn't really draw people together? How many people hang out with each other simply because they were born around the same time? Could a community's purpose be flexible enough to morph as the interest of its members changed? As ThirdAge's community members grew older, would the purpose of the site change to reflect their changing needs? These have been the social challenges of communities since the beginning of humankind. The Internet is simply a new sandbox.

In the Internet's relatively short life span, Web community experts have begun to translate these principles into concrete guidelines. In *Community Building on the Web,* Amy Jo Kim presents the following tactical blueprint for virtual community builders:

- Define and articulate your purpose.
- Build flexible, extensible gathering places.
- Create meaningful and evolving member profiles.
- Design for a range of roles.
- Develop a strong leadership program.
- Encourage appropriate etiquette.
- Promote cyclical events.
- Integrate the rituals of community life.
- Facilitate member-run subgroups.[6]

In a *Business 2.0* article, "Talk Is Cheap. And Good for Sales Too," Brian Caulfield recommends six rules for successful communities:[7]

- Define your goals.
- Start simple.
- Don't put marketing in charge.
- Allow users to express their points of view.
- Answer posts within twenty-four hours.
- Reward your posters.

Yet with all the attention and analysis, in the scheme of community building, virtual communities are very, very young. Much has yet to be learned. It's important to note, though, that a solid foundation honed over centuries is in place. Even though there is and will be variance from e-community to e-community, some elements will remain constant—clarity of purpose, individual identity, clear leadership, multifaceted communication, and the ability to subdivide into microcommunities. The important thing to keep in mind is that community is based on tenets, not technology. Understand your customer-community dynamic and then apply design, infrastructure, and management to support it.

Summary

Today's customer-community architects have a hefty guidebook constructed from two decades of customer-centric business trends, age-old fundamental community-building principles, and a sea of Web communities built during the Internet boom years. In addition, there are a number of initial customer-communities from which to learn.

In the next three chapters, we will showcase many examples of various customer-community approaches. As you will see, some initial steps that have a big potential payoff are relatively easy to take. They may be as simple as opening up a customer-to-customer-communication channel and paying attention to the customer-community that forms naturally within your current customer base. Then you can choose whether you want to go further to build an even stronger, more loyal, more collaborative customer-community that partners with you for the success of your business.

Chapter Four

Customer-Community Profiles

In this chapter, we group thirty-five of our most important cases into categories to provide an overview of customer-communities in action. Our ten categories are not meant to be comprehensive but rather to provide a lens through which to view the case studies. We present this aggregation to trigger your thinking about the wide array of customer-community applications that might work in your business. Note that our assignment of a company to a certain category is not intended to suggest that it exemplifies only that category. Most companies that have engaged their customer-communities have done so in a multidimensional manner. Our groupings are merely intended to make it easier to see specific customer-community principles in action.

Figure 4.1 provides a bird's-eye view of our ten categories, including the thirty-five representative companies cross-referenced to the twelve community principles detailed in Chapter Three and defined in Figure 4.2. We will build on these examples throughout the book.

Premier Customer-Communities

eBay, Amazon.com

Trust, Reputation, Integration, Infrastructure

Amazon.com and eBay lead our case study pack due to the innovative and comprehensive ways they both foster customer-communities. Amazon.com, the renowned virtual bookstore turned virtual department store, seamlessly weaves customer-community throughout

Figure 4.1 Customer-Community Pioneers

	1 Purpose	2 Identity	3 Reputation	4 Governance	5 Communication	6 Groups	7 Environment	8 Boundaries	9 Trust	10- Exchange	11 Expression	12 History
Premier Customer-Communities												
eBay	1	1	1*	1	2	1	1	1	1	1	1	3
Amazon.com	1	2	2	3	3	2	1*	2	2	1	3	3
Early Virtual Communities												
Usenet	2	1	2	2	2	1	3	2	2	2	1	1
The Well	3	1	1	1	1	1	2	1	2	2	1*	1
CompuServe	3	1	2	1	1	1	1	2	2	3	2	2
GeoCities	2	1	2	2	2	1	2	1	2	2	2	2
Portal Communities												
AOL	2	1	2	1*	1	1	2	1	2	2	2	2
Yahoo!	3	2	3	3	1	3	1	3	3	3	3	3
About.com	2	1	1	1	2	1*	1	2	1	1	2	3
Local Customer-Communities												
craigslist	1	1*	2	2	2	1	2	1	2	1	1	1
Mary Kay Cosmetics	1	3	3	3	3	3	2	3	1	1	3	3
Retail Customer-Communities												
Barnes & Noble	1	2	2	3	2	2	1	2	2	1	3	3
REI	1	1	3	3	2	2	2	1	1	1	2	2
Abercrombie & Fitch	1	3	3	3	3	3	2	3	3	1	2	3
Advisory Customer-Communities												
The Motley Fool	1	1	1	2	1*	1	1	1	2	1	1	2
E*Trade	1	1	1	2	2	1	1	1	2	1	1	2
Charles Schwab	1	3	3	1	3	1	3	3	1	2	3	3
Ask Jeeves	1	1	1	2	2	1	2	1	2	2	2	2
drkoop.com	1	1	1	2	2	1	2	1	1	1*	2	2

Customer "Cults"

	1	2	3	4	5	6	7	8	9	10	11
Apple	1	2	2	1	1	1	1	1	1	1	1
Odwalla	3	3	3	3	3	3	3	1	3	3	1
Palm	1	2	2	2	2	2	1	2	2	2	2
Electronic Arts (ea.com)	1	1	2	1	1	2	1	2	1	1	1
Zippo	2	2	3	3	2	2	3	3	2	2	1*

Unlikely Communities

	1	2	3	4	5	6	7	8	9	10	11
MCI (Friends and Family)	1	3	3	3	3	3	3	2	1	2	3
Saturn	3	3	3	3	3	3	3	3	2	2	3
Holiday Inn	2	1	3	3	3	3	3	3	1	3	3
Safeway	2	3	3	3	3	2	3	3	1	3	3

Peer-to-Peer Customer Service

	1	2	3	4	5	6	7	8	9	10	11
Hewlett-Packard (ITRC)	1	1	1	2	1	2	1	1*	1	1	1
Oracle	1	2	2	1	1	1	1	2	1	1	1

Professional Marketplaces and Business-to-Business Communities

	1	2	3	4	5	6	7	8	9	10	11
Monster.com	1*	1	2	1	1	1	1	1	1	1	2
ELance	1	2	2	2	2	2	2	1	1	1	2
VerticalNet	1	2	2	2	1	1	1*	1	1	1	2
BizLand	1	2	2	1	1	1	1	1	1	1	2
IBM	1	2	2	2	1	1	1	2	1	1	1
PeopleSoft	1	2	2	2	1	1	1	2	1	1	1

Notes: Numbers indicate to what level each site has integrated the specified community-building principle: 1 = high, 2 = medium, 3 = low.

* Identifies the best example for the community-building element indicated. See Figure 4.2 for a description of why each site was chosen as the representative example.

Figure 4.2 The Twelve Principles of Civilization: Definitions and Example Sites

1. Purpose	Community performs a necessary and useful function for members.	Monster.com's purpose is not only obvious to the general audience, but there is a prominent "First Timers Start Here" button that more clearly describes Monster to newcomers.
2. Identity	Members can identify each other and build relationships.	When posting to a craigslist message board, the member is directed to give specific details. This rigor creates much richer identities within the craigslist community.
3. Reputation	Members have reputation based on their activity and the expressed opinions of others.	eBay pioneered peer-to-peer commerce reputation building through aggregating customer and seller approval ratings.
4. Governance	The facilitators and members of the community assign management duties to each other, allowing the community to grow. Members agree that their behavior can be regulated according to shared or stated values.	AOL has paved the governance way by defining a community leadership structure that includes both volunteers and paid community leaders.
5. Communication	Members must be able to interact with each other, to share information and ideas.	Threaded dialogue ability was so important to The Motley Fool that it built its own message board infrastructure.
6. Groups	Community members can segment themselves according to specific interests or tasks. Members can relate to each other in small numbers.	About.com's topical index is one of the most sophisticated nested group structures on the Internet.

7. Environment	A synergistic environment helps members achieve their purpose.	Amazon.com's environment is so integrated that there is seamless flow from perusal to purchase.
8. Boundaries	The community knows why it exists and who is outside and inside.	Each of VerticalNet's marketplaces has its own completely separate, independent Web site that is simply linked in to the VerticalNet main site.
9. Trust	Members must be able to build trust over time with other members and the community facilitators. Members know with whom they are dealing and that it is safe to do so.	The Hewlett-Packard Information Technology Resource Center (HP ITRC) customer-community problem-solving forums yield trust not only because of the peer-level interaction but also because responses that have been validated as correct are indicated with a "magic answer" icon.
10. Exchange	The community recognizes an exchange of value, from knowledge and ideas to goods and services. Members can easily indicate their preferences and opinions.	drkoop.com's members understand that their medical insight can be of great value to others—so much so that drkoop.com elevates "A Day in My Life" member stories, which are first person accounts of what it is like to live with a condition or disease.
11. Expression	The community has a recognizable character, and members are aware of what other community members are doing.	The Well has a distinct sense of place. Its "About" section describes an "online gathering place like no other—remarkably uninhibited, intelligent, and iconoclastic."
12. History	The community remembers what has happened and reacts and changes in response.	Zippo.com's "About" section details the rich Zippo legacy from the founder to the Zippo lighter timeline to the history of the "Zippo Car."

everything it does. eBay, the online auction and marketplace site, embeds elements derived directly from fundamental community-building principles.

eBay is a customer-community natural. Collectors are community folk. Their similar interests are extremely well defined. They scour thrift stores, go to auctions, are the first to arrive at garage sales, and travel back roads just in case there's an unenlightened homeowner with and old shed or barn full of valuable collectibles. They know each other. They commune. At flea markets, they chat at sunrise while waiting for the coffee wagon to open. They exchange small talk with their favorite vendors. They discuss *Antiques Road Show*. One unique attribute of this tight community is that its central purpose is commerce. There may be no clearer online example of a group of consumers who interact collectively as members of a community.

In September 1995, when eBay decided to open its virtual doors, there was an understanding that it was catering to a customer-community rather than individual customers. eBay used this awareness to develop an advanced *infrastructure* that addresses some of the problematic issues in a commerce-oriented community. While most e-communities were concerned solely with the critical triad of communication tools (e-mail, message boards, and chat), eBay focused on the issue of how to create *trust* within a virtual peer-to-peer commerce environment. eBay has addressed this issue with a rating system that builds a public profile of the seller. How obvious, you may say to yourself. In truth, it was neither obvious nor easy; yet its beauty lies in the fact that it appears to be so intuitive. Sites all over the Web that deal with peer-to-peer exchange have now mimicked these *reputation*-building techniques. eBay challenged other virtual communities to think about more than communication tools. With its expansion of infrastructure, services, and the business landscape, eBay has continued to evolve beyond its online auction roots to build the premier customer-to-customer marketplace on the Web. For example, until eBay acquired Half.com, one of the Internet's fastest-growing peer-based secondhand or discount bazaars, eBay commerce had been primarily collectible auctioning and negotiated pricing. With Half.com, eBay augmented its customer-community by adding a new ability for fixed-priced, mass-market, peer-to-peer commerce. According to Mary Lou Song, former senior manager of community strategy at eBay, "We have a process that really involves working with our community to create a vibrant marketplace, and we stick to it faithfully. It is good for business and it is good for our users."[1]

Amazon.com publicly opened shop just two months prior to eBay. Why its founders chose to invest so much in virtual community practices and infrastructure is not as obvious. For the most part, virtual bookselling is not a community-oriented business. There may be some small precedent for community book buying. Certainly there are book buyers who shop in local bookstores, who spend hours browsing shelves for the book that will be the perfect read for a rainy Saturday. There are also book owners who form book clubs and discuss character flaws and plot lines in groups. Many local bookstores have played directly into this community book-buying psychology by creating a warm and cozy atmosphere that is inviting to the meandering bookworm. But that is a small subset of the book-buying community. Bookselling these days is a volume business. The obvious advantage of online bookselling is not virtual community; it is expanded customer reach, price competitiveness, and efficient distribution.

While eBay propelled its customer-community with peer-to-peer exchange, Amazon.com led with an inclusive, intimate approach to customer service. From the start, Amazon.com embraced its customer base as a part of the extended Amazon.com family. In fact, as Amazon.com attempts its challenging low-price-point volume business model, it subtly weaves community into everything it does. It has built a comprehensive backbone that fully *integrates* virtual community elements, from peer advice to subtle product advocacy. From enabling customers to share book reviews with each other to a customer service organization that has led the way in personalized electronic service, Amazon.com's community elements are so subtle that most Amazon.com customers, unlike eBay customers, probably do not consider themselves part of a community. Yet they have their favorite reviewers. They pay attention when Amazon.com entices additional purchases by showcasing what similar customers have bought. They read Amazon.com's Listmania! which highlights recommendations by random customers. They may go first to Amazon.com before barnesandnoble.com or borders.com.

It is this fluid integration of the customer-community that sets Amazon.com apart from other online retailers. In the last couple of years, many e-commerce sites have copied Amazon.com's customer-community techniques. Will its business model be strong enough to weather the competition? Will it stay around and continue to innovate, creating customer-community norms that other e-tailers emulate? The jury is still out, but Amazon.com has single-handedly changed online commerce regardless.

Early Virtual Communities

Usenet, The Well, CompuServe, GeoCities
Threaded Dialogue, Web Community Craze

The virtual community was founded long before the mid-1990s explosion of the Internet. From the early 1970s to the early 1990s, members of Usenet, The Well, CompuServe, Prodigy, and a handful of other electronic communication networks basically architected the *threaded dialogue* landscape that still today sustains communication within virtual communities. This rich experimentation in virtual group dialogue was the basis for discussion board technology. These communities explored self-governance, created netiquette norms of virtual interaction, contrasted moderated and nonmoderated discussions, experimented with appropriate thresholds of microcommunity segmentation, and perfected interfaces that enabled members to intuitively navigate the complex, three-dimensional virtual communication expanse. These pioneers brought into being a new form of human interaction. They provided varying degrees and depths of conversation threading within a vast number of discussion groups, each with multiple levels of subgroup segmentation.

And then came the Web. GeoCities was one of the earliest notable communities that started out first on the Web (that is, it didn't migrate to the Web from a virtual bulletin board). In 1994, GeoCities was founded with a unique offering that enabled its members to build their own personal pages.[2] The dramatically swift membership growth of GeoCities was a significant driver for the financial community's backing of the myriad of community sites that sprang up in the mid- and late 1990s. It was Yahoo!'s 1998 purchase of GeoCities in a stock deal worth about $3.5 billion and $1 billion in options that shifted the *Web community craze* into high gear, a period that lasted until mid-2000, when valuation metrics turned away from membership and toward profitability. Portals and niche sites of all shapes and sizes sprouted and claimed to be "the one-stop shop on the Web" for whatever it was they were offering. You name it, there was a community Web site for it—and usually a dot-com company started to support it.

Portal Communities

AOL, Yahoo!, About.com
"Need"-Based Communities, Microcommunities, Community Leadership, Virtual Volunteers and Employees, Community Ghettos, Relinquishing Control

In the mid-1990s, the portal path became one of the roads most traveled for Internet entrepreneurs. Sparked by the Yahoo! phenomenon and the inflation of portal valuations, new portals were introduced left and right. There were community portals centered around demographics (Women.com, MyPrimeTime, PlanetOut, Bolt), around communication tools (Ecircles, Egroups), around specific interests (for photography, Zing; for genealogy: Genealogy.com; for spirituality, Beliefnet); there were community portals created around just about any hobby, pastime, or characteristic that would compel people to come together. Many of these sites, due mostly to unprofitable business models, have been folded into other companies or have disappeared altogether. But during their tenure, much was learned about virtual community building. In this book, we refer to various community portals to showcase important community attributes. Three that have made significant contributions to the world of e-business are AOL, Yahoo!, and About.com.

AOL is a unique portal because the central purpose of the community is a revenue-generating service that has evolved in most global societies from a luxury to an amenity to a *need*. With AOL's Internet Service Provider (ISP) subscription foundation, AOL has a commerce cornerstone and subsequent leg up on other community portals. From its inception in 1985, AOL basically happened into community through its communication technologies, around which members began to aggregate. As the AOL community grew, AOL began to experiment with various ways to sustain and manage the community. AOL perfected the ability for communities to naturally segment into *microcommunities*. AOL also experimented with community empowerment, with a leadership structure that consists of *volunteers* and paid *community leaders*. Through AOL's costly discovery (several First Amendment and exploitation class-action lawsuits have been filed against AOL) have come many lessons about Internet boundaries of free speech and employment law.

Like AOL, Yahoo! created an Internet service that evolved into a need. Yahoo! basically invented the "one-stop" portal. Before Yahoo! taxonomy, information architecture and search techniques were an unappreciated domain. Yahoo! changed that overnight. Unlike AOL, Yahoo! didn't build a business model that charged for its required service. Also, Yahoo! didn't put community front and center. It focused on individual efficiency. "My Yahoo!" introduced personalization to millions of people and squarely positioned Yahoo! as the portal for the individual. Yahoo! did invest in community (for example, Yahoo! groups and the previously mentioned GeoCities acquisition) yet Yahoo! *ghettoized* (segmented or segregated) its community folk in a way that other sites copied to try to achieve the benefits of community membership growth without a central commitment to community. Yahoo!'s services—especially the Yahoo! e-mail service—have secured a Yahoo! installed base, but one without a central commercial purpose and with low switching barriers. This poses a significant challenge for Yahoo!. It will be difficult for Yahoo! to independently withstand the early 2000s Internet shakeout.

About.com was one of the many information portals that appeared in the mid-1990s. About learned from AOL's community leadership experiments and took the concept of *virtual employees* to a new level by attempting to patent its business model, which paid its community members to become About.com guides who "owned" About.com topic areas. These guides helped cost-effectively create a wealth of content. About.com didn't stop there. In an attempt to expand its content and reach even further, About began to *relinquish some control* over its site expansion and ultimately the user experience. Unlike Amazon.com, eBay, Yahoo!, and AOL, About was more flexible in outsourcing and creating partnerships where it did not need to own specific infrastructure or content. About.com was one of the first Internet sites to start an affiliate where any "mom-and-pop" site could get paid to direct links from its personal Web pages to the About.com network. The consistency of user experience versus the breadth of content and reach became one of the central issues with which portals grappled as they developed their growth strategy. To develop, outsource, partner, or acquire— that was the question.

Local Customer-Communities

craigslist, Mary Kay Cosmetics
Geographical Proximity, Personal Touch

Contrary to what virtual community extremists would have us believe, the Web did not eliminate *geographical proximity* as a community-building factor. In fact, some companies have used the Internet specifically for regional customer-community building, and others have used it to augment their current local business.

Craig Newmark was an early virtual community advocate and a proponent of the peer-to-peer way in which knowledge was shared via these networks. In 1995, Craig started www.craigslist.org to inform people about interesting events in and around San Francisco. Over time, people started posting items on the list in different areas: jobs, items for sale, and apartments (these in response to San Francisco's housing shortage). Soon craigslist became a virtual Bay Area swap meet and clearinghouse. This transformed the central purpose of craigslist from connection to commerce. A customer-community was born. Unlike eBay, craigslist did not skim anything off the top—there were no membership or finder's fees. Also, craigslist was one of the few sites that had no advertising and hence no advertising revenue. From a philosophical perspective, craigslist reflected its antiestablishment, technolibertarian roots. craigslist remains a vibrant San Francisco exchange-focused community. Its challenge will be maintaining some level of egalitarian purity while translating the central commercial purpose of its members into a profitable business.

Mary Kay Cosmetics is renowned for its door-to-door direct-sales business model. In the mid 1990s, when e-mail became broadly accepted as a new powerful business-to-customer communication medium and the Internet revolutionized distribution efficiency, Mary Kay's executive team questioned whether the company's local-territory, *personal touch* edge would still be a viable switching barrier for the Mary Kay customer base.

Instead of seeing this challenge as an "either-or," Mary Kay looked for ways to use the Internet to augment the existing territorial model. Mary Kay reacted and transformed its local beauty consultants (BCs) into Internet entrepreneurs. By mid-2000, Mary Kay was setting up hundreds of independent dot-com businesses every week, managed by its independent BCs. With only 3,600 employees on the corporate payroll but over 850,000 BCs worldwide, Mary Kay is a market leader in direct sales and the most active in e-commerce.[3] Many Mary Kay beauty consultants still retain their local door-to-door territories and simply use their new Internet network with its suite of new communication tools as a way to eliminate geographical distribution issues and expand territorial boundaries.

Even on the Web, the local Bailey Building & Loan–like customer-community works. No technology has ever completely eliminated the importance of physical closeness. No matter what level of virtual communication we are able to achieve, at times we still need to physically interact with one another. But that doesn't preclude using the Internet to help support local customer-community development and growth.

Retail Customer-Communities

Barnes & Noble, REI, Abercrombie & Fitch
*Shared Consumer Interests, Online Community, Environment,
Integrating Offline and Online, Demographic Communities*

It's one thing for a dot-com site to embrace virtual community or for a business to use the Internet to augment its communication tools and distribution reach. It's quite another for a traditional brick-and-mortar retail business to embrace the Internet, let alone virtual community. And anyway, do retail customers really want to bond with each other?

Barnes & Noble, confronting the Amazon.com phenomenon, had to decide how to play in the Internet bookselling space. B&N could have played it safe, simply using the Internet as a distribution arm, but instead decided to embrace the B&N customer-community. To be competitive in the new market environment, Barnes & Noble decided to leverage its brick-and-mortar status to build local customer-communities. In 1993, B&N had already completed incorporating Starbucks cafés into many of its locations[4] to make B&N more inviting as community gathering spots. How could the company translate this online? Build an *online comfortable community environment*. With B&N University, B&N radio, and a front-page link to an instant messaging tool, Barnes & Noble "has built an online community reflective of the casual reading-room atmosphere its real stores are known for—sans coffee bar and overstuffed chairs."[5] In addition, by *linking online and offline events*, the company has done an excellent job at tying its virtual activities into its brick-and-mortar storefronts. The strategy has paid off: Barnes & Noble now has a substantial share of the online book market.

When REI created www.rei.com, the company realized that the *shared consumer interest* of its customer base was a natural for virtual community. The "Learn & Share" section of the site enables REI customers—"a lively bunch of outdoor enthusiasts just like you, full of questions, ideas and opinions about outdoor gear and activities"[6]—to commune. Dennis Madsen, REI's president and CEO, states that "REI.com is seen as the complete resource for the outdoor enthusiast, and Learn & Share is part of this proposition and the Internet equivalent to the expertise provided by our store staff. Our sense is that providing this type of resource, combined with quality products and dedicated customer service, does inspire the customer loyalty that is an REI hallmark."[7]

In 1997, when Abercrombie & Fitch changed its image from conservative East Coast outdoorsmen fashion to hip college attire, total net sales grew to $522 million, up 56 percent in just a year's time.[8] With this makeover came a clearly defined *demographic profile* that A&F targeted with a beautifully crafted $5 *A&F Quarterly* that was far more akin to a coffee-table book than a mail-order catalogue. On www.abercrombie.com, A&F has created many community-bonding agents—a mailing list, A&F Mail, A&F TV, A&F Music, Postcards, Screen Savers, and even a fictitious A&F University with a campus map—to transform this target demographic into a customer-community.

Advisory Customer-Communities

The Motley Fool, E*Trade, Charles Schwab, Ask Jeeves, drkoop.com
Legal Complexities, Peer-to-Peer Advice, Cannibalization of Existing Services

Some professional communities have adopted advisory stances. For certain professions, as in the financial trading or medical world, the concept of virtual community is fraught with challenges. There are *legal complexities* through which you must wade to determine what information can be exchanged or endorsed by a brokerage house.

In 1993, David and Tom Gardner launched The Motley Fool, establishing the "Fool Portfolio" of stocks funded with $50,000 of their own money. Fools around the world were invited to learn from the Gardners' investing successes and mistakes. Investors using The Motley Fool's proprietary discussion boards could comment on the portfolio's track record and exchange *peer-to-peer advice*. Since The Motley Fool was not a brokerage house, it was not as heavily bound by legal constraints. In under a year, membership soared, positioning David and Tom Gardner as financial wizards and enabling them to publish four financial management books that all climbed *BusinessWeek*'s bestseller list.[9] But like craigslist, the central commerce purpose of The Motley Fool provided no direct revenue stream to the company itself. The challenge for The Fool will be the same as craigslist but on a much larger scale. At least within The Fool's customer-community, profit is not viewed as inherently anticommunity.

E*Trade was founded as a service bureau in 1982 by Bill Porter to provide online quotation and trading services to Fidelity, Charles Schwab, and Quick & Reilly. Over the years, it morphed into the premier online discount brokerage house. E*Trade experimented with customer-community dialogue and was very careful about delineating its own brokerage services from intercustomer information exchange. In April 1999, when E*Trade purchased financial community site ClearStation, E*Trade bet aggressively on community. Jeff Tidwell, former E*Trade senior product manager, said that Christos Cotsakos, chairman and CEO, got net gain fever and wanted to build E*Trade into the largest online financial community.[10] Since E*Trade was a company whose primary offerings were fee-based financial services, this move into virtual community clearly targeted a collective customer base. In fact, E*Trade's community "Customer & Member" login screen is one of the few that use the term *customer*.

Although Charles Schwab was the brick-and-mortar broker-age to most quickly move into the Internet space, it was a bit slower in the realm of customer-community. Why was Schwab sluggish here? Conservative roots? Fear of liability resulting from customers advising one another? The desire to avoid a day-trading reputation? Or was it the perception that customer-to-customer interaction would *cannibalize existing fee-based financial advising services?* When Schwab did begin to experiment with customer-to-customer contact, it kept very tight control over customer discussions. The company assigned qualified "registered representatives" ("Schwab reps") to oversee all community discussions and respond with Schwab authority to any financial question raised by a customer-community member. It was sort of like a community gathering where you had to raise your hand and be called on by the official in charge.

The evolution of financial customer-communities will be unique because of the extremely private, self-focused, and competitive and legal nature of personal finances. Financial services could indeed be an area where community bonding is not as much about building relationships but more about discovering the best deal. That could mean that the customer-community loyalty bond may not be as strong.

Two other exemplary advisory customer-communities are Ask Jeeves (www.askjeeves.com) and drkoop.com. Both opened new doors to searching the Internet's seemingly infinite data banks of information. Ask Jeeves allows people to type in any question, and then the Ask Jeeves "natural language interpreter" or an Ask Jeeves Answer Point Enthusiast will search the Web for you. Because of its instant popularity, Ask Jeeves's 1999 initial public offering (IPO) was one of the most remarkable on record. Its opening stock price rocketed up more than 364 percent, closing at $64.9375 and garnering a market value of more than $1.6 billion by the close its first day as a public company.[11]

Medical information sites were another type of advisory site that brought a glint to venture capitalists' eyes because of the vast number of people who need medical advice of some sort. drkoop. com led the way. drkoop.com's 1999 IPO, though not as stellar as that of Ask Jeeves, rose 83 percent to close at $16.4375 to create a market value of $509 million.[12] Although Ask Jeeves has had some success in licensing its infrastructure, neither company has found a way to turn its user community into a paying customer-community. Not surprisingly, both companies' dramatic market devaluation reflects this.

Customer "Cults"
Apple, Odwalla, Palm, Electronic Arts, Zippo
Advocacy and Evangelism, Loyalty Through Crisis,
Early Adopter Communities

According to *Entrepreneur's Start-Ups* magazine, you can "develop your own cult following. From underground phenomenon to national icon, your business can be a leader in its own right."[13] Some companies create customer "cults" that are almost irrationally loyal. In the mid-1990s, many of SGI's customers were so obsessively addicted to the company's leading-edge visualization technology that a simple employee could inspire awe simply by regaling SGI insider stories to cultish customer fans.

Just try to get a loyal Apple customer to use a PC. Fat chance. In the mid-1990s, Apple's customer loyalty sustained the company through a brush with almost certain death. Why? From the get-go, Apple focused on usability and addressed unique customer needs for certain computing segments like primary education, graphic art, and desktop publishing. By listening closely to the needs of those industries, the company garnered a loyal following. Apple has attracted a base of customers who, on their own, are driven to *advocate* and even *evangelize* for Apple, often even trying to convert friends who use competitors' products.

On Odwalla's home page, www.odwalla.com, it is stated that "Odwalla was founded on the belief that good business helps make the world a better place."[14] Like the Vermont-based ice-cream mavens Ben and Jerry, Odwalla has promoted its values-centric business practices and has earned respect from its customers— customers who rushed to support the company when a highly publicized *E. coli* outbreak was linked to nonpasteurized Odwalla juices. *Customer-community loyalty* pulled Odwalla through this crisis.

When the handheld Palm hit the market in 1996, there were many personal digital assistants (PDAs) on the market. Somehow the Palm Pilot was singled out by an extremely credible and well-networked *early adopter community* within the computer industry. For people working in Silicon Valley companies, the peer pressure to have a Palm Pilot became overwhelming. Was this the perfect PDA, luck, or timing? The immediate and widespread adoption in this market created a customer-community on which Palm was quick to capitalize. In response, Palm has enabled rich customer-to-customer networking at www.palm.com.

Video gaming enthusiasts have always been a fanatic sort. Gaming sites are some of the few community sites that have been able to achieve a significant community of individuals who will pay a subscription fee. Because of this, many Internet gaming sites have sustained their viability. One good example is ea.com, the Internet gaming presence of parent Electronic Arts, developer of computer-based entertainment systems like PlayStation and Nintendo. The exclusive ea.com, pogo.com (a "games for everyone" site), and AOL Games Channel programming all attract the most devoted of Internet gamers. The ea.com site is even able to segment its subscription customer-community into two tiers: "Sports Service" and "Platinum Service."

Though smoking is out of vogue in many parts of the United States, Zippo customers have great devotion to their clicking metal lighters. Zippo.com capitalizes on this collector psychology. The sight is a visual and auditory feast that showcases the Zippo car, a Zippo Day, Hollywood Zippo sightings, and more.

How do you create this type of customer cult? Or if you sense a customer cult in the making, how do you sustain it? It is especially here, at the first sign of customer "addiction," where you need to swiftly catalyze your customer-community.

Unlikely Customer-Communities

Saturn, MCI, Holiday Inn, Safeway
Leveraging Existing Infrastructure and Existing Offline Communities,
Membership, Exclusivity, Offline Gatherings

Do Saturn owners really travel across the country to go to a Saturn owners' picnic? Who imagined that an automobile manufacture could build such a loyal customer-community? Obviously someone did, for Saturn somehow managed to secure a loyal, repeat-purchasing customer-community.

Can customers of the same long-distance service truly form a community? Maybe not, but MCI turned this question around and asked, "Why not *market our services to an existing community?*" MCI's "Friends and Family" program, launched in 1990, offered discounts to customers who made calls to others within their designated "Friends and Family" circle as an incentive to encourage customers to recruit their frequently called friends and family members to switch to MCI. For a while, MCI was able to sustain this competitive advantage because the company *leveraged its existing integrated customer database*, a strategy that created a substantial entry barrier because at the time neither AT&T nor Sprint had such database capabilities.[15]

Holiday Inn's Priority Club is a common type of *membership program* with rewards linked to frequency of visits. But Holiday Inn is creative in how it constructs an *exclusive* community out of the most loyal of these customers. Twice a year since 1989, Holiday Inn has enticed five hundred to one thousand of its most frequent guests to bring themselves and their families to a *gathering* at a resort property for a weekend of hobnobbing, recreation, and roundtable discussions with hotel management.

In 1999, Safeway launched a customer intimacy program. New store layouts enabled more customer interaction, in-store Starbucks kiosks were added, checkers were trained to call customers by name (pulled from the existing Safeway Club database). All of a sudden, the Safeway shopping experience seemed much more friendly.

Cars, long-distance telephone plans, hotels, and grocery stores—why would they inspire us, their customers, to bond with one another? How are these companies able to pull it off? They have been creative about leveraging the social aspects of their customers. When thinking about whether or not your company or products can attract a customer-community, look past the obvious.

Peer-to-Peer Customer Service

Hewlett-Packard, Oracle
User Groups, Peer-to-Peer Support, Testimonials

The more complex and flexible the product line, the more challenging the customer service. Computer servers that are networked into a heterogeneous environment or massive databases that can be configured in an unlimited number of ways can create customer service nightmares.

With such complex product environments, why not recruit your customers into the service process? Enable them to help each other. Many companies, like IBM, Oracle, and Hewlett-Packard, have long had sophisticated approaches to creating customer *user groups* that facilitate information exchange between company and customers and between customers themselves. Most of these periodic user group meetings allow customers to interact with each other and learn more about upcoming products. MacWorld Expos are massive user conferences drawing Apple enthusiasts from all over the world. With Apple's loyal following, a MacWorld Expo can have the passionate vibrancy of a *Star Trek* convention. User groups can be easily leveraged for *peer-to-peer support*. Customers with similar product environments are often in a perfect position to suggest solutions and resolve specific service challenges. With peer support taking some pressure off the customer service department, it might be possible to simultaneously save customer service expense and build customer loyalty. Customer-to-customer service develops a rich pipeline of reference accounts, which are very important in the selling process of complex and expensive products. Who is a potential customer more likely to believe: a corporately massaged marketing pitch or a peer-to-peer *testimonial* from a customer who has similar challenges?

Customer, developer, and partner communities are prominently positioned on the www.oracle.com navigation bar. In fact, these community areas are the richest part of the site. One specific customer-community program is Club Oracle (offering two tiers of membership—the Gold tier is fee-based), which "was created as a means to bring people together, making them part of the exciting and innovative community that forms the core foundation of Oracle."[16] Oracle clearly understands the value of its customers' bonding into a community.

Hewlett-Packard has adopted the customer-community concept to such a level that the company has integrated eBay-like profile feature within its Information Technology Resource Center (www.itrc.hp.com). An HP IT customer can not only connect with other IT customers to ask questions or get recommendations but also actually scan various customers' profiles to find similar customers who are respected within the customer-community for solving service issues.

Because of the quantifiable customer service cost savings, engaging customers in *peer-to-peer service* will be one of the most advanced breeding grounds for customer-community concepts.

Marketplaces and Business-to-Business Communities

Monster.com, eLance, VerticalNet, BizLand, IBM, PeopleSoft Developer and Partner Communities, B2B Portals

In a manner of speaking, the Internet is the world's largest marketplace. Some very strong customer-communities have formed as industry- or service-specific marketplaces. Monster.com is "the leading global online network for careers, connecting the most progressive companies with the most qualified career-minded individuals."[17]

Monster's commission and fee model, like AOL's subscription model, positions it squarely as a community of commerce. Although one could easily argue that Monster's community is even more commerce-centric than AOL's because in addition to Monster's being fee-based, its community members are interacting within a marketplace for commerce-related reasons.

ELance.com is "the world's largest professional services market-place for small businesses."[18] Beerud Sheth, cofounder and general manager of ELance, believes in bringing the customer as far into the business as possible. He views the customer-community as "an extension of the ELance family" and expects all ELance executives to monitor the customer dialogues that take place in the community area of the site.[19] Sheth has gone so far as to host "Talk Live with ELance" message board discussion sessions with eLance customers.

Another vibrant breeding ground for customer-communities is the business-to-business landscape. Far more than consumer companies, the B2B world is about peer-to-peer information exchange. There are trade associations, conventions, conferences, and exchanges all geared toward hooking B2B folk together. Internet-based customer-communities are a natural outgrowth.

The same companies with complex product lines that embrace user groups almost always support *developer and partner communities* to the same or even higher levels, especially if those companies depend on those developers and partners as key components of their value proposition to the customer. Take computer hardware companies. IBM has been able to sustain its wide customer base because of its strength with software partners. The www.ibm.com Web site gives prominent space to support developers and partner communities.

The same developer and partner argument goes for much of the computer software industry as well. Microsoft, Oracle, and PeopleSoft all have stand-alone product lines, but key to each company's success is the way its software integrates with other software environments. PeopleSoft shot ahead of well-entrenched competitors mostly because PeopleSoft chose to create a substantial preferred partnership program rather than write all of its own application software. Such a program requires linking partners in a well-supported partner community.

Business-to-business vendors also come together on their own. The high demand for B2B peer-level information exchange has opened the door for *B2B portals*. VerticalNet, whose tag line is "Leading Business to E-Business," is a B2B community portal striving "to build and manage dynamic, industry-focused communities that provide the most innovative online information resources, communication vehicles, and e-commerce channels for industrial, professional and technology-based companies."[20] Small business portals, like BizLand and Microsoft's bCentral, have a similar opportunity. Small business owners, because of their inexperience and resource constraints, can greatly benefit from a community portal that not only links them into valuable information and offers services targeted at their needs but also connects them into a community of like-minded entrepreneurs so they can exchange ideas, tips, and best practices.

B2B customer-communities will assuredly continue to expand their offline efforts into the online dimension. Over the next decade, if only for cost efficiency, more and more information and service exchange will migrate to the Internet.

Corporate Customer-Communities

The customer-community concept can also be applied to any intra-company provider-to-customer department. Service functions in large organizations, especially those in large intranet-linked organizations, can address their internal "customers" as an employee-as-customer. For example, an IS department may catalyze a community of employees who use the company's financial database. This corporate employee-community will help guide support levels and prioritize future product enhancement decisions. Because organizations clearly understand the value of aligning employees, the internal corporate employee-community can be more palatable as a first experiment in empowering customer-communities.

Summary

Don't constrain your virtual community thinking to current norms and precedents; examine your current customer base to determine if a community bond is viable. You may be surprised by the amount your customers are already interacting with one another. In this book, we will continue to build on the examples presented here as well as others that shed light on the power of the customer-community. Let's now shift gears and examine how customer-communities can help with two of the most significant business challenges: growing and sustaining a loyal customer base.

Chapter Five

Growing Your Community

For most communities and businesses, growth indicates health. A large community has a louder, more forceful voice; a growing business usually results in increased revenue and most likely increased profit as well. Flat or negative growth means maturity, stagnation, or the beginning of the end. This chapter will show how the Internet has created new opportunities for community and business growth. We will also show how the combination of the two—the customer-community—can enable an e-business to efficiently scale even larger.

The Internet has lifted size restrictions on some businesses and transactions. With augmented communication abilities and the possibility of community leadership, virtual communities can swell far beyond than their nonvirtual counterparts. Simultaneously, through customer reach and distribution efficiencies, businesses are finally realizing scale possibilities within the global economy. Even "mom-and-pop" businesses can grow to an immense size. Bluemountain.com, a small family-owned virtual greeting card company, claimed 5.5 million users when it was purchased by Excite in October 1999 for $780 million; it was then one of the world's twenty most-trafficked Web sites.[1]

But the Internet has not eliminated all barriers to business growth. Scaling high-touch personalized customer service has become an even greater challenge with geographically dispersed customers. Many companies try to achieve customer efficiency service through voice mail answering systems (known as interactive voice response, or IVR) and e-mail response systems. But effective high-touch service often requires human intervention, which means real live people answering customer questions. This is extremely difficult to scale cost-effectively. Here is one area where your customer-community can directly help. Engaging your customers in peer-to-peer service activities can augment your customer service efforts. Your customers will receive the benefit of personal service, but you don't have to incur all of the employee-related expense. Before examining direct customer-community benefits, let's discuss the fundamentals of Internet-enabled community and business growth. We will examine growth opportunities resulting from three interrelated factors: the network effect of interconnected systems, intrinsic collective thresholds, and more expansive ability to communicate.

The Network Effect

As communities first form, there is a focus on meeting the individual community members' needs. Often early community growth reflects this individualism, and members are convinced to join one at a time. But once they expand beyond a certain critical size, communities become viral, almost contagious. They grow organically without conscious effort. Once a community passes this stage, it scales much faster and with less effort than a smaller community. Pyramid marketing schemes manipulate this momentum: "If one friend tells two friends, and those two friends each tell two other friends, . . ." This accelerated expansion of the community reaps a much higher return per member and yields more per member—provided that the community is prepared to handle the growth.

Bob Metcalf, inventor of the Ethernet, is known for a prediction called Metcalf's law that along with Moore's law[2] is widely credited as the explanation behind the stunning growth of Internet connectivity. Metcalf's law predicts that the total value of a communication network increases in proportion to the square of the number of nodes on the network. David Reed, former professor of computer science and engineering at the MIT Laboratory for Computer Science and former vice president and chief scientist for Lotus Development Corporation, expanded this idea to create Reed's law. Reed's law dictates that networks supporting the construction of communicating groups create value that scales exponentially with network size. In plain English, this means that networked communities grow much more rapidly than networked individuals.

According to Reed:

> Even if it's not your business to supply communications services, your business participates in many networks—perhaps the most important are supply networks that allow access to and bidding among suppliers and distribution networks that allow access to and competition among customers. The structure of these networks or market spaces, especially the value of the connectivity and relationships produced in these networks, can play a crucial role in defining the value of your business. If you can manage or influence the networks that connect you to suppliers and customers to create more value for all concerned, that extra value can be used as a competitive weapon. So paying attention to network value is a crucial strategic issue, especially as businesses move their customer and supplier relationships into the "net."[3]

Reed goes on to say, "In networks like the Internet, Group Forming Networks (GFNs) are an important additional kind of network capability. A GFN has functionality that directly enables and supports affiliations (such as interest groups, clubs, meetings, communities) among subsets of its customers." Basically Reed is saying that there is immense value in connecting and creating community among your suppliers, distributors, and customers. On his Web site, www.reed.com, Reed goes into further scientific depth about why he believes paying attention to these linkages is critical for Internet-enabled businesses.

Intrinsic Collective Size Thresholds

Sociological and psychological dynamics support the natural formation of small communities and create challenges for those communities to scale beyond an approximate range. Most groups in social animal species—flocks of birds, schools of fish, gaggles of geese—grow naturally to a certain size. They can't naturally maintain the same structure if inherent size limits are broken. If the collective grows much bigger than the average size for the species, a natural Darwinian downsizing occurs to keep the size below some natural threshold.

Much has been written about how size and growth affect a community. From urban planning to organizational design, strategists have pondered various growth plans and size thresholds to maintain optimal operating efficiency within an expanding system. Organizational experts will dictate relative size guidelines for teams, departments, business units, and entire organizations. They will recommend how to grow so that small teams and microcommunities can be, on one hand, independent enough to achieve entrepreneurial efficiency and, on the other hand, well tethered to the parent organization so that the broader organizational needs and mission are met.

Depending on the goals of the organization and the degree of autonomy required at the smaller levels, this balance can be quite tricky. It can make or break a company. Many large companies overburden individual business units with corporate bureaucracy. This can dampen innovation and slow the cycle time from concept to implementation and distribution. The smaller, more nimble competitors bypass these sluggish giants. Other companies give too much autonomy at the individual group level and are then unable to operationalize these disparate teams. Chaos reigns. Process-efficient competitors win out. Often organizational structure theories pivot around the optimal size of human communities and microcommunities. They dance between chaos and order. In fact, the most adept organizations will know when they need to shift in one direction or another when the size of the population dictates more or less autonomy. "Familiar order and chaotic order are laminated like bands."[4] The challenge beneath the pendulum swing is the persistent assumption in the minds of almost everyone in business: "Grow we must." Customer-communities are not as tightly interwoven as employee communities, but various size and growth constraints still exist, depending on the business's goals. High-end vendors will frequently develop pricing models that exclude many potential customers, forcing slow customer growth and creating an image of exclusivity. This type of slow-growth strategy favors long-term success through higher margins and a sustainable image over short-term profit from transient volume.

Is it all science, then? Are human communities bound to certain size thresholds that need to be considered when building cities, organizations, and customer-communities? Can you simply create an equation or, better, an automatic natural trigger that lets management or the community know when it's time to subdivide? Or is it better to just let the community decide and self-organize?

There are many factors that influence optimal community size. In Chapter Six, we discuss bonding strength as it affects sustainability, but the intensity of the customer relationship can also affect size constraints. Stronger glue not only holds longer but can also bond together larger items. The same is true of bonding agents between people. Often the more passionate the community interest, the larger the community can grow. For example, major social concerns like the economy or defense can strengthen a national community. Religious affiliations can grow to an immense size because the shared interest is one that is at the core of the human psyche and because religious leaders often cultivate this shared interest on a local community level. Yet sometimes too much intensity can be offputting to new members. Overly passionate communities can sometimes seem elite, exclusionary, or intimidating. How much inherent intensity is there in your customer base?

Another significant size-related bonding force is culture. In general, individualistic cultures like the United States have a harder time building and sustaining large communities than some of the more communal Eastern cultures. Is there a shared culture in your customer base? Or one that you want to create? Does the primary culture of your customer base affect the optimal size of a community?

Expansion Though Communication

A community's ability to communicate effectively is a key component of its scalability. The Internet has dramatically expanded intracommunity communication. E-communities are therefore able to coalesce and grow at faster rates and to larger sizes. This communicability not only affects the growth of existing communities but also enables communities to form that could never have existed otherwise. One Web phenomenon is that a community can form around uncommon interests. Before the Web, it was more difficult for people interested in some obscurity to find others who share the interest. The Web's search capabilities and pervasive interconnections have completely obliterated this barrier. Now anyone interested in the most arcane topics can find similar-minded others and self-organize. Such communities could never have aggregated much collective interest before the Web. People who collect French postcards from the late 1800s, Bongo funerary posts from Africa, antique Die-Cast pencil sharpeners, or models and prototypes of the Pennsylvania Railroad can easily find and bond with other people who share these interests.

As we noted in Chapter Three, communication is one of the foundational principles of communities. Each member relies on the other members to communicate not only to individual members but also to the collective whole. You could theorize that the communication ability of various species has sociologically created their natural collective size thresholds. We know that as technologies have allowed humans to communicate more effectively, many communities have been able to grow beyond previous size constraints. Many businesses no longer require colocation of key offices or functions for growth. Individuals are often better able to sustain and even broaden their circles of friends. It is now easy to create an e-mail distribution list and stay in touch with your entire extended family.

Infrastructure that enables effective communication is the most essential requirement for community growth, and it is also possibly the most controllable and malleable factor. In our first book, *Beyond Spin*, we discuss the how an intranet enables effective communications within large knowledge organizations.[5] Before the intranet, corporate communications were limited to interoffice memos, companywide meetings, and the trickle-down theory: the CEO communicated to the executive team, who communicated to direct reports, and so on down the chain until every employee had some variation of the original message—often some inaccurate and conflicting variation. Intranet communication not only supports top-down but also cross-organizational messaging. Where would today's organizations be without voice mail or e-mail? Even very large organizations are able to shift on a dime if they can effectively harness the abilities provided by these communication technologies.

It's obvious that the Internet enables this same type of communication to, from, and between your customers. But it is not so obvious how to harness this power. Before the Internet, the only way to interact with your customers was in person, on the phone, or through direct mail. There was no real forum for customers to interact with each other unless they were standing next to each other in a physical store. Sometimes like-minded customers talked with each other about a specific product. "You have an iMac, right? Do you know how to . . . ?" But this type of intercustomer-communication was infrequent. With the Internet, the potential for vendor-to-customer, customer-to-vendor, and customer-to-customer-communication has grown exponentially and in a dimension that remains largely untapped. It is this connectivity that has given the customer-community new life. It is not simply that communication opportunities have increased; specific communication capabilities have dramatically enhanced group communication. Let's take a look at some of them.

Low Barrier to One-on-One Dialogue

E-mail has dramatically lowered the intimidation barrier for person-to-person virtual communication. Contacting someone, whether a friend or a stranger, is much easier than before the Web—both logistically and psychologically. Entering feedback via an electronic form takes less effort than completing a paper form. So does dashing off an e-mail customer service request. In general, e-mail can be much more efficient than the telephone—especially since logistically, getting an e-mail account is worlds better than in the Internet's formative years, when connectivity was difficult and systems didn't always talk to each other. Once you are connected and you start receiving e-mail, all you have to do is simply "reply." No need to pick up a handset, remember the number, or dial. Psychologically, you can communicate through e-mail without rising, so to speak, to the social occasion. Also because communication tools like e-mail and Instant Messenger (IM) are written instead of oral, ongoing complex dialogues can be more easily sustained over time. Finally, communicating via the Internet is more affordable than the telephone. Most Internet communication services have no per-message charge, and this eliminates one more barrier to ongoing communication.

Anonymity

Often people lurk anonymously on the fringes of a community before joining. This can be difficult in the real world. How do you sneak into a meeting without being noticed? In most e-communities, anonymity is simple. You can hang out in the virtual shadows until you get a sense as to whether you want to participate. Anonymity also lowers the intimidation factor. If you are communicating with someone you don't really know—say, to another customer—it's much easier to communicate through a medium where you can partly shield your identity. With e-mail, you can be as anonymous or as personal as you want to be. Certainly you can also be anonymous on the telephone, but for many people, communicating voice to voice carries a level of intimacy that can be intrusive or intimidating.

Varying Levels of Asynchronicity: More "Pull"

Asynchronicity means there is some span of time in between the moment that you communicate something and the moment that the person to whom you have communicated replies. Before the Internet, there was real-time communication in a live meeting or the phone, and there was asynchronous communication of written messages, letters, or the answering machine. There wasn't much in between.

The Internet has showcased the importance of varying degrees of asynchronicity. Sometimes people want immediate responses; sometimes they would like a bit more time before they hear back. E-mail and discussion boards enable a broad span of "uncomplicated" asynchronicity, from near real time to time spans that are greater than postal letters. Telephone technology also offers the same time options (right away or later response), but the difference is that near-real-time phone tag is logistically challenging—it takes time to pick up the phone, dial, wait, . . . Why not just have a live conversation? Conversely, since telephone messages are not threaded (it's not easy to review all related phone messages on your machine; we'll come back to this matter shortly), too much of a time span between voice messages can be disorienting or out of context. Asynchronous variability allows many different types of non-real-time dialogue that are tough to orchestrate without the Internet. For example, we now have a much greater variety of "pull" communication tools.

With "push" communications like direct mail, phone messages, and e-mail, the communication recipient has no option but to "deal with" the communication. Such communications have a low annoyance threshold. The more effort it takes to deal with unwanted push communications, the lower the threshold. For example, e-mail "spam" (mass-marketed e-mail) is easier to delete than unwanted telemarketing calls. Therefore, in general, recipients are less frustrated by high levels of e-mail spam than they are by high numbers of telemarketing calls.

"Pull" communications, like message boards and chat rooms, require a conscious choice to communicate. Obviously, a customer who consciously chooses to communicate with you and other customers will be more open to listening to what you have to say.

Moderated Dialogue

Moderated dialogue has long been used in political debates, talk shows, and industry conferences. Moderation allows many people to converse without risking tangential discussions that meander off from the original direction. In real life, it is limiting because moderated dialogues require formal structures. A real-time moderated dialogue can seem like a chaperoned date. Discussion boards and chat software make moderation much less formal and more accessible. This enables massive group-focused dialogue, a key ingredient of community growth.

Multilogue

The most important communication functionality needed to support community growth is effective many-to-many communication, dubbed "multilogue." Richard Cross and Janet Smith underscore this: "'Multilogue' is essential to community bonding."[6] Real-time communications have a definite multilogue threshold. People talk over each other. Even moderated real-time discussions are challenging for large groups. Often people get ignored, which leads to disinterest and disengagement. It is this dynamic that encourages small classroom sizes for effective learning. Both variable asynchronicity and informal moderation make multilogue more effective. A Web-based distance-learning program can achieve effective learning with a much larger class size.

Multilogue is not just about large group communication; it is also about being able to define and communicate to and between groups of variable size. E-mail group aliases—or listservs—have created the first quick, easy, and inexpensive way to communicate to a select and updatable group. Before listservs (a single e-mail address for a select group of recipients), communicating to a select group was fraught with difficulties. Telephone or video conference calls can handle multilogue within small groups, but the etiquette required for a true dialogue is overwhelming. Conference calls can also be very expensive, especially if you are interested in video-conferences. Now you can simply create an e-mail alias. This one functionality spawned companies like Egroups and Ecircles that made forming and maintaining listservs even easier. Today many people who use e-mail have created at least one e-mail alias—all friends or all family—which they use to broadcast personal announcements like address changes or holiday greetings.

Conversation Threading

Threading conversations means keeping track of and participating in multiple parallel conversations. Enhanced conversation threading is unique to the Internet. In a live conversation, only a very few conversational threads can be discussed or followed at one time. Even at a large party or conference with various groups of people starting multiple conversations, it is hard to maintain those conversations for any length of time. Through large-scale conversation threading, message board technologies have completely changed group communication as we know it. With message board technologies, communities can begin as many conversations as they want and maintain them for as long as they want. Some of CompuServe's forums that were started in the late 1970s and early 1980s are still going strong and continue to catalyze community interactivity.

Subdividing into Microcommunities

Subdivision is a natural reaction to community growth. Look at any large community, and you find offshoots or slices of that community that have been spawned during that community's evolution. One of the major challenges for urban architects is creating a plan that is flexible enough to allow for the natural subdivisions that occur with growth. All community architects have the same challenge. Before Internet-based communication technologies, community subdividing often meant that smaller separate groups would completely split away from the larger community. This was true because there was no easy way to communicate between and among communities. A community member needed to decide whether to stay with the larger community, join the new smaller one, or expend the extra effort required to be members of both. Flexible architecture, dynamic indexing, hyperlinking, and threaded dialogue make it easy to introduce semipermeable boundaries for separate spaces or subcommunities that are both independent and interconnected to the parent community. Simple conversations can occur in distinct communities, yet at the same time, these distinct communities can easily remain linked back to the overarching community. You no longer need to choose between the two; you can easily navigate from a discussion about *The Ring of the Niebelungen* in a microcommunity formed around Wagner's early years to a discussion about divas in the broader opera lover's community. This natural bifurcation allows virtual communities to grow very quickly and to massive sizes that were impossible before the Internet.

Archiving

Many businesses of long standing like AT&T, Kodak, and IBM understand the community-building value of history and have invested in company archives and even museums that serve both the employee community and the customer-community. This history can be important for member retention as well as the orientation of new community initiates. The ability to archive Internet-related communication media allows a virtual community to build a history of itself. Also, most discussion board technologies include a search functionality that helps members locate archived information. For a customer-community, this could mean the ability to find replacement parts or support information for discontinued products. A rich archive that is easily explored also enables new members to research context so that they can knowledgably join ongoing conversations. This functionality helps moderate the ebb and flow of participants, a natural fluctuation that helps maintain the evolving bond as the community grows and changes over time.

In-Context or Dual Communication Features

With the Internet, people can communicate directly within the content that they are reading or the online transaction that they are completing. You can e-mail Web pages to a friend or participate in a discussion on an article that you just read. E-tailers can integrate customer service e-mail links throughout their e-commerce transaction pages. Just think if you could as effectively communicate context in a nonvirtual commerce setting. What if, while in a department store, you could contact your spouse miles away and ask, "I was thinking about getting this sweater for you; do you like it?"

Parallel Communication

The myriad of online synchronous and asynchronous communication tools allow you to participate in many simultaneous communications. You can be having a brainstorming session with one group via an e-mail list, debate an issue brought up on a message board, e-mail a friend a confirmation for dinner, and discuss some issues on a real-time IM session—all at nearly the same time. Although such parallel communication can be overwhelming, it can also be incredibly empowering. On the Internet, you can easily sustain intimate contact with several different circles. You don't have to constrain yourself to one or two communities. You can stay tightly or loosely connected to many at once. Today, as a customer of a particular company, you may not have any interest in communicating with other customers because you have too many other communication obligations. But consider this: being part of a customer-community may simply mean that you occasionally listen to what other customers like you think. This doesn't have to be overwhelming because there is no required commitment.

There are many other communications that have been activated by the Web. You can Evite people to an event; your e-calendar can trigger you with a reminder; you can visually brainstorm through an electronic whiteboard; you can annotate your e-mail with video so that you can see someone. With this myriad of communication abilities, people with common interests can quickly find one another; they can anonymously listen in; they can communicate to one another and to the larger community without being intimidated; and they can easily form subcommunities while still linked into the larger parent community. It was for these very reasons that many large virtual communities were formed so quickly after the introduction of the World Wide Web.

Other Growth-Related Factors

Advancements on other community-building fronts have also made impacts on the scalability of virtual communities. In the community-building principles delineated in Chapter Three and Figure 4.2, we see many powerful changes. The ease and possibilities of Internet architecture have made rich community environments much easier to build and change. Profiling has allowed individual reputations to be formed even within very large e-communities. Large-scale peer-to-peer exchange has become possible with database-driven transactions and distribution expansion. Electronic leadership and self-governance can scale much more effectively due to the required structural foundation of virtual communities. But it was the broadening of communication abilities that sparked the e-community revolution. This new potential not only ignited the fire but also enabled community growth beyond what was ever before possible.

We do not intend to imply that this growth comes easy. Maintaining order within and satisfaction among large groups of people always poses some challenges. Lots of people require lots of communication and lots of listening. A large customer-community also requires adequate infrastructure. Many a popular Web site has faltered during peak usage levels. Some never fully recover. Also even with additional communication abilities, can large communities sustain the intimacy required to bond the community together? Let's now turn to some of the challenges that remain for large-scale businesses. One in particular—scaling high-touch customer service—is one that we will explore in depth and one for which we will recommend a potential customer-community solution.

The Intimacy Challenge of Large-Scale Communities

In *It's a Wonderful Life*, Bedford Falls was a relatively small town. People knew each other by virtue of proximity and the natural constraints of small-town living. They saw each other as they went about their daily lives. They might have gone to the same church, shopped at the same stores, and banked at Bailey Building and Loan. The limited selection of retail and service venues means that people in small towns have a shared interest to ensure that local establishments meet their individual needs. In such a case of limited choices, where everyone is relying on the same service institutions, meeting individuals' needs also means meeting the collective's needs. Therefore, the small size of the town actually propelled frequent interaction and common interests and created an ideal atmosphere for community to develop.

As a community grows, service institutions multiply and become less proximate. In a large community, you don't run into the same community members as often. It becomes harder and harder to know each other. The whole of the community becomes less personal.

For Mary Kay Cosmetics, becoming less personal would mean abandoning a significant competitive edge. But not embracing the Internet would be shortsighted. Mary Kay wanted both e-growth and personal touch, so the company electronically empowered its local beauty consultants. Beauty consultant Hope Pratt who, before 1987 had never seen a keyboard and now runs her own e-commerce Web site, says, "The human touch is still central." Yet she has used the Internet to grow her client base and "retain her clients when they (or she) moved out of her territory." She still periodically phones her long-distance clients just for the intimacy of voice contact.[7]

Maintaining customer intimacy is one of the key challenges of business growth. Most businesses don't have a localized sales model that they can easily leverage. As they scale, they lose personal touch with their customers. E-business intimacy is even more challenging due to the virtual nature of interaction.

Scaling High-Touch Customer Service

Some companies have managed to grow their business while retaining a personal touch, but overall, has the Internet enabled high-touch service to scale? Many observers believe that the introduction of interactive voice response (IVR) systems and Internet submission forms has actually caused service to deteriorate. Business journalists lament the technological impact on customer service. Business 2.0 even had a June 2001 cover article with headlines that screamed, "ARRGH! Is Bad Customer Service Driving You Crazy? Technology Was Supposed to Make Customer Service Easy. Why is scaling customer service so hard?" How can your customer-community help?

Anyone who has telephoned a company for service and spent the first two minutes navigating a seemingly endless IVR system knows how alienating technocentric customer service can be. But no one can deny that over the past decade, great strides have been made in technology-enabled "personal touch." Today's customer service organizations can provide individualized service to a disparate customer base far more effectively with Internet communication. Amazon.com is brilliant at using the Internet communications tools to achieve timely, high-quality, personal customer service. In *The Eng@ged Customer,* Hans Peter Brondmo specifically prescribes e-mail strategies to develop an intimate customer relationship: e-mail newsletter campaigns, automated yet personalized e-mail reply systems, e-mail alert systems, and a variety of other e-mail techniques to "personally" engage the customer.[8]

But technology can be pushed only so far. Eventually companies are still going run into a "customer service representatives per customers served" ratio threshold. Unless e-tailers are going to copy the offline retail world and position their products as luxury goods or premium services and subsequently pass the high-touch customer service expense on to their customers, they will have to find even better ways to scale high-touch. How? How do you find the e-service sweet spot (see Figure 5.1)—the ability to achieve low product price and low customer service cost—and still maintain high-touch service?

Is the Internet's expanded potential for business growth limited by the inability to cost-effectively scale high-touch customer service? This is where a connected customer base can help. Virtual community growth potential overlaid on business growth potential equals a customer-community that can lend a hand. And since scaling personalized service is one of the most significant challenges to growing businesses, let's explore this customer-community benefit further.

Peer-to-Peer Service

People like giving advice. Customers like giving advice to other customers. The Amazon.com customer-community freely reviews products. Motley Fool community members give each other investment tips. AOL community members help AOL newbies out. There are challenges to engaging your customers as virtual customer service

Figure 5.1 E-Service Sweet Spot

Customer E-Service Cost ↑	Unprofitable	Luxury item, premium service
	E-service sweet spot	Noncompetitive

Product Price →

representatives. There are consistency issues, liability issues, and the potential for negative advocacy. But these issues are resolvable. In fact, you need to resolve them anyway in order to do business on the Web. You may magnify the issues somewhat by formalizing communication channels between your customers, but we believe that the ensuing cost savings and resulting loyalty are worth it.

Peer-to-peer service doesn't have to be formal. Community message boards are often an excellent conduit for people helping each other out. It is natural for customer-community members to post customer service–type questions. Look at ELance's Water Cooler message boards, where eLancers discuss the optimal way to use ELance.com site and its services.

Or you can go a step further and help customers who have problems find other customers with solutions. Hewlett-Packard's Information Technology Resource Center has an incredibly rich peer-to-peer service component. On www.itrc.hp.com, HP Information Technology customers can log into the forums section of the site—"the gathering place for IT Professionals to solve problems, exchange ideas, and learn lessons from the 500,000 fellow peers who also use the IT Resource Center"[9]—and ask other customers questions. They can then award accuracy points to whoever responds to their query. Like eBay, this peer-based profiling system allows customers to build a point-ranked reputation within the customer-community. As you accrue points, you are rated as a "pro," "graduate," "wizard," or "royalty."

Jeff Siegle, manager for HP's Online Community, indicates that in the beginning, he was worried that the profiling systems might alienate customers who were generously volunteering their time to advise other customers but then got rated poorly. The model had some flaws because HP was assessing the value of the advice that the community member was contributing over time. What he witnessed has been the exact opposite. Today, community members, not HP, rate each other on the importance of the advice they receive. "Customers appreciate knowing if their advice was helpful or not."[10] Glen Van Lehn, a network engineer at City College of San Francisco who manages the college's intranet, is an HP ITRC customer. He says that the profiling system is extremely helpful as he researches specific questions (there is "magical answer" icon annotating correct answers to customer queries) or looks for someone who can answer questions for the type of heterogeneous intranet environment that he manages.[11]

You will most likely want to reward your customer volunteers. HP recognizes customer-community members who reach various status tiers. Over the history of the site, HP has awarded monetary gifts as well as offered public recognition and appreciation to top ITRC community members. You can go as far as AOL and develop a comprehensive incentive structure that includes hiring customers and paying them as customer service representatives. You can even, like AOL, provide a training program to improve the consistency and quality of peer-level service. "America Online enlists the help of more than 10,000 volunteers to patrol its bulletin board and employs approximately 100 subscribers (known as the Community Action Team) to determine when comments are unacceptable."[12]

Jim Griffith is an eBay legend. He was a part of the eBay customer-community from the outset. He started answering questions for other customers and began to build his reputation as Uncle Griff, the wise sage you turn to for advice on eBay. He developed a following, and eventually eBay hired Uncle Griff as supervisor of customer service. He was then promoted to manager of training and customer support for all of eBay's internal employees. Not only does he host a Q&A column on the site called "Dear Uncle Griff and Dear Aunt Flossie," but he is also a regular contributor to eBay's monthly print magazine.[13]

Turning customer-community members into more "formal" volunteers or hiring them as employees is not easy. There are many lessons to be learned regarding training, quality assurance, liability, incentives, advocacy, and content integration. There is no doubt that assigning any responsibility to customers will raise challenges. Is the payoff worth the effort? From what we can see with early cases, the answer is unequivocally yes. You don't need to start with a full customer-community employee conversion program in place, but give customers some skin in the game—leverage their support to acquire and retain other customers. Start with a nominal incentive plan, and work your way up.

Inherent Differences Between Customer Service and Community Building

When first considering the possibility of customer-community service, you should start by simply recognizing some inherent philosophical and practical contradictions between customer service and community building:

- The drive toward technologically enabled economies of scale coupled with high attrition levels in customer service have led to customer service departments' becoming more general and impersonal in their communications. Community building teaches us that the more personal the interaction, the greater the bonding potential.

- Information-driven customer service has shown us that the more information we have about customers, the better we can individualize their needs. Community-building practices have underscored the need for individual privacy and trust.

- Customer service organizations have leveraged direct marketing techniques to maximize customer reach. Successful community building dictates that most communication should be among and between community members and that one-way communication from the organization to the community should be kept to a minimum.

- To achieve consistently high levels of customer service, customer service departments need to retain a high degree of control over the entire customer service process. Relinquishing some control and allowing for dynamic cocreation can be much more cost-effective and create deeply engendered community loyalty in the process.

- Customer service departments, to protect the corporate image, often hide the existence of bugs and problems, addressing them only reluctantly when they arise. Communities proactively warn members about known issues, good or bad.

- Customer service focuses solely on improving service levels in the present and the future. Community architects are also interested in the history of community evolution.

These differences can lead to tensions between traditional customer service types and virtual community builders. These are exacerbated by the fact that at the core, customer service departments are first and foremost company advocates while customer-communities are first and foremost customer advocates. This dichotomy creates a philosophical divide—one that needs to be bridged for a successful implementation. But then both customer service and community building have always been about building bridges.

Larger Voice, Louder Voice

Finally, let's reiterate one benefit of your customer-community that is directly related to its connectedness. In general, most of the benefits of growing your customer base are the same whether the customers talk to each other or not—with one exception: the voice of an interconnected e-community grows louder with size. A large group of disparate customers don't have a loud collective voice; a large customer-community does. The bigger your customer-community grows; the louder and more powerful its voice becomes. Most often bigger communities are more powerful than smaller ones. Look at the relative electoral power of large states in the U.S. political system. Who will forget the year 2000 presidential race? If it had been Delaware where the vote was so close, the three electoral votes wouldn't have affected the outcome. But Florida's twenty-five electoral votes—4.6 percent of the entire U.S. electoral pool—mattered quite a lot. Past a certain point of critical mass, size matters more and more. A very large community's power gets even stronger and gains much greater influence because people notice and listen to an expansive, unified crowd. Consider the strength of AARP (the former American Association of Retired Persons) and the National Rifle Association—two of the largest and most powerful lobbying groups in the United States. A unified customer base can yield this type of power. What would happen if all customers of Coca-Cola came together in a unified voice (as they did in rejecting New Coke so vehemently and quickly)— would they like to buy the world a Coke? They could certainly afford to.

The power of a large community can be either positive or negative, or it can flip from one to the other in the blink of an eye. Nationalism can shift to xenophobia; religious faith can turn to zealotry and judgmentalism; customer advocacy can morph into customer boycotts. Intensely passionate communities make the headlines and the history books. Determining a way to stay aware of and potentially direct this energy is, in and of itself, a reason to pay attention. Instead of a surprise attack from a customer badmouthing on epinions.com or a boycott orchestrated on badbusinessbureau.com, imagine your customers with an AARP-type of force vocally supporting your business goals.

Summary

Growing your customer base requires expanding beyond local or geographical boundaries. A large customer base means that customers are disconnected, don't know each other, and don't personally interact. That was true until the Internet came along. Now a large-scale customer base can once again commingle. They can build a customer-community. This community can grow extremely large and still maintain a sense of connectedness. Because of the introduction of new communication tools and other functionalities that affect core community-building concepts, virtual communities can scale far beyond their nonvirtual relatives. A large customer-community not only yields increased revenue and profitability resulting from economies of scale but also results in a loud unified voice that can augment your marketing and branding efforts. It can also help you scale other parts of your business. In this chapter, we have underscored peer-to-peer customer service for two reasons: the difficulty in scaling high-touch customer service and the willingness and effectiveness of customers helping each other out. In Chapter Seven, we will detail many other operational ways that a customer-community can help you scale cost-effectively—content development, product feedback, testing, research, and even development.

Although customer growth will happen naturally, it needs to be managed. An adequate infrastructure needs to be built and an appropriate leadership structure developed. Not surprisingly, the size of a customer-community does matter to the bottom line, especially if growth is architecturally anticipated and effectively managed. Yet surprisingly, if you stay aware, catalyze, and maintain the inherent bonding within your customer-community, this growth is not contradictory to sustainable customer loyalty.

Chapter Six

Understanding Community Bonds

Creating a customer-community is one thing; keeping it going is something else altogether. This chapter will examine some of the elements that keep customers attached, or bonded, to a company or community. Just as the reasons that lie behind customer loyalty and the power of brand are difficult to quantify or pin down, so too are the reasons customers engage in and return to community interactions. Despite the fact that some of the psychological bonds that pull people together may be less concrete, we will highlight a number of possible reasons why you can attempt to turn up the volume on sustainability of customer-communities. We will examine five specific bonding agents that will yield powerful insights into potential intensity and longevity of online communities.

Think of your own consumer habits. How do you choose a service provider? Why do you eat at a specific café or shop at a particular store? More than likely, your selection involves one or more of the following: convenience, habit, price, brand name, product quality, product selection, service efficiency, service quality, or a less discrete reason like the overall pleasure of the experience. You can probably mentally rank how each of these affects your choice. Now, think of what makes you return to that same restaurant or store. What makes you return frequently? What makes you loyal? A brand of product may be the primary reason you choose a retailer, but product quality could be what keeps you coming back. Are the other customers a factor in your decision? Convenience may drive you to try a new restaurant in your neighborhood, but the "see and be seen" clientele may get you to return. Can you truly pinpoint the reason for your patronage? It may be much easier to identify what precipitated a first-time visit than to define the roots of your loyalty.

Throughout the years of management analysis, experts have deconstructed concepts like branding, quality consistency, cost effectiveness, and sustainable high-touch customer service to increase competitiveness. The resulting strategies usually focus on discrete controllable actions that, once implemented, lead to a predictable, desired outcome. Unfortunately, the collective force of your customer base is not so controllable or predictable. But that does not mean that the desired outcome is not there. It can be. Your first step in catalyzing this outcome is understanding the intrinsic potential bonds between your customers.

Bonds between people are sticky and durable. Especially peer-based bonds. Get customers knowing each other, and they are going to come back. The boating industry has boat shows; some restaurants are closing down one night a week to offer cooking classes; Saturn has its Homecoming, which draws thousands of owners back to "Saturn family" events in the main manufacturing plant in Spring Hill, Tennessee. What, if anything, attracts your customers to each other? What causes them to form relationships?

Some communities last a lifetime; others come together and dissipate in the blink of an eye. Why? Why do we stay in touch with some who were distant childhood friends yet not with others who were our best buddies? Why do we go to the same hairstylist for years and then suddenly switch? Human ties ebb and flow over time. Some evolve and change; others don't. Though there is no cookie-cutter approach that ensures sustainable human relationships, there are some underlying building blocks that influence the bonding strength and durability of community connections. In this chapter, we will explore ways to sustain human bonds online, specifically the bonds that can emerge between customers.

Just as there are numerous types and strengths of glue at the hardware store, there are many elements that determine how sticky and durable a community bond can be. We will discuss six: need, demographics and culture, proximity, habit, brand awareness and frequency of interaction, and shared interests (including emotions, beliefs, skills, goals, causes, and so on).

We believe that understanding and strategizing with these six bonding agents will yield powerful customer-communities. You may need a community to provide some essentials for living. You may be part of an ongoing community because of your demographic profile or cultural norms of institutions with which you were raised. You may participate in a community simply out of proximity or habit. You may consciously join a community of shared interest. Or you may get swept up in a whirlwind that keeps you connected to a community that you merely happened into. More than likely, a community is bound and sustained by not just one but a combination of these forces.

Need-Based Communities

Need-based communities form psychologically pure community bonds. We've taken you on a graduated inside look of Maslow's hierarchy of needs as they relate to online community needs. In Chapter Two, we explore Maslow's eight needs levels that drive human motivation, ranging from physiological to transcendent. In an urban environment, you need a doctor, a grocer, a banker, and some other services to support a healthy, holistic existence within that community. Individuals who choose a specific service provider may form a community based on the common need that the service fulfills. The strength of this community can be enriched if the service also meets the social need of the community members to interact with one another—as in a local flea market.

Need-based communities are the underlying foundation of a small-town environment. Merchandisers and service providers have few competitors and service the needs of their local communities. Small-town institutions are ordinarily less automated than their larger urban counterparts, and by default, this more personalized service forces customers upon one another. In the idyllic small-town setting, community members interact as they are walking to the store or to the dentist or while waiting in line for the same banking teller with whom they have done business for years. This need, frequency, and familiarity builds a durable community bond.

Need-based communities are strongest if no competitors exist to offer alternative services. With competitors, the need-based communities are actually weaker than culture-based or habit-based communities. In today's global economy, there are always competitors. If not now, there will be in the near future. It is therefore risky for a company to focus solely on need within its customer-community. IBM did this with its PC market, thereby opening a wide door for Apple and Dell. Even within a high-switching-barrier B2B space, you should not rely on the assumption that your installed base will always need your products or services.

Market leaders often fall prey to the illusion that their customers will need them forever. They become smug. Instead of this arrogant complacency that often accompanies a significant market share, an industry leader should understand the need-based bond within the customer base and constantly work to maintain that bond. This is done by staying aware of the customers' evolving needs and meeting these needs ahead of the competitive pack. Whatever can be said about Microsoft's corporate culture, one thing is certain: the company is obsessive about staying aware of its customers' needs and paranoid of any potential competitors beating it to the punch or meeting a customer need first.

What exactly is a customer-community need? Community-defined needs change as the community evolves. Is gasoline a need? As U.S. cities have expanded their suburban reach without effective public transportation, the automobile has become a necessity for most Americans. Gasoline is therefore now considered a need by most Americans. What about a second car? As American families have evolved from one- to two-income households, so has the need for a second car. Ongoing analyses of demographic data and trends have helped companies uncover and predict new community needs.

When does a product or service evolve from a luxury to an amenity to a need? Is it always the community that drives this need? Is it product or service availability? Is it brilliant marketing? Let's consider the evolution of the two-car household. Was it the suburban sprawl and rising cost of living that drove this need, or was it the automobile availability that enabled cities to sprawl without public transportation? Which came first—or does it matter? It does matter because product availability and product marketing can even greatly stretch the concept of physiological needs where consumers actually believe they need a product or a service to survive within their community. And as that perception becomes a cultural norm, it does evolve into an actual need. Consider cellular telephones. Luxury or need? How much has the marketing of cellular telephones driven this need? A good marketing campaign can create a psychological perception of need and drive that perception toward a cultural norm.

As we indicated, it is difficult for a business to leverage this need factor alone because for need-based products and services, there is usually much competition. In most of today's societies, consumers are rarely forced to select a unique, monopolistic service provider. Yet a business can stretch the concept of "need" to the point that it becomes a highly leverageable factor. How many times have you heard your children say, "I *need* this" or "I *need* that"? As we've shown, need is a psychological factor as well as a physiological one. Marketing departments are very effective at manipulating the psychological needs on higher rungs of Maslow's hierarchy: esteem, cognitive, aesthetic, self-actualization, transcendence. Does one ever *need* a certain brand? Is the need a physical or a self-esteem need? Think about the businesses that have been spawned by human need for an aesthetic surrounding—the *need* for home improvement, gardening, or interior decorating.

Strong communities form around needs. Look at AOL and Yahoo! ISP and e-mail service are now considered needs in many parts of the world. AOL and Yahoo! have done an effective job of making those needs synonymous with their services. If, on top of fulfilling these needs, they also create significant switching costs for their customer-community, they have secured a loyal customer base. AOL has achieved this; the jury is still out on Yahoo!

Demographic and Cultural Communities

Some communities are held together because of demographic or cultural similarities. Sociocultural norms, religious denomination, and workplace all define culture-based communities to which you might belong. Demographic communities are formed around shared traits like ethnicity, age, gender, or sexual orientation. Such shared traits usually lead to a shared experience that can then lead to community bonding. Women's universities, youth groups, and friendships between parents with similarly aged children are examples of demographic community bonds.

Such bonds can be especially strong if the shared experience is negative. Fear and anger, though not necessarily sustainable over time, are significant bonding agents that can trigger memories and hence connections over long periods of time. Demographic communities with a history of oppression or persecution often have extremely intense and durable bonds. There is an intimate recognition between survivors of the Holocaust or the World Trade Center attacks. Consider the instantaneous bond that can develop if a group of people is stuck on an elevator in a momentary power outage.

Specific demographic targeting has long been the media and marketing strategy to lure individual members of gender or ethnocultural groups, and demographic customer-communities can be fiercely loyal (for example, students at women-only colleges, teenagers who frequent the same video arcade, and readers of *Ebony* magazine). The early virtual community boom years of the Web brought about many demographic portals like Women.com, Net-Noir, Gospel.com, Gay.com, and Latina.com. But few e-tailers were slicing their audiences in a way to build demographic customer-communities. Most companies could (and do) easily segment their customer base, but they don't do much to enable demographic communities to emerge. There are exceptions. Department store sites like Macys.com, JCPenney.com, Nordstrom.com, and Gap.com target gender and age groups with product categorization and site indexing. Top-level categories include "Women," "Men," "Boys," "Girls," and "Baby." Most of these companies also identify and market to various ethnic communities. Yet none of these companies interconnects the members of its consumer microcommunities with each other. Boo.com, by comparison, targets a specific younger profile and offers the "Boo Party" for members to interact with one another. Boo even develops the personality of "Miss Boo," who uses storytelling—a classic community-culling technique—to engage her youthful entourage. Boo has some significant challenges to overcome, including convincing customers that it can survive this second incarnation (the original Boo.com, focused more on technology than on profitability, quickly collapsed and shut down for a brief time in 2000) and building a brand recognition that doesn't hinge on the image, now tarnished, of e-commerce businesses who use the Internet as their solitary sales and distribution channel. But if e-commerce-only companies survive, Boo has a good chance at rallying a loyal customer-community following.

Bonding over cultural similarities can be a nearly identical dynamic to bonding over shared demographic traits (in fact, some of the most effective demographic marketing targets some identifiable cultural trait of the target demography—for example, the beauty industry is notorious for targeting women's image-consciousness). Cultural bonding can be obvious, as in some tightly knit immigrant communities, or so subtle as to be unrecognizable, even sometimes by the members of the community. The shared essence of most cultures is assumed, and community forms naturally around it. In most culture-driven communities, there is no actual mandate to join or belong to a specific community; it just happens to be an accepted norm.

Familial, ethnocentric, nationalistic, religious, and workplace cultures create attachments between those who are members of the same culture. When considering the possibility of customer segmentation, don't just focus on the broad, obvious cultural communities.

Some narrow cultures can be surprisingly powerful. Take, for example, the cultural bond of the technolibertarian purists who pervaded virtual communities in the early Usenet days. Coming late into the search engine game, Google was able to corral this community. Certainly part of the attraction was Google's PageRanking technology, which was deemed superior by many, but Google also drew in this extremely vociferous group by supplying a bare-bones, undiluted, unbannered, uncompromised technology solution. Google's rise to become the Web's premier search engine was blazingly fast. It is not surprising that Google added "Google Groups"—Usenet discussion forums—as one of only eleven links on its front page and is orchestrating an effort to "compile the most complete archive possible of Usenet posts." It's as if Google is creating the e-equivalent of a war memorial or activity center to honor and support a community of technology veterans who fought the early Internet battles for the freedoms that we have today.

Retailers have long experimented with cultural bonding. There are niche stores for every viable cultural customer base. You can shop at stores for religious art, astrological paraphernalia, ethnic food—you name it. If a cultural product selection can be amassed in such a way as to bring a profit, there's a store for it. You would think that owing to the direct link of culture and community, it would be an obvious strategy for retailers of cultural commerce to create customer-communities. In fact, customer-community building does indeed happen more frequently within cultural or demographic e-commerce. For example, www.christianbooks.com, one of the largest e-tailers of Christian products, offers a "coffeehouse" on its site complete with a broad selection of discussion boards, a daily devotional, Bible study, and Christian oriented electronic greeting cards. Rubashkin's is primarily a wholesaler (in fact, rubashkin.com has no direct B2C e-commerce component), yet the personality-infused rubashkin.com is obviously attempting to attract customer-community by reflecting the rich familial and culture-based nature of its Jewish target audience. Lane Bryant, the most widely recognized name in plus-size women's fashion, has a "chick chat" area of lanebryant.com where customers discuss issues relevant to the microculture of large-size, fashion-oriented women.

Although niche cultural sites that play to a blatant communal psychology may accrue the benefits in creating a customer-community, broader, more general e-commerce sites have an opportunity here as well. Imagine if you discovered that a large percentage of your customers purchased your product or service to improve their efficiency as they commuted to and from work. Could you tap into the commuting culture and leverage the resulting bond? What if you connected these customers and let them trade best practices on commuting efficiency?

Palm, the company known for its handheld personal Pilot organizers, noticed that community recommendations and tip swapping led to the dramatic growth in these handheld devices. With this realization, Palm built a "Community" section of palm.com where end users can connect directly with other Palm users, peruse "Cool User Stories," and join in live chat sessions with Palm experts. Palm developers have their own palm.com communities complete with a checklist for beginning programmers to develop a software or hardware solution. This developer community includes discussion boards, a suite of online documentation, event announcements, a full training curriculum, and a "partner alliance program" that grants access to an online "resource pavilion" that contains "technical and marketing information, pre-release development tools, a hardware purchase discount program, and other opportunities available to Partner Alliance members."[1] Palm is enabling the cultural connection and business bonds of its customer and developer communities. As a result, the Palm customer-community is, like Mac users, one loyal bunch.

Proximity

Many people join communities because they are close and accessible. It's just plain easy to shop at stores along your regular travel path. People join churches that are nearby and bond with other people who live in the same neighborhood. Physical closeness definitely influences communal choices. Often this proximity forces frequent interactions and encourages shared interests. If you pass your neighbor gardening every day, chances are that you may periodically stop, chat, and even discover some interests that you share. Neighborhood communities form naturally because neighbors share the common interests of safety, convenience, beautification, and environment.

Proximity is such a discrete community factor that it's hard for companies to manipulate proximity-based communities. People that are close to your store or service are close to you. People that aren't, aren't. Obviously, this is the reason retailers select specific sites near large target-customer-communities. McDonald's and Starbucks are both famous for their siting strategies, which have garnered them large local customer bases. There are stories of McDonald's founder Ray Kroc himself flying over various parcels to select the most appropriate site for new restaurants. Mary Kay of Mary Kay Inc. believed in the proximity factor so much that she crafted a sales force of local beauty consultants that went door to door selling Mary Kay cosmetics. You can't get more proximate than that.

You could argue that the Internet has obliterated distribution boundaries and has eliminated proximity as a commercial decision-making factor. This is obviously true to some degree, and as people get more comfortable shopping for basic products online, proximity may become less and less of a factor in the future. But there are still products we go to our local stores to buy.

So what's a business to do in light of our premise that online customer-communities are powerful? Use the Internet to extend the proximity borders. Mary Kay beauty consultant Hope Pratt extended her customer reach by adding e-mail to her communication tool chest. This "made it easier to retain her clients when they (or she) moved out of her territory." But even with the Internet, it was still hard for Pratt to compete without being truly local. "I had to do everything in my power to make it appealing for [my clients] to stay with me rather than buying from someone else down the block. I told them that if they e-mail me by 9 a.m., I'll get their order out by 1 p.m. and they'll get it the next day or the day after, depending on where they live."[2] Her postage bill grew but her phone bill dropped with the advent of the Web. Although proximity is a pretty immutable factor, the Internet entrepreneur can make communal bonding inroads even here.

Habit

Habit-based communities are a blend of culture and proximity. Proximity creates habit, and what is culture other than institutionalized habit? Communities of habit are built around frequency and the familiarity derived from it. Neighborhoods, schools, and workplaces encourage habit-based communities. Habit is one driver of community that a business can influence to create a competitive switching barrier. A person who forms a habit is likely to stick around, especially if building that habit involved a learning curve. In the personal finance arena, Intuit Corporation had a several-year head start on Microsoft. When the software giant tried to enter the market and pull loyal Intuit customers over, it failed because customers had mastered and were comfortable with their Intuit software and had invested time to enter their personal data. Most software companies have an advantage in this regard, especially because document and data conversion also creates a disincentive for people to switch. The steeper the learning curve and the more cumbersome the conversion logistics, the higher the switching barrier. This is why the concept of an installed customer base is so important to these companies. An existing customer will most likely buy upgrade packages and future versions.

People don't like learning new habits, nor do they like breaking established ones. Get a customer in the habit of coming to your store or using your service, and you've won a loyalty battle. Most businesses understand this switching barrier, which is why they spend so much effort on attracting first-time customers. If a company can get someone to purchase once, a habit can begin to form. Most statistics show that a customer who has purchased once satisfactorily from a company is often more likely to purchase again. The second purchase continues to pull a customer down the habit path. Many stores have created store-specific credit cards or repeat purchase discount cards for a more powerful incentive to turn a first-time buyer into a loyal customer. Most e-companies also encourage habitual use by making repeat shopping easier and easier. In addition to the general familiarity with the site offerings, atmosphere, navigation, and ordering process, the repeat customer receives more customized and faster service. These e-companies build individual customer profiles that track a customer's personal data and usage pattern. This benefits the customer, who gets individually targeted promotions and the convenience of one-click shopping. This consumer-profile-enabled shopping habit makes it difficult for a customer to walk away because of the time it would take to build a usage profile at some other company.

Communal habits can be the easiest to develop and the most difficult to sever, especially if interacting leads to better buying experiences. Again, consider Apple's and Palm's customer bases and partners who have built affinity with each other by sharing Macintosh and Palm handheld usage and development tips. Amazon.com customers, with their repeat usage profiles and their favorite reviewers, are difficult to recruit away. Get your customers talking, and if they like each other, they will habitually return just to chat . . . and buy.

Brand Awareness and Frequency of Interaction

Two related psychological factors that help sustain a customer-community are a positive brand awareness and frequent vendor-to-customer interaction. Brand allegiance can definitely strengthen a customer-community bond, and conversely, a customer-community can be integral in an ongoing brand awareness campaign. Especially in B2B communities, news about products, designs, and features is spread much faster by word of mouth through the partner and user community than it would if entirely dependent on the product's marketing departments to create and distribute promotional materials. Some companies engage customers directly in their branding campaigns. What if you held a customer-community contest in which winners were chosen to be spokespeople for your product or might possibly even appear in your advertisements? You can imagine the resulting customer loyalty, not only from the winners but also from your entire customer-community.

Frequency of interaction is tricky. Too much forced communication can turn a customer away. Customer relationship management (CRM) experts have become incredibly data-driven and savvy about appropriate communication thresholds. They communicate just enough to keep customers psychologically tethered but not enough to annoy them. Even so, with the advent of e-mail and increased uses of telemarketing, junk communication has risen to the point that many customers don't pay attention or don't believe any communications from retailers, regardless of whether or not they are loyal customers. In an article, "Getting to Know You," Yankelovich and Partners claim that consumers have confidence in what corporations tell them only 6 percent of the time. Only 5 percent believe advertising claims, and 4 percent believe what car salespeople tell them.[3]

Frequent customer-community communication is more effective because most intercustomer-communication is "pull" communication as opposed to "push." Basically, this means that customers choose to communicate as opposed to having junk mail pushed at them. If a business can develop a strategy that keeps its customers frequently communicating with one another, it can achieve an adequate level of interaction that influences loyalty and minimizes the backlash that can result from overpushing communication at customers. A loyalty strategy that leverages customer-to-customer-communication can also potentially lower the cost of direct-mail and telemarketing campaigns.

Shared Interests

"Shared interests" is generic for the all of the other commonalities that can bind a community. These various interests often don't have the intrinsic longevity that need, culture, or habit do and are therefore more dynamic and flexible. People convene around shared hobbies, skills, goals, leisure pursuits—almost anything. What is the longevity of these communities? Interests change, goals shift, skills improve, and the supporting communities will either mutate or dissipate with these changes. By understanding the fluid nature of these bonds, you can create structures and norms that prolong durability, support change, and reinvigorate dying communities. Some communities, like the Elks Club, for example, infuse a community of interest with culture and habit. Others, like community centers, design enough flexibility so that interests can shift within the community structure. Sustaining shared-interest communities is an art.

Common interests can lead to loyal community consumerism. Consider maternity and baby product consumers. Expectant and new parents experience an intense community bond. Mothers with one-year-olds often form instant relationships with other mothers of similarly aged infants. Tips and advice are swapped moments after meeting each other for the first time. They discuss what toys distract their toddlers for the longest period of time and what clothes are the most practical. Maternity and baby product retailers are in a prime position to leverage this bond. Technology customers have obvious shared interests around the best way to maximize the specific technology they have purchased. Vertical-interest stores—those that sell sporting equipment, musical instruments, specialized antiques—clearly have customer-community potential. REI has tapped into the shared athletic interests of its customer base with the "Learn and Share" portion of www.rei.com, which links a community of outdoor enthusiasts. To entice customers to participate in these forums, REI advertises:

Wondering where to go? What to bring? Want to learn about fixing a flat on your bike or how a carabiner works? You've come to the right place. For more than 60 years, REI members and employees have been in the great outdoors doing what we love. REI has combined all of this expertise into a series of comprehensive clinics, checklists, shopping help and quick tips. Check it out![4]

Shared-interest customer-communities are not new. Traditionally, offline companies have created community activities around the shared interests of their customer base. Often customers like to sit down and relax with a drink or a bite to eat after their shopping day. For much of the twentieth century in America, every small town had a drugstore with a soda fountain. Today Barnes & Noble bookstores incorporate Starbucks coffee shops, large discount retailers like Target and Wal-Mart often have fast-food counters, and exclusive stores like Emporio Armani and Paris's Collette have posh in-store cafés. Self-improvement and entertainment interests have further been associated with consumerism. Nordstrom has created a very successful spa in its San Francisco store. Some McDonald's have playgrounds that have kids clamoring to eat under the Golden Arches. At Chuck-E-Cheese pizza parlors, one could even argue that entertainment takes precedence over the food. Home Depot offers home repair classes; some wine shops have regular tastings, and major department stores mount annual celebrity fashion shows and fundraising events. What are the shared interests of your customers? Can you leverage these interests into a community activity that will lead to customer loyalty?

The Rise of Shared-Interest Communities

A few things happened over the past two hundred years that dramatically shifted the community landscape. First, transportation technologies like the railroad and automobile led to a more transient society. Communities resulting from geographical proximity were affected by this increased mobility. Second, communication technologies like the telegraph, radio, television, and the Internet allowed people to easily communicate with others who shared commonalities. Third, automation technologies like bank ATMs and Internet-enabled e-commerce eliminated the need for people to interact with each other in procuring specific services. Fourth, distribution improvements opened up choices for all need-based services, meaning that monopolistic institutions could no longer dominate the options. Finally, many culturally based communal institutions waned—the family unit became far less stable, as evidenced by higher divorce, cohabitation, and spousal abuse rates; religious participation decreased; and military participation by average citizens diminished, especially after the end of the Cold War.

All of these factors contributed to the rise of shared-interest communities. Communities of practice (shared skills), cause-based communities, communities of shared experience, and other common-interest groups now account for a substantial percentage of community groups. You need only look quickly at Yahoo! Clubs to see millions of people dynamically organizing around shared interests to understand how pervasive these virtual communities can be.

We highlight this shift in the community landscape because, as we mentioned earlier, shared-interest communities are much more volatile than other types and much more susceptible to variations in community norms and structures. Community organizers therefore have much more control to ignite, influence, and develop a shared-interest community.

When *Fast Company* magazine was launched by Alan Webber and Bill Taylor in November 1995, it won an immediate following. Thousands of readers jumped on the *Fast Company* bandwagon, excited that someone was addressing the blistering new pace of the business world and the human response to it. Heath Row, self-proclaimed *Fast Company* "social capitalist," noticed that *Fast Company* readers had a shared intensity that reached beyond the pages of the magazine. He convinced Webber and Taylor to form the Company of Friends (CoF), "*Fast Company* magazine's global readers' network."[5] By the autumn of 2001, www.fastcompany.com noted that "more than 39,000 business people, thought leaders, and change agents have signed up in more than 150 urban areas around the world. From Auckland, New Zealand, to Washington, D.C., *Fast Company* readers are self-organizing local discussion groups, mentoring and networking organizations, and creative problem-solving teams."[6] Who would have thought that readers of a magazine could form such a rich community?

The bottom line is basically that the rise of shared-interest communities means that people are bonding over interests that require some level of ongoing consumerism. Take those who love sports or technology, home design enthusiasts, or collectors. There has never been an easier time to coalesce broad customer-communities and Web communities, all of which will have purchasing patterns centered around one interest or another.

Multiple Bonds

Most community bonds are a mixture of two or more of these bonding agents. For example, PlanetOut Partners aligns the demographic and cultural bond of its gay and lesbian target audience. Yet in doing so, PlanetOut Partners has focused on the specific needs of this community. Megan Smith, vice chairman of PlanetOut Partners, notes that isolation is a major issue for many gays and lesbians and that this has increased their need to meet others in their broader community. PlanetOut Partners' strategy is therefore developed with the understanding that its target audience is a need-based community.[7] The executive team is fully aware that in adequately addressing this need, PlanetOut Partners achieves a stronger and more durable community bond.

Margaret Spencer, vice president of Martha Stewart's wedding registry and former COO of The Wedding List, notes that the strategy of The Wedding List is to efficiently meet the needs of soon-to-be-married couples. The executive team realized that wedding gift giving is not simply about efficient registry and purchase processes.

Spencer notes, "Weddings are rich in tradition, and in most cultures, couples getting married want to touch and feel products and imagine them in their own home environment."[8] For this reason, The Wedding List offers highly personalized service and has pursued a multichannel strategy, opening local storefronts in New York, Boston, and London. The stores attract local clients and reflect the rich traditions of wedding gift giving. Spencer adds that "stores are used for events—providing a forum for brides to come together."[9] With this localized strategy, The Wedding List creates intertwined customer bonds of need, proximity, and culture.

Stronger Bonds Through Intensity and Vulnerability

You can't predict how sustainable a community will be simply by the types of bonds that hold it together. Other variables come into play. Two of the most important are intensity and vulnerability. Shared intensity or shared vulnerability can affect the duration of a community positively or negatively. Take wartime comrades, survivors of a shared near-death experience, or members of a political activist organization. Less death-defying but intense nonetheless are the emotions that come with getting married, graduating, or having children.

Intensity and vulnerability are transient, so to take advantage of these magnifiers, you'll need to pay close attention to their movement within the community. Boston's Filene's Basement, realizing the intensity of brides-to-be who are desperate for the perfect wedding dress, offers a one-day-only wedding gown sale where daughters and mothers gather in line before dawn and flood the store the moment the doors open. This annual event needs little advertising as the intensity of the experience gives rise to widespread word-of-mouth promotion.

Often these intense, vulnerable experiences lead to lifelong relationships; at other times they lead to burnout and defection. Community builders who create passionate communities are experts at enabling participation with continual intensity as well as recruiting new members to replace those who leave the community. Is this level of awareness needed in a customer-community? Sometimes. When a company is in crisis—as Odwalla was during the *E. coli* scare or the near-death experience of Apple in the mid-1990s—the company's leadership must stay acutely aware of customer reactions. If managed effectively, supportive customers through tough times will likely be even more loyal as a result of the shared vulnerability.

It is most likely that intensity and vulnerability will come into play during interactions between individual customers or between individual customers and customer service representatives. A customer may have a bad product or service experience. The emotional reaction may begin as anger focused toward the retailer of the product. If the customer service representative can effectively solve the customer's problem, that negative intensity can be turned around into a more durable positive bond. Michael Lowenstein, coauthor of *Customer Winback* and managing director of Customer Retention Associates, indicates that when analyzing results from positive resolution of customer service complaints, you often discover that statistically "customers are more loyal than they would have been if they had never made a complaint."[10] It's probably not a good idea to orchestrate intensity and vulnerability (as some military training does) just to increase the customer-community bond, but customer service representatives should be aware that when dealing with emotionally charged customers, they have an opportunity to engender a deeper and more lasting customer loyalty.

Summary

In the end, how can you ensure the sustainability of your customer base? Can you determine what will attract and bond your customers to your company and product or service offerings? It is this type of assessment that yields business opportunities. But after you choose your product, distribution, and customer service strategy, put on the customer's hat. What will make your customers *need* your products? What will make your customers form a habit of buying from you? Do your customers share any interests or cultural traits that are tied to consumption? What will bring your customers back again and again? Most important, how do you get them to spend again and again? How do you create, grow, and sustain customer-community value?

Part Three

Customer-Community and the Bottom Line

Chapter Seven

Creating Value
from Customer-Communities

In 1999 and 2000 as the financial community began to demand a return on its massive Internet investment, you could hear the question ring through virtual dot-com ventures: "How can we monetize community?" Virtual shopping channels were quickly erected on community sites. Membership programs were developed. Advertising became more and more targeted and provocative. And still the profits did not roll in.

City planners don't ask how they can "monetize community." Rather, they honor the two needs—they balance social living spaces with commercial areas that support the community. Witnessing the natural swells and flows of community patterns, it becomes obvious where to put businesses and gathering places that make money *and* forge healthy communities.

In urban commercial areas, there are two types of potential shoppers milling about: *reactives*, those who come primarily to hang out and possibly buy something, and *proactives*, those who come to shop and possibly enjoy hanging out between purchases. Certainly the city planner would not design a commercial zone entirely for reactives while ignoring proactives and then wonder why subsequent revenue generated couldn't support the cost of commerce. Yet that is exactly the path we've taken with virtual community development. Is it any wonder that community sites created for reactives can't turn a profit? In contrast, the commerce-oriented city or Web site architect should design spaces that leverage the psychology of the reactives while focusing most energy on creating a compelling environment for the proactives. In this chapter, we examine communities rooted in proactive commerce and contend that they are stronger over longer periods of time and have a far greater potential for profitability.

Remember, too, that the primary focus of this book is not how to entice a community to spend money but rather how to engender customer loyalty by building a community out of your current customer base. The widespread belief that community and commerce don't mix is based on the approach that says community members drawn to commune will buy something. We suggest turning this around and measuring the value of customers who are first drawn to an e-business by commerce and then participate in a customer-community.

The "Monetizing Community" Trap

Starbucks has built an empire intertwining commerce and community. The company is now tackling the Web in the same community-leveraging way. "Starbucks is tying its online efforts closely to its central mission: building customer loyalty around cappuccinos, lattes, and other fancy beverages." The company is rolling out high-speed wireless connections in its physical stores in a way that maximizes connection with people and the traditional café experience. Though skeptics wonder if he will be encouraging people who loiter but don't purchase anything, Chairman Howard Schultz claims, "Our most successful stores turn out to be the ones with the most loitering. We think it's great if people want to stay awhile. It creates a sense of community."[1] We believe that this philosophy translates to online loitering and purchase patterns as well.

Note that Starbucks is not creating a virtual Starbucks community. The company has not fallen into the generic "monetizing community" trap but has instead targeted its current customer base by creating an additional community draw. To do this, it used virtual technologies to generate more revenue from customers who commune.

To understand customer-community value, we need to move beyond inadequate virtual community definitions and metrics.

Joseph Cothrel, vice president of Participate.com, makes some broad claims about the monetary success of online communities. Focusing on B2B commerce-based communities, he points out that "the usual metrics we choose for communities—page views, unique visitors, etc.—are really measures of the overall health of the community, not its ROI [return on investment]." Cothrel is a strong proponent that community will, in fact, catalyze online commerce. He cites statistics indicating that "traditional" online community members are 36 percent more likely to buy something at a site than nonmembers. Overall, community use shows a high correlation with both heavy marketplace use and high-value transactions. According to Cothrel, community members transact more in Net marketplaces and are more likely than nonmembers to purchase higher-ticket items.[2] "More likely to buy," "heavier marketplace use," and "higher-value transactions" all translate directly into higher monetary value.

The Almighty Click-Through

When commercial Web sites burst on the scene, media companies and buyers alike were initially elated because the medium allowed ways to instantaneously measure and quantify the consumer reaction in the form of the almighty click-through. Following the deeply entrenched standards of classic media advertising strategies and buys, Web marketing was segmented into the same categories, and the click-through quickly became the established yardstick by which banner ads and Web revenue were evaluated. We are just beginning to recognize the folly in this.

What went wrong? Let's deconstruct this thinking. Figure 7.1 provides a simplistic look at how a business generates revenue through the transformation of a prospect into a loyal customer.

A, B, C, and D are the business elements that drive customer behavior. A consists of features that attract new customers, such as store location, brand identity, and marketing and promotion. B elements help induce a first-time purchase—product line quality

Figure 7.1 The Pathway from Prospect to Loyal Customer

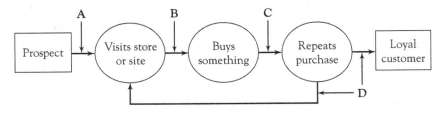

and breadth, presentation and atmosphere, and competitive pricing and sales efforts. C gets the customer to return; it is the sum of A plus B plus customer service plus repeat purchase incentives plus general customer satisfaction. Notice as you continue down this path, the activities become more varied and interwoven. D features induce loyalty—the Holy Grail and the most complex. D is A plus B plus C plus membership incentives plus all the bonding elements discussed in Chapter Six that lead to customer loyalty. Basically, D is just about everything your company does—or doesn't do.

For e-business, Figure 7.1 is generally the same, which is why early Internet valuations were based on extrapolations of traditional offline business success metrics. Certainly there were different e-techniques to drive customer behavior: A on the Internet achieves click-through and includes new marketing programs like banner advertisements, viral marketing, and affiliation. Important attributes of B online were navigation, transaction functionality, and distribution efficiency. For the most part, the general behavioral concepts remained the same as in the offline world. But there were two *huge* differences that were not fully considered. First, because clicking onto a Web site is so darned easy and not always intentional or commercially inspired, the statistical percentage of people who visit a site and are then converted to buyers is vastly smaller than in the offline world. Let's call this difference *conversion*. Second, because of the efficiency of the Internet marketplace, *loyalty* is much more difficult to achieve and sustain. These two elements led to misevaluations, misuses, and poor design of virtual communities.

Let's talk about that conversion problem for a minute. In the offline world, the prospects you attract through the front door are a pretty consistent bunch. Not to mention the fact that they are likely already in a consuming frame of mind. It takes both physical and psychological effort to get to a store, walk in, meander the aisles, and interact with salespeople. Conversion rates of these folk are predicable. This is not the case for conversion on the Web. There is enormous conversion variance between active e-shoppers, people drawn to a Web site through a promotion, and people acquired through a forced membership acquisition (a merger of two sites, for example). Yet early Web valuations treated site "visitors" the same and were therefore based on page views and click-throughs. Subsequently, marketers promoted "come one, come all" incentives and indiscriminately attracted hordes of "unqualified visitors" to their sites. It is not so surprising that visitation numbers have not been consistent predictors of revenue generation or profitability.

Regarding e-loyalty, there has been an understanding that a "member" is more loyal than a visitor. But unfortunately, the concept of "member" was divorced from that of "customer," and subsequently the "member" definition was oversegmented until it was ripped to shreds. This resulted in both customer and business confusion and dissatisfaction. Many sites have registered users, affiliates, community members, marketing program members, and membership program members. Community members can either join or be acquired through a merger with another site. Registered users often register only because they are forced to enter a sweepstakes or use a feature like e-mail. They never visited again. Marketing program members got more promotional communications than the other types of members and often couldn't remember how or why they signed up to be continually spammed. Membership program members were treated with more respect because they spent more money. Often people accidentally signed up for more than one type of membership and then were confused by noncoordinated communications. Also, benefits didn't cross membership boundaries. Membership program members got nothing additional in the community area of the site—no membership-only discussion board or chat room. And it seemed like the more valuable members were not as loyal. E-businesses were disgruntled that high-maintenance, non-profit-generating community members stuck around while membership program members would switch allegiance with the click of a mouse. This confusion led to the perception that e-membership doesn't lead to e-loyalty and therefore has no significant value.

When you analyze both of these misperceptions, the opportunity for customer-community becomes quite clear. First, the customer-community concept converts current e-customers into more loyal e-customers. The behavior of an e-customer who has already purchased is much more predictable than that of a random visitor to your site. Second, in the analysis of the e-membership quagmire, there is evidence that virtual community does engender loyalty.[3] Put these two revelations together, and you have predicable purchasing patterns and potentially increased loyalty to your site. That spells value.

A Fresh Look at the Customer-Community Value Proposition

Let's take a fresh look at how a customer-community effort can pay off. Customer-community success should be quantified not by membership acquisition but instead by customer loyalty metrics similar to those used to measure customer service. Arthur Armstrong and John Hagel, in a groundbreaking virtual community article in the *Harvard Business Review*, wrote, "We believe that commercial success in the on-line arena will belong to those businesses that organize electronic communities to meet multiple social and commercial needs. By creating strong online communities, businesses will be able to build customer loyalty to a degree that today's marketers can only dream of."[4] Businesses should therefore judge the effectiveness of customer-community efforts through the following types of loyalty-related cost savings and revenue generation:

- Decreased cost of customer retention
- Higher purchases by community customers than by non-community customers
- Higher frequency of repeat purchases
- Lower cost of customer service (due to repeat customer familiarity and potentially engaging customers as virtual customer service representatives)
- Increased customer satisfaction (per standard metrics)

Second-tier benefits include these:

- Decreased cost of customer acquisition due to customer-community advocacy (customer acquisition, *not* member acquisition)
- Lower cost of product development (if feedback loop is created between customer-community and product development)

In *Net.gain*, Hagel and Armstrong present an extensive argument for the potential value created in commercially focused virtual communities. Although *Net.gain* is about virtual communities in the broader sense (Hagel and Armstrong focused on deriving value from large virtual communities of shared interest rather than commerce-centric communities) and their value metrics hinge on membership aggregation, they explore many important nuances of value creation relevant to customer-communities. As they dissect membership value, they highlight three points: "First, community members are likely to evolve in their role and economic contribution to the community. Second, not all members are equal in terms of their economic potential for the community. Third, as in all service businesses, some key variables significantly shape the overall economic performance: the cost of member acquisition, the net profit generated by each member during his or her lifetime as a member, and the average churn rate, which determines the average length of membership."[5] Hagel and Armstrong focus on the economic contribution of Internet communities. Let's drill a bit deeper and look at actual customer-community activities or outcomes that contribute to the bottom line.

Sixteen Bottom-Line Possibilities

Leveraging customer-community loyalty into economic value will vary, depending on the commercial goals of the organization and how the interests of the customer-community evolve. For Amazon. com, customer-generated reviews entice additional sales; for eBay, buyer and seller profiling secures trust in the purchase process; for REI, customers' "sharing and learning" helps www.rei.com serve as the "complete resource for the outdoor enthusiast" and thus engenders lasting loyalty. There are many other ways in which your customer-community can add value to your bottom line. In Chapter One, we generalized eight customer-community business benefits: customer loyalty, a collective customer voice supporting you and your brand identity, broader marketing reach through customer advocacy, focused product input, peer-to-peer customer service, partnership development support, additional revenue generation possibilities, and lower operational costs from drawing your customers into your business operations. Here we will get more specific about customer-community value creation. Figure 7.2 presents a matrix of potential customer-community value and the inherent bottom-line contribution as a mix of increased customer loyalty, direct revenue generation, and decreased operational expense.

Figure 7.2 Contributors to Customer-Community Value

Source of Contribution	Customer Loyalty	Direct Revenue	Lower Operational Expense
Customer Data			
Personalize	•		
Enhance efficiency	•		•
Target market	•	•	•
Provide access	•		•
Sell market research		•	
Sell customer data	X[a]	•	
Fees			
Incoming user fees			
Subscription	•	•	
Usage		•	
Transaction		•	
Incoming partner fees			
Advertising		•	
Content licensing		•	
Outgoing user fees			
Referral	•		•
Royalties	•		•
Outgoing partner fees			
Click-throughs			•
Impressions			•
Advocacy or Pass-Through Revenue	•	•	•
Group Discounts	•	•	
Affiliation	•	•	
Customer-to-Customer Commerce	•	•	
Incubation	•	•	
Offline Events	•	•	
Competitive Research	•		•
Product Testing	•		•
Product Feedback	•		•
Product Development	•	•	•
Peer-to-Peer Customer Service	•		•
Virtual Employees	•		•
Other Operational Savings	•		•
Membership	•	•	

[a]Possible loyalty loss.

Customer Data

Any marketer will tell you that customer information is money. The Internet has been a dream come true in terms of customer data collection. Some businesses have realized many new avenues for the collection and use of data, while others have limited themselves to pre-Internet marketing strategies. We call out six different ways to leverage customer data: personalize the experience, enhance efficiency, target the market, provide customer access, sell market research, and sell personal data.

Personalize the Experience. Customers have always liked individual treatment and will pay for it. Offline, a personal experience requires a one-to-one relationship between the sales or service representative and the customer. Online, individual service can be placed squarely in the domain of the individual. When Yahoo! first introduced customized Web pages with "My Yahoo!" other portals soon followed. After an extensive usage study showed that "people who have registered for personalized portals are also likely to stay online for a longer time,"[6] mimic technologies were being introduced right and left. Today personalization has grown to mean so much more than customized pages; it means any technology or strategy that helps provide a more individualized customer experience. E-businesses can proactively track customer usage patterns and can then feed these data into a system that constantly hones the individual experience. "Personalization will breed familiarity between customers and merchants. Many consumers are willing to 'spend' their personal data in return for time or money savings. Leaders will build a central data repository."[7]

Customization doesn't have to be limited to individualization. You can also offer group personalization. What if a customer microcommunity relinquished personalization control to one leader who would personalize the commerce experience for an entire microcommunity? Imagine a computer-literate son facilitating and standardizing the e-commerce experience for his entire family or a bride-to-be easing the wedding gift purchase experience for all of her guests. Evite.com allows one party planner to customize an invitation "experience" for all invitees to a particular event. This group customization concept could easily and effectively be adopted by e-tailers.

Enhance Efficiency. Most e-commerce sites have realized that they can translate data from individual customer transactions into more efficiency for future customers. If you collect payment preferences and "bill to" information once, you can make the second purchase a one-click process. Build a database of "ship to" addresses for customers to click, or better yet, offer the customer an easy way to import information from an electronic address book or personal database.

Target Market. Pinpointed target marketing can push a customer further down the loyalty path, or it can overwhelm and turn a customer away. The difference between those two diametrically opposed outcomes involves subtlety and frequency. Many companies choose to target customers with annoying telemarketing calls, direct junk mail, and e-mail spam. They statistically know how many vendor-to-customer communications will yield a sale. They also know how many times they can spam a customer without ticking the customer off. Businesses often use this knowledge in a limited fashion, indiscriminately broadcasting messages at a frequency just below the alienation threshold to deliver short-term results at the expense of long-term loyalty. With more Web-enabled integrated targeting techniques, marketers can achieve both, especially if they focus on results that truly add value to the customer experience instead of efforts that are designed merely to not make the customer mad.

Both retailers and e-tailers have learned that targeting can be more effective when a customer gives you time frames for being contacted. The Internet has made this far easier. For example, prompting a customer to enter special dates like birthdays and anniversaries when he or she wants to be notified of targeted purchase opportunities can yield far higher hit rates and can lead to customer appreciation rather than annoyance.

Some sites have learned from Amazon.com that targeting can often be subtler and more powerful if coupled directly with the transacting process. A return customer who is already shopping is not likely to be annoyed at customized suggestions. In fact, combining historical individual purchase data with aggregate customer-community data can expand target opportunities. Amazon.com analyzes what a customer has previously purchased, researches similar purchase histories for other Amazon.com customers, and statistically aggregates the most frequently related purchase to targeted customers. This is spot on. The process often adds value for the customer because the nongeneric, customized recommendations are directly in line with purchase preferences as well as mindset. But often such consumption targeting is more complex than simple behavioral extrapolation.

Kim Daus, one of the authors, explains:

> I have wide-ranging and unusual book-buying patterns. I am a consultant to companies on leadership development and strategic communications. I am also studying for a master's degree in theology and ethics. Additionally I am a black-and-white photographer and a gardener. Can you imagine the confusion I must cause to Amazon.com's database? Should the company target me with leadership, photography, theology, or technology topics? What does this blend of interests tell Amazon about me that would help it serve me better? What if it could begin to predict what interest mindset or mood I'm in when I enter the site? Can it know whether a purchase was a reflection of my own taste (bought for myself) or not (bought as a gift)? I do not have children, but I've purchased gifts from the Baby Center. E-mails targeted to me on the basis of past behavioral data could be irrelevant. Could advanced data analyses decipher and make sense of my consumerism, subsequently offering relevant recommendations?

Clearly, even Amazon.com has more to learn.

Finally, it is an obvious leap from targeting an individual to targeting a microcustomer-community. The sport-specific forums of rei.com are ideal venues for narrowing marketing promotions. As an avid rock climber, wouldn't you want to see specific climbing gear discounts promoted on your discussion board?

Provide Customer Access. American Express was one of the first companies to produce yearly purchase summaries for its customers. American Express simply uses data that it already collects to directly benefit the individual customer. You can imagine that this type of summary would be perceived as useful and result in customer loyalty. It might also, like membership programs, result in more repeat usage because of the customer's desire to get more out of the summary. If a customer restricts his or her credit card usage to American Express, the yearly account summary will provide a comprehensive and therefore more useful detail to help manage personal finances.

Combining these data with aggregate customer-community data might also be useful to the customer. For example, wouldn't it be nice to know how others in the American Express customer-community use their cards? What percentage of the average customer-community member's expenditure goes to restaurants? With online access, you wouldn't have to confine customer data access to a yearly summary. Customers could access their purchase histories at any time. If a yearly summary can bind a customer, just think what providing real-time access to a comprehensive customer activity history could do.

Showing real-time customer-community activity could also be helpful. Let customers know how many people are simultaneously shopping so that they feel comforted by choosing a popular shopping venue or so that they can query another shopper for advice. Collect data to understand what purchases are associated with the need for customer interaction and proactively offer customer interaction venues for those purchases. For example, when you are purchasing computer products online, it can be confusing to know whether you are buying the right product. In a store, you may turn to the shopper next to you and ask, "Do you know anything about . . . ?" In a virtual store, this should be a whole lot easier. Use customer aggregate data to predict these decision points and intercustomer dialogue opportunities that can encourage a purchase.

Sell Market Research. Consumer companies pay big money for market research. Sales of Web site analysis and data-mining software are expected to climb from $29 million in 1998 to $132 million by 2001, according to International Data Corporation.[8] A customer-community is a defined market, and aggregate data on this community can be very valuable. By definition, attitudinal and behavioral data captured by Women.com is about Internet-enabled women. If Women.com can prove that a statistically significant percentage of Internet-enabled women frequent its site, imagine the data it could sell. What would Revlon pay to discover what Internet-enabled women claim as their biggest cosmetic issue? Your customer-community may prove to be a valuable demographic slice. For example, wouldn't the behavioral patterns and discussions of www.tiffany.com's customers be of interest to other luxury providers?

Sell Customer Data. *Don't do it*—unless your business model in no way, shape, or form depends on customer loyalty. It is so tempting to sell marketing lists, but it is extremely dangerous. If customers, especially Internet customers, discover that you've sold their contact data to a telemarketer or Internet marketer, your goose is cooked. DoubleClick became the poster child for this strategic boo-boo: when, in 1999, news of privacy problems broke, its stock instantly plummeted.

Fees

There are various fee-based revenue streams to consider, especially for service companies. Fees for nonservice companies can be trickier, and a business must show the customer sufficient value to justify the fee. The landscape of Internet fees is still in flux. In the boom days, Internet fees were considered at odds with the "open access" philosophical foundation on which e-business was built. As dot-coms continue to fold due to their inability to turn a profit, fees will likely begin appearing more frequently. It is wise to analyze your business to determine potential fee opportunities and then remain aware as industry acceptance of various fees begins to emerge.

Here is a brief overview of some possible fees.

Incoming User Fees

Subscriptions and memberships: Payment for ongoing benefit or right (example: AOL monthly subscription)

Usage: Cost based on amount of use (example: query fees on research sites)

Transactions fees: Cost for transactions carried out (example: cost for a wire transfer of funds)

Incoming Partner Fees

Advertising: Rates based on number of viewers, readers, or users for delivery to an audience (example: banner ads on many Web sites)

Content licensing and distribution deals: Income from content sold to media outfits (example: a news site paying for Reuter's news media content)

Outgoing User Fees

Referrals: Payment to customer for referring a new customer

Royalties: Commission paid when you deliver business to someone else (example: fees paid to Intuit Advisors when accountants sell Intuit software to their clients)

Outgoing Partner Fees

Click-throughs: Money paid to sites for the number of visitors who clicked an ad and were directed to your site (focus: membership acquisition and e-commerce)

Impressions: Money paid to sites for the number of people who viewed an ad (focus: brand recognition)

Some of these fee structures can be applied to customer-communities as well as individuals. You could discount membership and usage fees for community leaders or customers who maintain a certain level of activity in the customer-community. Or you could offer referral benefits to the customer microcommunity that grew the fastest or produced the most yearly revenue.

Group Discounts and Benefits

Local service companies like the hotel and rental car industry are clearly aware of group loyalty and reward this loyalty through group or affinity discounts. You could reward segments of your customer-community in the same fashion. What if a customer microcommunity formed around a certain type of product? For example, what if a group of Californian Zinfandel-loving Wine.com customers formed a group and decided to try a new Zinfandel every month if they received a group purchase discount? Imagine the potential loyalty that could result.

Advocacy or Pass-Through Revenue

We've discussed the power of advocacy. It is one of the only customer-community benefits that can simultaneously achieve customer loyalty, revenue generation, and operational savings. Therefore, it is ever so tempting to provide incentives for this behavior. Paid advocacy, or pass-through, revenue can be a catch-22. Such referral programs can work, especially if financial reimbursement is not secretive or if there are benefits to both the referred party and the referring party. But often the discredit associated with monetary payments can outweigh the increased referral activity prompted by the incentive. Once someone is paid to say something nice, the testimonial is no longer impartial and therefore possibly less effective. Nonfinancial advocacy incentives and facilitation may be a better approach. The "e-mail this to a friend" functionality is an example of facilitated viral marketing.

When Chrysler introduced the PT Cruiser, the carmaker decided to let its customers do some of its marketing. Jay Friedman, vice president of marketing for LiveWorld, which provides interactive online services for businesses, explained: "We used several [approaches]. . . . We did online chats with Chrysler people and customers about the PT Cruiser. And then we let customers talk with each other through discussion boards. It allowed Chrysler to draw an audience to create some good buzz about the PT Cruiser and I think it helped a lot of people get interested in the car."[9]

Customer-communities can be advocacy engines, even if not given incentives or prompted. You can monitor customer-community dialogues, pull quotes and get customers' permissions to use them, and even direct potential customers to these dialogues. You may be surprised at the prospect-to-customer conversion potential.

Affiliation

On the Internet, affiliate programs are easy to start. Affiliates are usually paid to direct traffic from their Web sites to yours. AOL's affiliate network entices potential affiliates: "Maximize your website's potential to generate revenue for you. Just add a 'Try AOL' ad banner to your website and start making money!"[10] You can research and recruit affiliates to improve your reach and customer transition ratio. You can create a special landing "welcome" for potential customers who came to your site from an affiliate location. You can develop joint promotions with your affiliates, or you could simply outsource affiliate logistics and then enjoy a lower cost of extending your marketing reach and branding efforts.

You can also let your customer-community handle some of the affiliate strategy for you. For example, if Amazon.com makes it easy for authors to create their own promotional Web pages and gives them a percentage of the profit, authors will direct potential book buyers back to Amazon.com.

Customer-to-Customer Commerce

Customer-to-customer commerce and incubation are two ways to give customers a significant stake in your site. Both are deviations from most traditional businesses' e-commerce strategies. Therefore, if you are considering either, the value proposition needs to be explored in light of your core business strategy.

The Internet is the ideal marketplace for peer-to-peer commerce. Companies that uniquely facilitate lay sellers finding lay buyers, as well as the selling transaction logistics, are in a position to score a steady stream of commission revenue. eBay and ELance are good examples. Both have targeted specific marketplaces using unique functionalities to secure loyal customer-to-customer commerce communities.

How would a business catalyze commerce between members of its customer-community? The shopping channel on www.disney.com includes both DisneyStore and Disney Auctions. A customer of Disney can easily search collectibles from Disney-controlled "disneyauctioneers" or link directly into eBay to become a customer-to-customer buyer or seller of a Disney collectible. www.cocacolastore.com has its own collectible shopping area. It would be easy for Coca-Cola to augment this marketplace with customer-to-customer commerce as well. The Zippo Manufacturing Company ardently leverages the collectible status of its cigarette lighters. There's a national Zippo Day, a Zippo car, and even a Zippo museum. Zippo proactively engages its customer-community, showcasing an international calendar of community swap meets and a complete listing with contact information for local Zippo clubs around the world.

We can imagine different types of customer-to-customer commerce besides collectibles. What if a company allowed its customers to sell accessory product lines? What if a virtual furniture store created a customer-to-customer home accents marketplace or a clothing e-commerce shop allowed its customer-community to sell handmade jewelry? Certainly there are product genres that lend themselves to peer-to-peer commerce more than others, but this arena has just begun to be tapped. E-businesses where customers are already shopping have a built-in e-commerce infrastructure and an installed customer base that so that they can create peer marketplaces quickly.

Incubation

In the late 1990s, Idealabs paved the way for Internet incubation companies. When Idealabs "hatched such online companies as eToys and Eve.com, raking in nearly $1 billion in the process,"[11] many other incubators popped up out of nowhere. Incubation holding companies scouted out the best and brightest Internet entrepreneurs and coddled them until they were independently successful. For this effort, the incubating parent takes a piece of equity that it hopes, when combined with other equity stakes in other incubated children companies, will add up to a nice chunk of change. Incubators joined venture capitalists in the Internet's lucrative "here's something to get you started, you can pay me later" game.

Customer-communities are fertile soil for incubation. In a customer-community, you have potential entrepreneurs who are already associated with the parent company. The parent company need only provide guidelines, some infrastructure assistance, and access to the rest of the customer-community to help a customer entrepreneur get off the ground.

If, for example, the anchor stores in a shopping mall owned the physical plant, made all the marketing decisions, and established the leasing guidelines, they could craft an overarching customer-community experience while at the same time leasing shopping spaces to community entrepreneurs. In this model, the primary vendor creates the central customer experience and then leverages the entrepreneurial customer-community members to round out this experience with ancillary commercial venues. The entrepreneurs get help launching their businesses, and the other customer-community members get more to choose from.

Helping to start a customer's business may create lucrative revenue streams and extreme customer loyalty. Obviously, incubation can be fraught with branding, quality, competitive, liability, and management challenges, but if it is thoroughly planned and supported, the payoff could be big. Once you have your legal guidelines in place, open the door to your customer-communities. Let them present you with ideas, concepts, and business plans. Choose carefully; start slowly, and measure your progress. For reasons of simplification, you may want to roll incubated customer businesses under the affiliate umbrella.

Offline Events

Virtual communities do not replace real-life interaction. Once people get to know each other online, they often want to meet live. Here is another revenue-generating, loyalty-creating opportunity: Do customers who go to the annual Saturn picnic purchase more Saturns or refer more people? Do the frequent guests that attend the semiannual Holiday Inn Priority Club event continue to stay at Holiday Inns? Do Barnes & Noble customers who convene at book signings shop more regularly at B&N? What do you think?

Customer-community events can garnish press, make customers feel like an exclusive group, provide event-generating revenue, and create significant customer bonds. Certainly events can be challenging to organize, but if they are orchestrated effectively, they can be very powerful. Business-to-business vendors whose customers need to network with each other have long understood the bonding power of live events. E-tailers whose customers may want to commingle could follow suit.

Events don't have to be expensive or logistically intense. They don't even have to be company-sponsored. Sometimes your customer-community will organize its own events. At ThirdAge Media, the ThirdAge.com community members organize their own local gatherings. Supporting these events by sending products, logos, giveaways, or even staff members is often greatly appreciated. Aveda franchisers pay to attend periodic seminars and become better Aveda salespeople in the process. eBay University gatherings are live events held across the United States and led by power sellers who help other community members "unleash the power of trading" on eBay.

Competitive Research

A customer that has chosen your products has likely done some competitive research and does so on a regular basis, sometimes even more than your employees, who are financially and psychologically committed to your company. Tap into this. Whom do your customers regard as your competitors? What do they see as your competitive advantage? Why do they stay? They know better than a marketing research company does, and you can access them a lot more quickly.

Product Testing

Customer-community testing will not replace the need for internal product testing, but it can certainly augment this effort in insightful ways. Often internal testers do not personally use the products they test, or their testing time may be skewed toward unused features. On the flipside, real customers are going to test the product features or elements that are important to them personally. Therefore, customer-community may yield far more pragmatic testing results. Customers who test will get the first crack at the product (and ideally a discount as well). This early access plays directly into an early-adopter psychology. If this group can influence the quality of your products and also buy them first, they could be your most loyal customers.

It saves money to test-market using the Internet. Procter & Gamble has made a religion out of product testing and now have its share of internal converts holding test-market studies on the Web. "Before rolling out a new product nationally, the company typically spends several months and millions of dollars to conduct field tests in a handful of midsize, middle-American cities. But the Internet has fostered new, more efficient ways to sound out customer attitudes toward product innovation. As A. G. Lafley told P&G shareholders, 'By doing a test online, we can do it for a tenth of the cost in a quarter of the time.'"[12] When they applied years-old product-testing skills to the Internet, the company began to experience higher than usual consumer conversion rates with new products—in some cases as much as 12 percent, "which is quadruple the rate at which most consumer Web sites are able to turn visitors into buyers."[13]

Product Feedback

Customers often know what they want. Let them tell you; then act on their advice when it is appropriate to do so and communicate when it is not. The result could be happier and more loyal customers.

Using your customer-community for product feedback is a no-brainer. Having an organized group of customers at your fingertips can save product development time and effort. Customer feedback not only lowers the cost of product research but also gives the customer-community a cocreator role in the product development process.

As an aside, let us reiterate that cocreation can be one of the psychologically strongest strategies for companies to achieve lasting customer loyalty. Some sites like AOL, eBay, and VerticalNet have engaged their customer-communities on a psychological, cocreation level. AOL's community leaders are truly members of the extended AOL family; eBay customers build a valuable reputation in the community; VerticalNet's marketplace would be nothing without its members' contributions. These customers belong to a customer-community that keeps them coming back again and again.

Sometimes customers just want to know that they are heard. Greg Icenhower, associate director of Procter & Gamble corporate communications, says, "So far, the biggest value of getting all of this feedback has been letting consumers know that we're listening."[14] P&G's call center for Reflect.com (a site that lets women "brand" their own versions of makeup, perfume, and other beauty products) is called a "concierge service," and the site's manager, Ranae Kline, admits, "We have not made a single change that hasn't started from a conversation with one of our consumers."[15]

Feedback can be more general, in the form of a business suggestion. Most companies talk about learning from their customers, but how many really do it? How many really give their customers a forum—one that can truly influence change—to bounce ideas back and forth among themselves and back into the company? ELance.com has created a customer-community discussion forum called the "Bug-Fix Board" so that customers can help ELance improve its site and subsequently improve the customer experience. This type of involvement is tantamount to giving customers as much say-so as product developers.

A final word of caution: don't ask for feedback if you never intend to use it or if you don't have the processes to support it. If customers don't see their recommendations acted on, they could become upset or apathetic. This is a communication challenge; nothing more. Loop back to customers and show the aggregate result of the feedback and product development decisions resulting from the feedback.

Product Development

Hallmark has engaged its customer-community directly in product development—not research, testing, or feedback but actual development. Hallmark launched an online message board where "200 preselected women, mostly with children under 12, gather to talk about their lives, hobbies, decorating ideas, and more. Hallmark mines the online conversations for product ideas and asks the participants to respond to queries about Hallmark's own product and promotion notions."[16]

According to *BusinessWeek*, Tom Brailsford, Hallmark's manager for knowledge leadership, commented, "We're trying to get outside the building here, trying to be connected to the marketplace. The principles of innovation are based on the belief that innovation occurs out there just as much as it does here."[17]

ELance has introduced a product proposal white paper process whereby the ELance customer-community can submit a business idea to the ELance executive team. Beerud Sheth, cofounder and general manager of ELance, is proud that ELance Charities originated from such white paper. "Our customer-community came up with this plan to facilitate its charitable pro bono work. ELance gets to lend a helping hand while simultaneously attracting more nonprofit buyers and chartable ELancers. Everyone wins."[18]

Obviously loyalty and evangelism would result from a group of customers who saw their product idea selected and implemented.

Peer-to-Peer Customer Service

Terry Marasco, director for West Coast customer service for Terra Lycos, says that what his customers want are quick, accurate answers and that it doesn't matter how they get them. Customers often help each other out with customer service issues. This is especially the case with regard to complex product lines like computer equipment and narrowly focused niche products like mountain-climbing gear. If your products are such that your customers could benefit from each other's product setup, usage, troubleshooting, or maintenance expertise, it may make sense for you to create a "formal" program.

Consider Ace Hardware's partner community program, which allows Ace franchise owners to help solve each other's problems.

"To find answers to questions today, franchise owners are more likely to go to the message boards and chat at [password-protected] www.acehardware-acenet.com than call a live customer support line, saving Ace an additional $50,000 a year."[19] Ace's experience concurs with a McKinsey study published in 2000 that estimated that message boards and chat rooms where business customers exchange information can cut customer support costs by 25 percent.[20] Ace's unanticipated bonus is that the boards also serve as a clearinghouse for ideas among its dealers, not just the word from headquarters.

Peer-to-peer service might be the most tangible and quantifiable customer-community benefit because of the understood challenge of scaling efficient personalized customer service (see Chapter Five) as well the potential operational savings associated with decreased service call volumes.

Virtual Employees

In Chapter One, we briefly discussed turning your customer-community into customer service representatives or, like About.com, paid researchers. Turning customers into employees both saves money and creates customer loyalty. And customers who really use the product often make the best employees. It can be a win-win-win situation for the business, the customer, and the employee. Remember eBay's Uncle Griff (mentioned in Chapter Five)? He started as an eBay community member and is now a valuable customer service employee with a faithful customer-community following of his own. A formal program to hire customers is a big step, so start slowly. Once you connect your customers, volunteerism will begin naturally. Customers will help each other out. They will exchange tips and start advice forums. It will be tempting to capitalize on this and possibly even pay some customers for increasing their helpful efforts. If so, go for it, but be sure to research and implement the logistical and contractual requirements.

Other Operational Savings

Depending on your business, there may be many ways to pull your customer-community into your operations. Sites like MyFamily.com and Bolt.com publish member-generated content rather than expensive editorialized content. In some cases, customer product reviews can be much less expensive and more effective than paid marketing collateral. Companies who rely on developers or partners can create B2B communities that can greatly reduce partnership development and maintenance costs. Other operational savings ideas could be generated from inside the customer-community. Communicating groups often generate surprisingly innovative ideas. Your customers are going to talk about how you can supply them with better, cheaper, faster products. In doing so, they may offer to lend a hand in ways that you haven't envisioned. When you connect your customer-community, who knows what ideas may surface that could save you money.

Membership

Membership has enormous potential breadth. Membership can involve a singular benefit, like group discounts, or a complex incentive program. If attempting a comprehensive resource-intensive membership program, you need to think long and hard about its cost-effectiveness. Since the introduction of credit card membership and frequent flyer programs, much has been written about membership incentives. Does membership affiliation create a long-term competitive advantage, or does the quick adoption by competitors simply add operational costs into the business model with no derived advantage? Obviously, a lot depends on the incentives and the barrier to entry they create. Many membership experts believe that incentives need to be tied directly and securely to repeated and consistent use of the primary business offering. For example, frequent flyer incentives create sustainable customer loyalty because of the accrued benefits tied directly to repeat usage.

Customers don't want to give up accrued benefits on one airline to switch to another. If the benefits are purely financial or not linked to a company offering (for example, a car or a cash prize), psychological loyalty to the company is not as great. Michael Lowenstein, coauthor of *Customer Winback* and managing director of Customer Retention Associates, warns of the short-lived results from "loyalty points and prizes schemes." In "Dot-Coms and the Casanova Complex," he warns that "many companies devote considerably more energy and resources to winning or capturing customers than they do on keeping them" and recommends more individualized, affiliative loyalty tactics like personalization, which he says is the "heart of the 'relationship' in successful online CRM programs."[21]

Although financial incentives can be more immediate, psychological incentives can be longer-lasting. Many retail businesses use frequent buyer cards that encourage usage by giving away something after a certain number of repeat purchases (usually the same item that is being purchased repeatedly—for example, a free coffee after ten purchased coffees). The addition of a tangible object, such as a physical card, can increase the psychological bond. The television show *Seinfeld* made fun of this psychological bond once when central character, Elaine, spent an entire episode searching for a deli membership card she had that was one punch away from a free sandwich. As the spoof showed, she didn't even like the sandwiches, but because she was so close to the free one, she continued to buy there.

The early days of membership incentives on the Web were riddled with financial savings. Seemingly every site had contests with cash prizes. Win a trip. Win a car. "Sweepstakes—Enter Now!" Sweeps sites became some of the most frequently visited sites almost overnight. Yet once the financial incentives dried up, so did visitation to the site; there was no residue of customer loyalty. Consider AllAdvatage, which once advertised, "The Rules Have Changed. Get Paid to Surf the Web!" It claimed more than six million members and was among the top twenty on PC Data's list of most-visited Web sites. Now it has no members, and its Web site is a "File not found." Visitors are not members. And forcing a visitor to fill out a membership form to potentially win a prize does not create a true member. In the height of the dot-com venture craziness, there were rumors of Web site companies paying college students to visit their site repeatedly in the weeks before meetings with venture capitalists so that traffic would be higher. That is taking nonassociative visitation to the extreme.

Smarter e-businesses spent more time recruiting individual membership loyalty by providing a more efficient and individualized shopping experience. These sites asked members to complete profiles and monitored customer usage patterns. When customers returned for a second purchase, offerings were more targeted, and purchase logistics were easier. The more often the customer shopped at the site, the better the experience became. This membership tactic, if managed strategically, can continue to spiral upward, resulting in both heightened usage and efficiency. There is a tricky threshold here where members may feel you have too much information about them. Internet shoppers want efficiency and targeting but also privacy. Amazon.com is strategic and cautious here. With continued use, Amazon.com incorporates more and more customer information but keeps it at arm's length with regard to privacy.

Creativity and Honesty

Some companies have been extremely innovative in extracting revenue from their customer-communities. *Red Herring* reported one innovative fee charged by EzBoard, a discussion board application service provider (ASP) that claims that over 700,000 communities use its service: "While it offers a free service, it gets revenues from the communities that pay a small fee to turn off the pop-up ads, which are numerous and annoying, and probably serve more to get people to convert to paid than to generate income for the company."[22] In an offline world, would you pay a little extra money not to be bombarded by promotions when you shop? Is an "advertisement-free zone" one of the reasons some us will pay more money to shop at small boutiques instead of department stores?

You may think that there will be an outcry from your customers if you attempt such nontraditional revenue generation tactics. Possibly there will be, but in the end, customers are not naive; they know that businesses need to turn a profit in order to be viable. There should be no hiding the fact that your company needs to generate revenue. After the mid-1990s Internet craze, when venture funding quickly dissipated, many dot-coms had to scramble to determine appropriate revenue models. A few companies pulled their customers directly into the financial planning brainstorming. In determining new funding streams, Craig Newmark, founder of craigslist, wanted to honor the traditional community values on which craigslist was built. He decided to consult the craigslist community by posting a message headed "Paying the Bills" in which he asked for feedback on several new revenue-generating ideas. The ensuing healthy dialogue resulted in unique funding ideas and many appreciatory posts like this one from community member "nontoxic": "thank you cl management . . . for involving your community in the revenue discussion. It's so sane and considerate and cool. I don't know how it will all work out, but I love your attitude."[23]

Such honesty about the need to make money is refreshing, and so is the inclusiveness of Newmark's approach. As the dot-com bubble was bursting, Philip Kaplan launched a Web site named—pardon us but it is the name—FuckedCompany.com, "a game based on the classic deadpool, but instead of betting for (or against) people, you're betting on companies. The lines are a little blurred when dealing with companies because there is rarely a clean-cut death. To make up for this, FuckedCompany.com rates different levels of a company's demise and awards points based on the level of severity." It was wildly popular and became a site where the dot-com-disgruntled tattled on their companies. Kaplan says, "FuckedCompany.com has also pretty much turned into the source for news about dot-com companies. Bad news, that is."[24]

FuckedCompany's enormous popularity made him reconsider the potential for making money from it. How could he tell this to his extremely anticorporate followers, who often equated business profit with evil? Here's how he has done it on the "What is it?" page of his site:

> FuckedCompany.com is free. ~~I don't make—and don't plan to make—any money from it.~~ I could maybe make money doing this.

Instead of spinning the truth, Kaplan is upfront about his desire to turn a profit but admits that this is a change of heart. Customers are usually rational people who understand the business fundamentals and who also want to reward a good idea and hard work. When you communicate with your customers personally and honestly, most of them will understand.

On the Internet, membership loyalty is more important than in the pre-Internet days. So many other switching barriers have been eliminated that if you can't psychologically tie your members to your company, you are doomed to fighting the no-win Internet price wars. Luckily, the Internet has also provided better ways than ever to achieve membership loyalty: Personalize. Enhance individual efficiency. Target but don't invade privacy. Cocreate, affiliate, and incubate. Create a membership bond. Tie it to repeat usage. Be creative and honest. And then give customers something tangible in the process.

Summary

Though many past Web business models have failed to blend community and revenue growth, we believe that community strongly correlates with value-creating behaviors in the marketplace. Some observers might ask if virtual communities are passé—an experiment in a failed paradigm—but the problem has never been with the community concept but rather that sites tried to apply old media mentalities to a dramatically different medium. Many focused on trying to get the chicken to lay golden eggs instead of frying up the golden eggs already in the basket.

Successful Web business models will have community elements prevalent. The best business model will not be one that simply monetizes communities of interest but rather one that links customers who already have a commerce mindset. The result will be more loyal customers, more frequent transactions, and more referrals. Successful Web businesses won't just slap up old-fashioned marketing messages; they will behave in different ways, listen more, and connect customers better. Already there are some ways to achieve revenue gains from customer-communities— personalized and targeted customer data, product development, testing and feedback, and customer-to-customer commerce, to name a few. As with any business maturation process, more ways to evoke customer-community value will emerge as we continue through the e-business life cycle. To create and build from this opportunity, businesses will need to structure their organizations differently, or else their more nimble competitors will get there first. Let's now examine organizational issues required for implementing a customer-community program.

Chapter Eight

Organizational Issues and Roles

At Amazon.com, customer service is not the complaint department. The company is obsessive about the total customer experience. Bill Price is vice president of Amazon's global customer
service organization. "Amazon considers Price's outfit to be a research lab for discovering how to adjust and improve customer service."[1] All encounters with customers are considered vital to the
company's success, and Price's outfit is at the center of tracking
every single reason for every customer contact. The top ten reasons
are monitored daily, weekly, and monthly, and the team's job is to
constantly work to eliminate these reasons. You can't fake good
customer service. And you can't have an organizational structure
that doesn't support your strategic stance. Just building a customer-
community alone won't get you to significant bottom-line value. It
must be a strategic tenet of your company, and it must be reflected
in all areas of the company—internal and external. In this chapter,
we examine seven organizational issues to consider when migrat-
ing to a customer-community focus: strategy, organizational structure, communication, processes, infrastructure, outsourcing, and
community leadership.

Partnering Versus Building

Although dabbling in customer-community doesn't imply much
organizational work, a more emphatic effort does. You may decide
that even if you can benefit from a connected customer base, it is
better to partner than to build.

According to Brett E. Lauter, vice president and chief marketing officer for Wine.com by eVineyard, when eVineyard acquired Wine.com, it determined that Wine.com was involved in too many ancillary activities that distracted from focusing on retail efficiencies. Commenting on Wine.com by eVineyard's decision to partner rather than build, Lauter comments, "There are many wine discussion groups on the Net; we realized that it would be better to partner with these sites rather than create our own community."[2]

Many companies choose to build some customer relationship components and partner for others. Maybe you will choose to insource (that it, build or customize an off-the-shelf product) your message board system and outsource customer-community events. Or you may outsource the system and first-tier support but supply second-tier and escalation support. The build-customize-partner combinations are endless. You may even build and partner on the same piece of infrastructure. PlanetOut.com has built its own chat and message board engine but partners with AOL, which also has a chat and message board engine. A PlanetOut or AOL customer does not need to know if he or she is using AOL's or PlanetOut's infrastructure. According to Megan Smith, vice chairman of PlanetOut Partners, "Our goal is to provide a service to our customers wherever they are on the Web; we are often 'platform-agnostic' as to which infrastructure they use."[3]

To integrate vertically or not is an age-old business dilemma. There is no right or wrong answer except usually with regard to the extremes (no to insourcing everything and no to outsourcing everything). It comes down to which customer experience you want to control and which you will trust an outsourced partner to control. Which do you view as truly strategic?

Strategy

Strategically including customer-community requires that customer service be treated as a truly crucial function. It must not be barebones or regarded as damage control. Often companies pay lip service to customer service but when you look under the surface—and it doesn't take much searching—"there is no there there." Companies of this nature usually don't treat customer service as a competitive edge—adequate or subadequate service will suffice for their business model. Customer service investments will be a low priority. One key sign of a nonstrategic customer service stance is the way personnel investment dollars are spent: expenses will be skewed toward tacticians, and in-house customer service training will be limited. What is the unwritten internal view of the customer service division? Does your best talent want to work there, or is the perception that people who can't survive in other divisions get assigned to customer service?

It is not necessarily hard to connect a customer-community if your customer interactions are second-tier, but it will be hard to sustain a positive, healthy cost-beneficial one. In fact, it would be risky; connecting your poorly serviced customers might lead to negative advocacy.

It is not enough to view customer service as a valued function; to strategically embrace a customer-community approach, a company must believe in the competitive power of a connected customer base and be willing to relinquish some control to this collective. The executive team must believe like Rosabeth Moss Kanter in *Evolve!* that "one company's loyal community of empowered users is another one's biggest nemesis. One company's exciting opportunity is another company's death threat."[4] With this level of commitment, there can be a balanced discussion and decision-making process with regard to natural tensions that arise while deciding how to connect your customer base. Sacred cows will most likely need to be challenged, and you will have to be willing to barbecue some burgers. The customer service executive and the marketing executive should collaboratively determine how to approach branding consistency challenges resulting from customers' collective voice. Metrics should be put in place to prove the effectiveness of customer connectedness. Customer service tenets, like "The customer is always right" or "Our goal is to provide outstanding customer service" might even find their way into the formal corporate value system.

Community Strategist

An investment in strategic customer-community thinking needs to accompany an ongoing commitment to be strategic. Read that again. Far too often, companies try to shift strategically with a tactical implementation. Many companies believe that virtual community means opening a chat room, throwing up a bulletin board, and then hiring a couple of interns to monitor this new community and answer any questions members may have. It is no wonder that many of these virtual communities get siloed, simply discuss shared interests among themselves, and add nothing to the bottom line. John Hagel and Arthur Armstrong predict in *Net.gain* that it will be the commercially motivated community organizer who will be responsible for shifting virtual communities from a purist dialogue model to a bottom-line-oriented model in which both vendor and customer-community will benefit.[5] They are basically arguing that the community organizer must be aware and guide community development toward the profit goals of the company.

We will go further and say that it will be a commercially motivated, customer-oriented community strategist who will be responsible for this transition. Being "customer-oriented" is a simple clarification that the community organizer be completely aligned with the customers' needs. The change from "organizer" to "strategist" implies a different set of skill sets required in the employee driving this effort. You don't hire an organizer to craft and implement a strategy.

The customer-community strategist would ideally report directly to the head of customer service or whoever is responsible for the total customer experience. This person would also have matrix responsibilities to others like the CIO or marketing execs who handle branding, customer relationship management, voice of the customer, or PR. Since this position is not traditional, a less traditional organization structure will likely make more sense. The key is to make sure that the strategic vision is shared with the key constituents. This person's responsibility would be to analyze the customers' needs and determine the appropriate organizational structure, processes, infrastructure, and programs required to leverage the collective customer-community.

In addition to an overarching customer-community strategy position, you must consider strategic skill sets for key elements of your customer-community program. For example, if online training is to be a key differentiator for your company, it is not enough to link to a couple of courses and hire a facilitator to manage the virtual classroom logistics. Like offline education, online training is complex and requires a strategic approach to truly make it a differentiator. There is a reason why there are so many universities in the world yet so few of them are considered world-class. Likewise, there is a reason why so many companies spent dollars on e-learning but business impact has not been affected.

Customer service organizations have learned the strategy lesson and now understand that a bevy of telephone operators does not a customer service organization make. Nor is it cost-effective. If you are to differentiate customer service, you must hire a customer service leader who is a strategist, not a tactician. If you want bottom-line results, hire up, not down.

Community Information Analyst and Community Merchandiser

The best way to find out how to reap value from your customer-community is to connect customers and then listen. You can begin a customer-community analysis by simply having someone in charge of listening. In *Net.gain*, Hagel and Armstrong suggest different kinds of listeners. To extract value from a community, they recommend filling two separate positions: community information analyst and community merchandiser. The position of community information analyst is an advisory position similar to that of other departmental information analysts. Individuals in this position "will be responsible for managing members' profiles, the vast quantities of data generated by the recording of participant's clicks on the keyboard while inside the community's electronic boundaries. They must analyze members' patterns of behavior and deduce from these digital footprints what is important to members and what is not, what can be improved, and how."[6]

The position of community merchandiser has direct bottom-line responsibilities. "The community merchandiser is responsible for meeting the transactional needs of the community's members and . . . maximizing the revenue streams generated by the community."[7] Since Hagel and Armstrong were speaking of general communities, they focused on matching providers with community members' needs and "maximizing advertising and transactional revenues." Within a more focused customer-community, we would expand this role to also determining the right mix of revenue generation and expense saving measures that optimally benefit both the business and the customer-community. The merchandiser would constantly be listening for new revenue and savings opportunities as the community evolved. The community merchandiser is an advanced customer-community position. Start with a strategic information analyst and listen for the opportunity.

Organizational Structure

How many departments in your company touch the customer or potential customer? In a traditional brick-and-mortar company, that usually describes marketing, sales, and customer service, with other departments having only occasional focus group interactions with customers. Rarely do these three departments march to the beat of the same drummer. Most of the time there is overlap and confusion over who is responsible for what. Often the customer is the recipient of this confusion, shuffled around from one department or voice mail extension to the next. Yet as challenging as this separation can be, the marketing, sales, and customer service distinctions are clear enough to both the employees and the customers to justify this segmentation to achieve a tighter focus on the core of each of these roles. In the virtual realm, there is much less distinction to both the customer and the employee. The companies that organize to provide a seamless face to the customer will win here. To illustrate the challenge, let's compare general offline and online consumption.

The offline consumer process goes something like this:

1. I see an advertisement for or hear about a product I want to buy.
2. I drive to the store to buy it.
3. I call the customer service department when I get home if I have a question or there is something wrong with the product.

In this simplistic depiction, there are linear media, venue, behavioral, and timing boundaries between the marketing, sales, and service components. The integrated nature of the Internet world makes this separation much less distinct. On the Web, the process goes something like this:

1. I see an ad online or get an e-mail recommending a product.
2. I click to the Web site, browse marketing promotion for the product, and click over to an order process.
3. I click on another link to ask a question from either the service department or other customers who have purchased the same product.

One venue. One medium. No driving. No calling. No waiting. Because the process is tightly integrated and can handle nonlinearity, the Internet has revealed itself as one of the primary commerce and service venues of the foreseeable future. It requires businesses to organize differently or at least to communicate seamlessly across organizational boundaries and have incentives to do so.

Cross-Disciplinary Teams

To leverage this integration, you must rethink your organization structure. Should a content department that writes editorial promotions for products be separate from a commercial department that handles the order process? Should they both be separate from a marketing department that is trying to recruit potential customers through on-site advertisements? Who is responsible for in-context selling—content, marketing, or sales? How does this translate to an integrated experience for the customer? In 1999, both authors worked at ThirdAge Media. At that time, the marketing department was responsible for acquiring registered users and holding focus groups; the community department, for servicing registered community members; the client services department, for building a customer advisory council; and the membership department, for building a ThirdAge purchasing club with members. The content department tracked "eyeballs" and click-throughs, the sales department tracked ad clicks, and the marketing department focused on registration enticements. The person surfing the ThirdAge.com site was, unbeknown to him, entering a very different world and communicated with very different people, depending on which link he clicked. It often ended in a fragmented and frustrating user experience as well as confusion for the employees.

We are not advocating that all departments that touch the customer be merged into one. Obviously, this would muddy the waters, and various expertise would drown under too broad a focus. Organizations, by their very nature, must be structured. Employees in different departments will have specific responsibilities and boundaries. But the organization and its incentive structure should be designed to maximize the customer experience, which should be a much more holistic, efficient, individualized, and interactive experience than offline. The e-customer demand for integration will force companies to rethink the way they are managed. Incentives and communication between teams should reinforce this. Businesses will need to revisit the matrix structure and functional management. They will need to advocate fluid cross-functional incentives, processes, and communication. Outsourcing and integrated networks that expand functionality will exercise the organization's muscles as they train for the new customer service competition.

Consider what your primary goals and key differentiators of this experience will be. What will attract new customers and retain existing ones? Is there a need to distinguish between marketing and sales? Should customer-focused organizations be combined and organized under the umbrella of customer management? What do you see as the source of your competitive advantage—is it customer acquisition, customer service, or a tighter concept like the development loop between customer feedback and new products or features? Organize around that primary focus and the key core competencies to achieve those differentiators. Then ensure that fluid, cross-departmental strategies, relationships, and processes be institutionalized so that organizational boundaries can be as seamless as possible. The end result is that the customer experience is as integrated as the Web dictates it should be.

In this analysis, we recommend that you first consider the primary customer-to-company interaction points. Ensure at all turns (whether through your primary organization structure or via cross-functional teams) that you are constantly striving for a holistic, integrated customer experience. You must make sure that no one drops the ball in the middle of a customer experience and that all interactions look and feel like they are with the same company. Customer service leaders are like directors in a play. All employees who touch the customer are actors, makeup artists, grips, and crew, and the customers are the audience. Every actor and every stagehand knows what each other is doing, and the roles they play ensure that the customer-audience has the best experience possible. If one actor drops a line or forgets that the primary recipient of his performance is the customer-audience, the experience is broken, and the audience walks away disappointed. If a marketer draws a potential customer into a store or Web site because of an exciting new product or campaign but the store sales team knows nothing of the marketing campaign or the product (or it's hard to find on the Web), that dissatisfied noncustomer will not applaud and walk out and may even spread the word of being dissatisfied.

Let's look at the events in a holistic customer experience. Figure 8.1 traces a singular consumer experience from unawareness to postpurchase issue resolution.

Many companies trip over the purchase-to-fulfillment sequence. For a customer, this is the most important scene of the customer experience play. It's the crescendo to climax, the whodunit revelation, the boy-gets-girl kiss. The whole performance leads to this point. Any trip-up here, and the customer will walk away dissatisfied. Unfortunately, this exact experience is the one that many companies split across various functions. It is understandable that a company would want manufacturing, inventory management, and shipping split from sales, but most customers don't want to have three separate activities for purchasing an item, waiting to get the item from inventory, and waiting for delivery of that item.

To the customer, it's just one experience. Every employee who plays a role in that experience should intimately know the customer interaction history from start to finish. Therefore, no matter how many divisions are involved behind the scenes, you need smooth cross-functional processes; an integrated sales, fulfillment, and customer service infrastructure; and well-oiled communication to cross-functional teams.

Figure 8.1 The Customer Purchase Experience

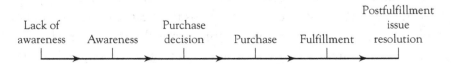

Figure 8.2 shows this consumer process augmenting with internal and external feedback loops of repeat purchase and membership acquisition.

Some companies also divorce the secondary processes of encouraging repeat purchases and membership recruitment from the primary consumption processes. No audience member wants to be sold a ticket for an upcoming play if the play she is watching right now is not yet over. If a membership coordinator unwittingly markets a membership program in the middle of a bad fulfillment experience, it can backfire, alienating the customer. Functions responsible for these secondary experiences also need to stay aware of customer history. Again, integrated infrastructure and interteam communication are crucial here.

Burnout

Consider one more important element in crafting the appropriate organizational structure—the high-burnout nature of the customer-community representative. This issue has long plagued customer service managers. The customer service representative's role is stressful, and the bulk of the time is spent with dissatisfied customers. Although many people resonate with this degree of customer interactivity, it often leads to burnout and higher than normal attrition. The subsequent rehiring and training are time-consuming, lead to

Figure 8.2 The E-Customer Purchase Experience

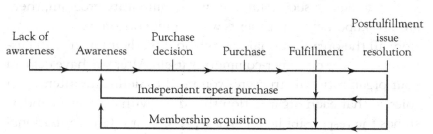

inconsistent service, and can be especially challenging in tight labor markets, where employees are more difficult to replace.

Customer service departments have developed many strategies for dealing with burnout: split project and service or sales responsibilities; investing in solid training and mentoring programs to shorten the learning curve for new employees; creative compensation structures; and growing the recruitment pipeline for faster replacement. It is important to accept the customer service burnout factor and plan around it as opposed to pretending that burnout doesn't exist or doesn't lead to attrition. Of course, the best way to make the employee's customer service job less stressful is to deliver a solid product in the first place. But even in a perfect world, service calls and irate e-mails will continue, and you should accept the inherent difficulties of the job, address them as best as processes will allow, tweak compensation programs when it makes sense to do so, listen to suggestions from customer service reps, systemically manage attrition, and "not be afraid to 'fire' overly taxing or abusive customers."[8]

Integrated Communication

Any time you are trying to achieve a joint goal in a departmental organizational structure, integrated communication becomes critical. Ask any software engineering manager who builds technologies with separate programmers piecing their code together or any automobile manufacturer who designs ergonomically efficient cars with separate design teams. Have you ever remodeled a home without using a general contractor to coordinate the efforts of all of the subcontractors? Don't.

To achieve a successful customer-community program, there are two important constituents who require ongoing communication: all the organizational teams who directly interact with customers and the customer-community itself. After you have defined your organizational structure, you need to delineate interaction roles so that each organization that deals with customers understands the responsibility and has a process for interorganizational communication. If there is no clear distinction between departmental responsibilities, inter- and intraorganizational confusion or competition can follow, which would result in even less communication rather than more. This dynamic often occurs when departments are vying for internal power. The customer loses in the process. If the roles are distinct and interdepartmental competition is minimized, channels will open and will perpetuate the right communication flow. There are many ways to structure such communication, including periodic interteam meetings, a customer-communication log, and weekly e-mail updates. The departmental heads should solidly support whatever communication strategy works best for the respective teams.

In actuality, your second constituency is broader than your customer-community—it's anyone who interacts with your site. You communicate to the prospect browsing your site through every color, architectural choice, and word on the site. This communication should be consistent and be fully cognizant of that person's history with you. Say someone surfing your site clicks on a link to contact you. Depending on what she has requested, she probably receives a response from your marketing department, your customer service department, your Web support department, your community department, a third party whose ad is marketed on your site, and on and on. Does the employee receiving the request know who the right person is to respond? Does that employee know who else has communicated with the customer? Does the response get logged? If there is no process or technology to route the request to the right person or to let others know the communication history of this customer, confusion will likely result.

It is not just your employees who communicate to your customers. To achieve the maximum consumer engagement, your Web site must be communicating to the customer through every virtual pore. The customer-communication strategy must take into account all elements of the Web site: the site design, the information architecture, the content flow, the transactional processes, third-party advertising and content, and every communication that is triggered by the customer browsing this site. Does someone at Amazon know your Amazon.com purchase history? No, but some database at Amazon.com does, and it uses that history to suggest potential purchases. Again, it's all one experience to the customer.

Standards, Documentation, and Processes

Hand in hand with effective integrated communication go standards, documentation, and processes (SD&Ps). SD&Ps ensure efficiency and consistency. Because e-business is technology-supported, there is a crystal-clear correlation between SD&Ps and effective customer interactions. Standard response times, documented service practices, and streamlined e-commerce processes are all blindingly visible to the customer. Unlike offline commerce, where you can hide a convoluted billing process, on the Web your customers will note any inefficiencies immediately. With this fishbowl exposure, the Web forces good business practices.

As much as possible, SD&Ps should be embedded directly in the infrastructure so that employees are triggered into doing the right thing. For example, standard e-mail responses should be programmed into your e-mail system so that a customer service representative can simply select the appropriate reply, add a personal touch, and send a reply that is perceived as efficient, consistent, and personal. We would also recommend using your intranet to codify and institutionalize the SD&Ps, or if your organization is large enough, you may want to consider a full-blown knowledge management or documentation system.

Infrastructure

The CIO and CTO roles have never been more important. Integrated, efficient, flexible, and personalizable infrastructure is integral to a differentiated customer experience. Online, every customer interacts with your technology. Your technical infrastructure is not the customer experience, but a technology flaw is. Even the most distant prospect who visits your site once interacts with an infra-structural representation of your company, the gestalt of which could influence him to become a customer or not. What do you want him to experience? You certainly don't want your customer to experience slow loading times or be greeted with "Sorry, our site is down. Please come back later."

Your Internet presence is built atop an interwoven set of tech-nologies. You have an order fulfillment system, a customer relationship management database, call management software, Web-publishing infrastructure, the search spider, an integrated application infrastruc-ture, a personalization engine, and whatever else is elemental within the core architecture that supports your e-strategy. On top of this foun-dation reside various other technologies and applications to handle this e-commerce transaction or that member interaction. Third-party noncore application outsourcing requires integration with other tech-nologies over which you have little control. Content licensing or advertising agreements extend your site beyond its borders to other sites that may have inconsistent, nonintegrated, and even incompati-ble infrastructures. We could go on and on.

How much of this can you or do you want to control? Do you, like AOL, try to control it by building a gated community to ensure that your customers stay within your proprietary technology envi-ronment? Do you, like many Web sites, link to many other sites and expect your customer to be Web-savvy and understand the fragmentation of leaping from one environment to the other? Or do you strive for something in the middle—some aspects of infra-structure that you build or control closely, some that you license in a more off-the-shelf fashion, and others that you connect to with third-party links? Do you guide your customer through www.your-site.com with clearly delineated levels of integration, or are there "loose" areas of your site? There may be many approaches to infra-structural integration. Architecturally, does your site support the best prospect and customer experiences possible?

Ask Jeeves pioneered the "wrapper" to import third-party con-tent pages into a page with an Ask Jeeves header. This makes all third-party content appear at least partly within Ask Jeeves's control. In doing so, Ask Jeeves achieves brand extension and navigational retention of customers without having to tightly integrate foreign technologies or partner sites. This wrapper strategy is very effective for Ask Jeeves because of the search engine–like nature of the site: the customer asks questions, and the Ask Jeeves engine points to various potential answers on the Internet. Other sites have adopted this wrapper strategy with much less success. iVillage.com created a network of sites that dramatically extended its content by offering a slew of third-party content. Growing content in this manner allowed iVillage to quickly ramp up its customer base through membership acquisition (adoption of people that were members of third-party sites that iVillage acquired and merged into the iVillage.com parent site) and new customers attracted to iVillage-wide offerings. Yet iVillage has struggled with quality control, branding confusion, and navigational confusion, and it takes a credibility hit when third-party content or infrastructure doesn't meet iVillage standards.

Regardless of your approach, the basic nature of the Internet dictates integrated infrastructure. Your customers will expect it. If there are problems with any technology linked into your site, they will look to you for answers. Put yourself in their shoes. How many times have you had a problem with your desktop computer and when you try to get it fixed, a tech support or IS person asks, "Is it a hardware problem, an operating system problem, or an application problem?" How should I know? The rich hyperlinked environment of the Internet exacerbates this problem tenfold. If something is linked into your site, it *is* your problem.

We do not mean to imply that infrastructure should always dictate process. In an ideal world, the opposite would be the case, but the world is not ideal. Regarding the interrelation of infrastructure and SD&Ps, it is too often forgotten that a company must pay attention to ensure that SD&Ps evolve as the business changes. It is often an infrastructure initiative that force SD&P reevaluation. Let's spend a moment on this important tangent.

Inevitably, there comes a time in the business growth cycle when a complete process overhaul is in order. If business leaders have attended to process analysis and revision along the way, this overhaul will be much less painful. All too often, a business moves forward but continues to use old processes to meet new demands. As the processes begin to fail, work-arounds are built to manipulate old square process into new round business holes. Standards lag even further behind. And documentation is a lap or two back, huffing and puffing to even stay in the race.

During the 1990s, many companies called on process consultants to come and make sense of things. Results were mixed. Why? If companies are not vigilant about process change, old, manipulated, and tangled processes become deeply rooted. Employees are bound to old processes even more than to their job descriptions. Changing them is very difficult and distracting. If this is the case, the best time to do a process overhaul is simultaneously with a major infrastructure implementation.

We recommend coordinated system implementation and process rework for three reasons:

1. *Deadlines must be met.* When a company financially commits to a major piece of infrastructure, there is a clear implementation schedule that forces process change. Missed deadlines have a quantifiable negative impact on business success. This risk often forces executives to do the right thing and support an SD&P overhaul within a discrete time frame.

2. *Change can be misinterpreted as criticism.* It is easier for an organization to adopt process changes caused by a new system implementation than process changes caused by a reengineering effort. A new system may be perceived as inevitable, whereas reengineering may be perceived as a criticism of the existing way of doing things. Thus a reengineering effort unconsciously points the finger of blame at the current members of the organization, and employees may be tempted to sabotage the effort, even unconsciously.

3. *Customization is costly.* Major infrastructure is usually built on
assumed or unquestioned processes. Although these processes
may not ideally map to your business, customizing infrastructure to meet your business is a bear. And then in a year or
two, when you need to upgrade, you have to go through the
entire customization process again. That is how implementation consultants stay in business. It is often better to tweak
your processes to fit the infrastructure. You can also then
easily embed "ticklers" (automatic reminders) to trigger
employees into following the right process.

Of course, we do not advocate ignoring process until you are
committed to a major system implementation. If bad processes are
causing business pain and loss, you need to address them as soon as
possible.

Outsourcing

"For . . . high-traffic sites, outsourcing is often an effective solution.
'The issues involved with successful communities are not only
complex, but unforgiving,' says Jim Cashel, coeditor of the *Online
Community Report.*[9]

"'Effective commercial communities require rigorous design,
constant tuning and updating, and the kind of content creation
that requires daily professional attention,' writes Wally Bock, editor of the e-mail newsletter *Briefing Memo,* in his white paper on
online commercial communities. 'It is not for the faint of heart.'"[10]

Should you outsource your customer-community infrastructure
and possibly even the community management? A good CIO (or
whoever it is who controls your Internet infrastructure) will help
determine the right balance between technology and human capital. A CIO innately understands this integration trade-off because
she has to consider it in every decision of her job. "Do I buy off-the-
shelf technology because it is cheaper and supported by a third
party, or do I build from scratch because it will be better integrated

with our environment and I can more effectively control the support issues? Or do I buy and customize? If I customize too much, will the vendor still support the product?" These questions need to be asked for every technology decision a CIO makes.

The general business rule of thumb—"If it's not a competitive core competency, outsource it"—does not always apply for IS infrastructure. Compare Internet infrastructure choices to the design and architecture decisions you make when you build a house. Do you outsource the foundation? Do you outsource the architecture, plumbing, or electrical wiring? Would you think differently about outsourcing a renovation that had structural implications versus one that had no structural changes? A renovation that had electrical and plumbing changes versus one that didn't? Do you outsource interior design? How about selection of home essentials like dishware and sheets? Services like gardening, cleaning, or cooking? Living in or visiting a home should be an integrated experience. It should not matter which pieces are outsourced and which aren't.

As a rule, the more you outsource, the more challenging it is to achieve an integrated experience. And often the more foundational and interlaced the infrastructure is—like plumbing and electricity—the more you want to outsource to experts. Finally, the more directly "tangible" an element is experienced by the customer, the more you want to control it. In our analogy, a homeowner will probably choose his or her own dishware; likewise, a business owner will not outsource product marketing. This comparison is not ideal by any means, but it does provide a general way to think about the pros and cons of infrastructure outsourcing.

Obviously, outsourcing technology can be much more difficult than outsourcing elements of home design. First of all, the purpose of a home does not evolve as quickly as that of a business. The foundation plumbing lines that you put in when you built the house will probably serve the house through its lifetime. That is not true for a business. A small company with an in-house financial management system turns into a medium-sized company running on a medium-sized financial package and then into a large company that relies on an Oracle financial database. Businesses evolve, sometimes dramatically. You may still want to outsource foundational business "plumbing," but it is ideal to have some level of internal support and customization expertise.

Second, there are three clear sets of constituents: employees, partners, and customers. Each constituent's effectiveness is maximized through an integrated experience with the company that needs to be prioritized in the company's best interest. For example, should a company outsource all HR infrastructure even if it leads to a less efficient experience for employees? To answer this question, the CIO needs to compare all options—build from scratch, buy and customize, outsource completely—and weigh these against her organization's ability to implement, integrate, and maintain these options vis-à-vis other IS priorities. It's no wonder that the CIO position can be the most difficult executive seat to fill.

One reliable truth about the Internet is that rarely can you completely outsource all customer-focused technology. Technology is a fundamental differentiator for a virtual environment. Amazon.com gained significant competitive advantage with its patented "1-Click" technology. eBay's rating functionality has become the standard in the virtual peer-to-peer marketplace. Fool.com's home-built message boards are superior to off-the-shelf options. Why has Yahoo! chosen to acquire technology companies rather than content sites? Outsourcing becomes increasingly risky the closer the technology is to the customer. Consider our home analogy—the choices that affect our day-to-day living, the choices that result in elements with which we or our family and friends frequently interact—these are the choices that we want to make personally. We select appliances, choose paint colors, and get closer to interior design than to structural architecture. In general, the same should go for technology decisions in your company. If your customer interacts with the technology, shouldn't that technology uniquely reflect your company and your commitment to that customer?

Some companies, though, do choose to completely outsource customer intimacy technologies like interactive voice response

(IVR) systems and virtual community infrastructure. We don't contend that outsourcing these technologies is always incorrect, but you should ensure that the manner in which these technologies touch your customers supports the virtual image that you are trying to create for yourself.

One more thing to keep in mind is the breadth of ancillary applications or developer programs associated with potential outsourcing vendors. Choosing multiple-siloed, best-of-breed technologies can turn into an integration and maintenance nightmare. Many community sites of the 1990s chose one vendor for e-mail, a different one for chat software, another for message boards, and another for the e-commerce backbone. Then they wondered why users complained about being confused and disoriented. They also wondered why their IS departments spent so much time on integration and maintenance. Often businesses choose the Microsoft suite of desktop products purely because of easy integration and support. Some would argue that Oracle is not the best financial database and PeopleSoft is not the best HR infrastructure, but their partner programs provide such extensive and supported suites of compatible applications that in the minds of many, the breadth of this application offering justifies some functionality trade-offs.

As you head down the customer-community path, you will definitely need to consider virtual community infrastructure. What level of investment are you willing to make? If you believe our thesis that a connected customer base is a loyal, revenue-generating customer-community, then you need to quantify potential increased revenue and decreased customer retention expense and compare this against the capital outlay (technology and human resources) for infrastructure purchases, development, implementation, and maintenance.

There is another financial reason to invest in customer-community infrastructure. There is often a direct correlation between investment in infrastructure and decreased labor costs. Throughout the 1980s and 1990s, traditional customer service departments invested in call management systems to leverage their customer service representatives. Similar investments in Internet dialogue management technologies will leverage Internet-oriented customer-community service departments. The challenge here, as in call management software, will be keeping the personal touch while automating pieces of the customer service representative's job.

Finally, we believe that far too many companies fully outsource community interaction infrastructure. This decision usually results in a community ghetto that is not integrated within the rest of the site. This approach is not only alienating to customers but also makes it difficult to maximize the commercial opportunities inherent in your customer-community. We believe that the companies that invest in development or customization efforts here will get the biggest revenue and loyalty bang for their buck.

Community Leadership

At various points in this book, we have mentioned community leadership as an essential element to customer-community growth. This leadership may be loosely structured or more formally prescribed. It may be completely insourced, staffed with full-time and part-time employees, or you may choose to involve your customer-community members in the governance structure. In general, as a customer-community grows, it will increasingly require a more structured, programmed leadership. A customer-community leadership program sounds potentially expensive and distracting, but it doesn't have to be. A moderated message board system has some level of customer-community leadership. Customer testimonials position some customers as advocacy "leaders." You don't need to create an extensive leadership structure to begin to instill community governance. If no structure is provided, a customer-community will appoint leaders on its own. Think of customer boycotts, for example—someone must lead them. Proactively thinking about and offering a leadership structure or formalizing volunteer roles could yield benefits in dramatic ways.

As you begin investigating customer leadership options, look at companies that have been there and done that, companies that blazed trails through this complex, uncharted territory. Study AOL. Study About.com. Both have engaged their customer-communities in a pseudo-employment or volunteer mode that has helped with immense scale challenges.

Customer leadership programs are indeed challenging. There are liability, training, management, and quality control to worry about. How many full-time employees manage how many leaders, who manage how many volunteers? Are volunteers responsible for topic areas or various dialogue technologies—or both? How do you control brand representation and quality of dialogue? How do you handle dispute resolution? What about security—can a disgruntled volunteer hack into your system? Can you fire a volunteer? What about the mob mentality that can turn against you? Is the risk worth taking? Customer-community leadership is an effective way to scale your customer-community without building a massive customer service department. Customer loyalty and advocacy are engendered as you engage your customer-community in cocreating a governance model. There are franchised businesses like Domino's Pizza or companies with independent sales consultants like Mary Kay Cosmetics that have similar offline growth strategies. Learn from these models as well. All in all, the benefits can greatly outweigh the challenges.

Summary

There are a few radical or transformational business strategies that you can try in small ways. Customer-community is one of them. You can begin gingerly, test the idea in a few ways that make sense for your customers, build a business case, and measure response. In the beginning, you may want to simply test the customer-community waters through experimentation that has little organizational impact—no organization structure changes, few infrastructure additions. If you already have a membership program, create a communication channel between members. But if you really want to strategically engage your customer-community, you will need to do more work. It is not enough to open a chat room or start a forum and hope for the best. That would be like touting a strategic approach to customer service and then setting up a poorly staffed information desk. You must strategically analyze your opportunity; design your organization; define, document, and streamline your processes; craft smooth communication channels and norms; systemically evaluate existing infrastructure; and invest in new technology. You should empower your customer-community to help you and create incentives for them to do so. The answers are not prescriptive—what works for one business may not work for another. To help you analyze and recommend your best strategic stance toward customer-community, we offer the final chapter, which will guide you through some further questions you may have.

Chapter Nine

Before You Start

If you sell on the Internet, your customers are connected. Actually, even if you don't, they're still connected. If your customers use the Internet; your customers are connected. Unless you do business only in the few remaining parts of the world without widespread Internet access, your customer base is growing more virtually connected all the time. The people who buy from you are talking to each other and are talking about you. You can ignore this, acknowledge this, or leverage this. This book is about leverage. A few companies are paving the way; learn from them. Dig beneath the flawed business models of certain dot-coms and learn how people are truly connecting online. Rich lessons are in store: virtual community building, personalization, transaction processing, online security, distribution efficiency, experiential commerce, dot dot dot.

Companies with solid businesses models will win in the end. But it will be those who look to the failures of the 1990s for lessons for the future that will win big. It won't be those who say, "See, I told you so," boasting of their surefootedness and business sense. It also won't be those whose only take-aways are negative: "Don't jump on an overhyped bandwagon." "Don't grow too fast." Don't, don't, don't. The big winners will be the companies that learn from both the don'ts and the dos.

Virtual community carries the baggage of a misguided, simplistic funding model that equated community growth with business success. Many embryonic industries start off on the wrong foot. Personal digital assistants like the Sony MagicLink and the Apple Newton came and went before Palm's Pilot finally ignited the industry. First-out-of-the-chute failures are common in business. The virtual community concept is not flawed; people still like to connect online, and those who do stick around longer than those who don't. This dynamic simply needs to be applied to the right business challenge. Helping to grow and sustain a loyal customer base is a bottom-line goal with indisputable value.

Not all business concepts allow you to experiment without huge momentum shifts or investment. The customer-community concept, however, allows you to start slowly and without much commitment. There is no need to throttle into high gear—unless your competitors beat you to the punch. If they get there first, that customer loyalty thing is hard to break. Just ask Barnes & Noble or IBM. Recruiting an Amazon customer-community member or an Apple Macintosh user away can be a bit of a challenge.

Before Starting Your Customer-Community

Answering the ten questions presented here should trigger some thoughts that will help you start in the best possible way for your business needs.

1. *Is your customer base currently connected? How? What are your customers saying?* You may be surprised at the number of ways in which your customers are already connected. Ask your customer service department. Do some searches for yourself online. Go to the top search engines and type in your company name or your lead product. The customer dialogue going on out there will amaze you. Not all of it is bad. Tune in and listen. Starting may be as easy as listening to communication channels already in place.

2. *Does your service or product or even your company image have inherent bonding possibilities?* Why did Coca-Cola choose a community branding campaign? "I'd like to buy the world a Coke." Who would have thought that people could bond around a soft drink? Coca-Cola's branding strategists certainly thought so. And how can you ignore Coke's market share stronghold? With other products, it may be much easier to determine community bonding pos-

sibilities. Books, music, food, sporting equipment, collectibles, fashion, computers—all have slightly different reasons that people form communities around them. What about your products? Don't just look for the obvious. What human emotions or needs make you think of your product or service? Think Nike. Think Coke.

3. *Are you currently organized around the optimal customer experience?* You should do this analysis whether you are considering engaging a customer-community or not. Internet customer adoption has forced this question onto center stage. A disjointed e-commerce experience is totally inadequate. An efficient holistic customer experience is required for success. Even if e-commerce is not a significant part of your business, customers who have experienced holistic, efficient e-shopping online are now expecting the same offline as well.

Take off your traditional organizational structure lenses and look at your organization. Is your organizational structure optimizing internal relationships or customer relationships? How many separate departments do you have that interact with customers? Do they all know what the others are doing? If not, are customers getting bounced from one department to another to another? Ask your customers. Look at your core values—are they centered on the employee or the customer? Both of us have spent much time in HR organizations of all shapes and sizes, and we certainly believe in optimizing employee efficiency. But why does your company exist— to hire employees or to serve customers? Are departments sufficiently encouraged and supported to communicate across organizational structures in a way that serves the customers' needs?

4. *Which department is best suited to "own" your customer-community strategy, development, and implementation?* This seems like an easy question, but depending on how connected the customer-interacting departments are, answering it can be very difficult. Does marketing own market research? Does customer service own direct customer interaction? Does a separate membership department deal with members? Does product engineering do its own customer testing? If you answer yes too many times, go back to

question 3. Given the size of your company, some fragmentation may be inevitable. So how do you decide?

The answer would lie in where you see the maximum value from your customer-community and in the best visionary to lead the effort. The first point far outweighs the second. In general, we believe that a customer-community effort should be part of the customer service organization, but if market research is your primary goal, you may want to have your CRM department take ownership. If customer loyalty is your primary focus, your customer service or membership department should lead. Whatever you choose, be sure to reevaluate as you monitor the customer-community evolution. You may discover that another primary benefit surfaces that is housed in a different department.

Remember that budgets can also affect this decision. From which department budget will these efforts be funded? What are the staffing implications for all divisions involved?

5. *At what level of commitment do you want to start?* Do you just want to dip your toe in the customer-community waters, or do you want to dive right in? If toe-dipping, be careful of how you start; don't communicate or implement in a way that will dishonor customers or make it difficult to pull back. An online discussion forum can be halted without too many disgruntled customers; an online incubation program is a different thing entirely. Customer product testing can go away; a customer-employee program is much more difficult to dismantle. Think about the level of commitment you are willing to begin and sustain. Be cautious about abandoning programs your customer-community has wholeheartedly bought into.

6. *Would a customer-community orientation affect any other programs?* The answer is yes. The real question is, Which ones? Many departments will want to know that you have set up formal lines for customers to talk to one another. These include sales, customer service, branding, marketing, and membership. There may already be formal customer groups in place for activities such as market research and product testing. Be proactive. Avoid confusion internally and externally. Let department leaders know. Create a list of all pro-

grams that directly touch customers. Have the customer-community strategist create communication that will clarify the distinctions between different customer programs. If difficulty is encountered in clarifying the distinction, should there be different programs?

7. *What other key players do you need to line up?* The combined answers to questions 3 through 6 should shed light here. If customer-community advocacy is a goal, marketing and branding departments need to buy in philosophically. If you are diving in to fully embrace your customer-community, IS leaders need to determine what infrastructure is best suited to interconnect your customer base. Without buy-in at all required levels, customer-community efforts will be either bootstrapped or sabotaged. Customers will be burned in the process.

8. *What is your first step?* Now decide what you want to do first. The answers to questions 1, 2, and 5 should guide you. Do you want to start a community dialogue forum? Set up an affiliation program? Organize a community event? Form a community product-testing group? Maybe you want to ask some customers how to proceed.

9. *How will you communicate your customer-community plans?* To your employees? To your customers? Consider creating a business plan or at least a strategic project plan. Ensure that key stakeholders have bought in before you get started. Have a thorough plan for ongoing communication—again, with both your customers and your employees. Communicate especially frequently with those internal constituents whose continued support is required for customer-community success and with those internal constituents making decisions about other customer programs.

10. *How will you determine success?* Metrics are always good. Loyalty metrics are like productivity metrics—hard to come by. That doesn't mean you should avoid aggregating what you can. In the *Information Week* article "Return on Interaction," Esther Schindler recommends that "community managers need to set goals for the site—goals that answer a site visitor's needs, reflect the company's mandate, and are measurable."[1] Determine quantitative measurements to showcase your primary goal. If it is product testing, did

customer-community efforts lower the cost of in-house testing? Did more quality issues come to the surface? Did the testing process go faster? Did customer satisfaction metrics increase? Quantify and compare the cost of customer-community programs.

Obviously, qualitative benefits should also be considered. Ask the customer-community members how they perceive the efforts. As a general rule when proving success, lead with quantitative metrics; follow with qualitative remarks.

Selecting a Customer-Community Leader

After answering our ten questions, you should have an idea of the scale and complexity of your initial customer-community trial. Now you need to select the appropriate person to lead the effort. This choice may be obvious. From question 4 you should have determined the department in which the trial should reside. Will the program be strategic or simply an isolated customer dialogue effort? Will you expect this team to oversee or influence overall site design, infrastructure decisions, membership acquisition and retention strategies, advocacy and testimonial communications, product-testing and feedback sessions, target-marketing efforts, developer and partnership development, the creation of a peer-level customer-to-customer service environment, community leadership structures that may include paid customer-employees, and affiliate and incubation programs?

Ensure that the leader you select can work with legal counsel and the human resource department to develop appropriate membership agreements, disclaimers, and, if appropriate, virtual volunteer and employment contracts. This leader may also need to work with the marketing department on all vendor-to-customer-communications and IS site design and infrastructure decisions. Given the possible impact of such a program, we recommend a creative, strategic, systems-thinking, customer- and bottom-line-oriented leader, a person who will not try to control the customer-community but views his or her role as a catalyst.

We may be overly ambitious in our profile of this leader, but we strongly believe that the historical relegation of virtual community management to tactical leadership has been a self-fulfilling underestimation of the leadership requirements for such an important role. In the past thirty years, the customer service executive profile has been elevated from tactician to strategist. In many cases, this raising of the bar has resulted in increased customer satisfaction, long-term operational savings, and even additional profit resulting from the development of fee-based professional services. Businesses have reaped fine harvests from the better seed they have sown. The same applies to your customer-community program. Do you want a virtual community ghetto that enables customers to chat with each other but doesn't really affect your business, or do you want to leverage your customer-community for all that it's worth?

Getting Started

Once you have selected your customer-community leader, the next steps are similar to any other customer program. (Your trial may be a complete program or an individual customer-communication feature. Obviously, the complexity and due diligence required in getting started depends on the scope and specifics of the trial.)

1. Flesh Out the Trial

- Determine a compelling, succinct, and crystal-clear purpose.
- Determine bottom-line impact goals.
- Determine resulting value for the customer.
- Determine scope.
- Determine the implementation time frame, evaluation dates, and success metrics.
- Determine communication channels.
- Identify other interrelated customer programs.

- Work with the legal department to develop appropriate guidelines, agreements, and disclaimers.
- Work with the IS and Internet design teams to design, develop, and integrate an intuitive environment that reflects the desired corporate image, the personality of the customer-community, and the goals of the trial.
- Work with marketing groups to create a communication plan (for communicating with leaders of other interrelated customer programs, general employees, and customers) and to mitigate branding risks.

2. Introduce the Program

- Execute the communication plan.
- Begin measuring success immediately.
- Monitor the customer-community response.

3. Evaluate Success

- On evaluation dates, compare success measures with goals.
- Correct your course as necessary.
- Proactively poll the customer-community for ideas to advance the success of the program.

4. Expand the Customer-Community

- Create a community leadership structure.
- Design for microcommunity segmentation.
- Acknowledge and reward community leaders for growth.
- Consider tiered membership incentives.
- Reward repeat purchasing.
- Develop additional exchange opportunities, such as affiliate and incubation programs, that benefit individual customers.

- Create exchange opportunities for specific microcommunities.

5. *Sustain Loyalty*

- Understand and leverage natural bonds within the community.
- Introduce new bonding agents.
- Create switching barriers tied to longevity—for example, profiles that increase in value with repeat usage or membership points tied to product discounts.
- Orchestrate cyclical live events online (and offline too, if possible).
- Facilitate local connections.
- Empower and reward community leaders for sustained membership.
- Create a community leader microcommunity to share best practices (and to sustain community leader loyalty).
- If possible, create a customer "cult."
- Communicate frequently.
- Don't kowtow to bad apples; enforce bylaws and guidelines.
- Have company representatives participate in customer-community interactions.
- Keep things fresh; introduce new content and activities.
- Acknowledge and reward both old-timers and new members.
- Don't fear turnover, but monitor and intervene if attrition is too high.
- Develop rituals.
- Maintain archives, and periodically and nostalgically reflect the community's history.

Next-Generation Customer-Communities

Over the next decade, Internet access will continue to grow, as will e-commerce and globalization. The collective customer base will be taken for granted. Customer-community concepts will become mainstream, much like the employee alignment concepts that have emerged since the networked workplace connected the disparate employee base. As much attention will be given toward leveraging the customer-community as has been given over the past few decades to empowering the individual customer. This trend may even increase as new technologies are introduced that help capitalize on collective customer interaction. Dialogue-mining technologies have already begun to emerge. "A new category of software called 'conversation trackers' can assemble the big picture from thousands of customer-comments in newsgroups, listservs, Web-based message boards, and big corporate e-mail threads."[2]

As value is extracted from group interaction, the dual individual and social needs of customers will become assumed, as will the bottom-line potential or customer personalization and community building. Programs that promote both will, like branding programs and firewall expenses, become common standard line items in corporate budgeting templates.

Companies that have a head start will secure competitive advantage. In the early days of brand awareness, while most were scoffing at the thought of spending money on psychologically bonding customers, companies like Coca-Cola and Levi Strauss barreled confidently ahead. They reaped the advantages of being first. Customer-community pioneers will have similar success. The community-building practices of eBay and Amazon.com will be emulated. It may well be the Amazon.com customer-community that gets Amazon through the difficult times ahead.

The future of the Web lies in what will happen organically when more and more people individually access the Internet as well as connect with each other in the natural course of their days. Access technologies have already become a standard part of the global infrastructure, much like electrical and telephone lines did during the adoption phases of those technologies. Communicating via the Internet, because of the myriad of communication possibilities, will be even more mainstream than the telephone. Internet companies, interactive technologies, and virtual spaces will continue to evolve to more fully meet our needs—our Maslow-identified needs—from the most basic to the most aspirational.

Summary

Your customer base is likely your most important asset. Helping it grow and sustaining its loyalty is your top priority. Think about loyalty for a moment. To what are you loyal? Your family? Your friends? Your country? Your church? Possibly your alma mater? What has engendered that loyalty—individual benefits or connections with others? Perhaps both. How about your loyalty as a consumer? To what vendors are you loyal? Which would you recommend to your friends and family? Which would you support over time, even through a business crisis? Local neighborhood stores? Certain restaurants? Why? Is your loyalty completely derived from product quality and individual efficiency, or does a personal connection with the vendor or habitual interaction with other customers affect your allegiance?

You may question whether this exercise applies to broad-scale e-commerce that does not foster the personal connections or engender commitment that neighborhood businesses do. When the telephone was introduced, many people argued that familial relationships and friendships could not be maintained over such an impersonal communication medium. How many of us now build and sustain our relationships via the telephone? Comparing Internet adoption rates over the past ten years to those of the telephone, you can see how much quicker Internet communication technologies have become mainstream. Think about the level of intimacy you achieved with e-mail, instant messaging, or chat software. Realize that voice and visual features will soon augment most Internet communication technologies. Couple this speed, level, and breadth of communication adoption with the integrated Internet landscape of transaction and distribution efficiency, personalization flexibility, and the ability to provide one-stop shopping for most consumer needs. In this analysis, the inevitable future of the customer-community is impossible to ignore. Will you, like Coke and Levi's in the branding revolution, be among the early pioneers? Or will you wait until customer-community approaches become more tried and tested?

Luckily, there is a wealth of history to use and apply. First, there are the fundamental principles that undergird community and have evolved over centuries of real-life social community building. Second, the past few decades of customer-centric business trends can be coupled directly with these principles to provide a solid foundation on which to build. Third, early virtual communities from the 1970s through the 1980s and the Web community craze of the 1990s have explored various technologies, leadership structures, and growth strategies. Finally, there are a few companies out there that have begun to build loyal Internet customer-communities.

What's next? What will the e-world bring? We will continue to mold technology advancement to meet the entire spectrum of human needs—not just individual efficiency, but our social and aspirational needs as well. Companies that understand and explore the full breadth of humanity will win. Distance will grow less relevant each day in the twenty-first century, and the September 2001 "attacks on New York and Washington will likely accelerate the trends that have businesses rethinking the necessity for in-person meetings."[3] As we strain to divine the future, high-tech tools make it possible to communicate and collaborate from nearly anywhere, and perceptions about the importance of physical location will likely shift as we all seek community.

In one of his last published articles, MIT luminary Michael Dertouzos discussed how future technologies will affect us—or more accurately, how we will affect the future of technology. "When we marvel at the exponential growth of an emerging technology, we must keep in mind the constancy of the human beings who will use it. . . . To render technology useful, we must blend it with humanity. This process will serve us best if, alongside our most promising technologies, we bring our full humanity, augmenting our rational powers with our feelings, our actions and our faith."[4] Commerce and community have always gone hand in hand. It's our nature. Most likely within our new globally connected world, the two will become more intertwined than ever.

Afterword:
Turning Customer-Communities
into Gold, Harry Potter Style

Community was a key original intent of the World Wide Web. The Internet enabled connections never before possible, thus making it significantly easier to facilitate ongoing interaction among people of similar interests. Somehow, amid the rush to develop e-commerce sites and attract and exploit customers, community has been given little attention among customer relationship management practitioners. On the Internet, where the opportunities for customer loss occur at warp speed, a recent McKinsey study, *ePerformance*, found that 98.7 percent of online visitors do not become repeat customers.[1] Another study determined that most sites will lose 60 percent of their first-time customers in a six-week period.[2] Most e-commerce companies are ill prepared to counter this. Most haven't studied or otherwise learned about the marketing and service opportunities represented by community.

The authors of this book showcase many examples of businesses that have leveraged their collective customer-community. Two additional ones that have caught my attention are eBags and eScout. Every product on eBags, a retailing site that sells luggage and related items, has a suite of customer testimonials and an aggregated customer rating. eScout is a B2B portal that iteratively focuses on the "trusted network" of its members and partners. eScout's tag line, "From Many, One," underscores the value the business places on collective membership and involvement.

These examples are, primarily, internally generated methods of endeavoring to create site, brand, or product loyalty through community. More fundamental is the building of community—and loyalty—around a concept or an idea (in addition to a service, product, or company). Control, in these instances, has passed from the company, or the sponsoring entity maintaining the community, to the community itself. The archetype of community loyalty is the almost cultlike Apple computer community of users.

There is another example of the customer-community concept that's even more impressive. The Harry Potter phenomenon can be considered a prime example of, as well as a metaphor for, what is possible with both online and offline customer-community building.

First, there are the Harry Potter books themselves. With just four books in the series, created by English author J. K. Rowling, each release of a new book has generated almost unparalleled excitement around the world. The first Harry Potter movie debuted in November 2001, and three more books have already been announced.

Interest and involvement are not limited to children. Parents and teachers have joined the ranks of readers enthralled by the fantasies of Hogwarts Wizardry School, Quidditch Teams, Golden Snitches, and such. The GeoCities Harry Potter portal site, sponsored by Yahoo!, has been visited more than three million times.

Warner Bros., in addition to offering Harry Potter gifts on its site, produced the movie and is now considering a Harry Potter theme park and a weekly TV cartoon show based on Harry's adventures. Potter enthusiasm extends well beyond all these things to an endless array of merchandise: toys, games, costumes, key chains, mugs, stationery, party kits (balloons, candles, hats, invitations, table covers, confetti, banners, cups, treat cups, and even thank-you notes), Christmas tree ornaments, and on and on. Fritz, an online gift and collectibles site carrying famous brand names like Hummel, Lenox, Swarovski, Waterford, and Lladró, offers close to thirty different Harry Potter collectible items.

More compelling than the physical evidence of the Harry Potter phenomenon is the way the enthusiasts have been formed, or formed themselves, into communities of interest and involvement regarding their fantasy hero and his fantasy world. There are official Potter fan sites, sponsored by companies like Warner and Scholastic. These sites feature discussion groups, trivia, and contests, plus the obligatory merchandise. Scholastic's site has discussion guides for teachers, and there are also links and content for parents.

But there are also many "unofficial" fan sites, in countries as varied as the United States, Turkey, Denmark, Poland, France, Russia, Japan, Spain, Switzerland, Ireland, and Hungary. This is where, perhaps more than anyplace else, the Harry Potter community of interest is most active.

The unofficial German site (www.hpfc.de), founded by two girls in Berlin, is especially noteworthy. Its objective is simple: to increase the fun with Harry Potter books. It offers an encyclopedia, online games, a forum for discussion, and cards to friends. Visitors become fan club members by passing an entrance exam based on their knowledge of book content. The site has received over a million page visits in the past year.

With all this community activity around the Harry Potter books, it's very clear that it has had a profound and positive commercial impact, both online and off. What are the implications and the lessons of this success, and the community largely responsible for it, for both consumer and business-to-business product and service marketers? The Internet has become the world's biggest marketplace. It offers buyers scale, distribution efficiencies, more efficient communication, and enhanced access to competitive offerings. At the same time, the costs and inconvenience of switching suppliers are dramatically lower. Companies, which in the offline world and carrying forward to the virtual world have focused on individual customers or customer segments, must also focus on the collective—the customer-community—to be successful.

Customers, generally speaking, can have both transactional encounters, which are short term, and relationships, which are longer lasting and firmer, with their suppliers.

Customers are social as well as individualistic. As discussed in Chapter Two, Abraham Maslow codified this in his hierarchy of needs when he identified higher-order esteem, cognition, aesthetic, self-actualization, and transcendence needs as human goals. Most companies, particularly on the Internet, have devoted much of their energy to increasing transactions by appealing to more essential customer needs. Just as communities of interest can bring people together who interact or relate on the basis of one or more shared values and interests (age, hobbies, and so on), these communities can be leveraged to facilitate buying and selling. In other words, community building is an essential element in loyalty building. It is a pillar of customer relationship management.

How is the Harry Potter phenomenon related to your business? It showcases the immense power of the collective. J. K. Rowling could never have predicted the community of readers her books would attract. Yet that customer-community has elevated her "products" to unimagined heights. You might not think your product line could ignite the same collective enthusiasm. Why not find out? Apple, Palm, REI, and Saturn are certainly good—and not all predictable—examples of customer-communities rallying around a company and a product line. Why not at least investigate the collective potential of your customers? You may be, like Harry Potter often was from his experimentations with wizardry, surprised and delighted by what you get.

Michael Lowenstein

Notes

Preface

1. Markos Kounalakis, Drew Banks, and Kim Daus, *Beyond Spin: The Power of Strategic Corporate Journalism* (San Francisco: Jossey-Bass, 1999).

Introduction

1. "At the Epicenter of the Revolution: Q&A with Steve Case," *Business Week*, Sept.16, 1999 [http://www.businessweek.com/ebiz/9909/916case.html].
2. Chaya Cooperberg, "Buy In to Buying Online," *Dell4Me*, Spring 2001 [http://www.dell.com/browser/article_0103_buy online.html].

Chapter One

1. Robert Spector and Patrick D. McCarthy, *The Nordstrom Way: The Inside Story of American's #1 Customer Service Company* (New York: Wiley, 1995).
2. "About Us" [http://www.nordstrom.com].
3. Howard Rheingold, *The Virtual Community* (Boston: Addison-Wesley, 1993), p. 5.
4. Jason Black, "Lean on Me," *Internet World*, May 15, 2001 [http://www.internetworld.com/051501/05.15.01ebusiness3.html].
5. Richard Cross and Janet Smith, *Customer Bonding: Pathway to*

Lasting Customer Loyalty (Lincolnwood, Ill.: NTC Business Books, 1995), p. 152.

6. Murray Raphel and Neil Raphel, *Up the Loyalty Ladder: Turning Sometime Customers into Full-Time Advocates of Your Business* (New York: HarperBusiness, 1995), p. 259.

7. Cross and Smith, *Customer Bonding*, p. 174.

8. Cross and Smith, *Customer Bonding*, p. 174.

9. Jeff Arcuri, personal interview, Sept. 17, 2001.

10. Beth A. Auerswald, "Restocking the Shelves: Recovering from a Recall," *Food Quality*, June-July 1999 [http://www.foodquality.com/jjcov99.html]; Kent Ord, "The Fad Is Over—The Next Wave Is Here, *Tactics*, June 1997 [http://www.prsa.org/juncom97.html].

11. Gómez.com [http://www.gomez.com/About/index.asp?subSect=overview].

12. Cross and Smith, *Customer Bonding*, p. 161.

13. Charles C. Mann, "Taming the Web," *MIT Technology Review*, Sept. 2001, pp. 44–51.

14. Ron Lieber, "We Won't Take a Backseat," *Fast Company*, Mar. 2001 [http://www.fastcompany.com/online/44/american.html].

15. Lieber, "We Won't Take a Backseat."

16. Terry Marasco, personal interview, August 22, 2001.

Chapter Two

1. On the low end, NielsonNetRatings claimed that the North American online population surpassed 100 million people in May 1999, which accounts for 38 percent of the overall population; Steve Hopkins, "Evaluating Image and Brand Positioning on the Internet," *Edge Research* [http://edgeresearch.com/research_1.html]. And on the high end, eTForecasts reports that 414 million people were online in 2000, a number that will increase to 1.17 billion by 2005; Euro RSCG Worldwide, *Wired and Wireless: High-Tech Capitals Now and Next* (New York: Euro RSCG Worldwide), p. 1.

2. Hopkins, "Evaluating Image and Brand Positioning."

3. Chris Michel, personal interview, Sept. 20, 2001.

4. [http://www.nod.org/adaessay.html].

5. Rachel Konrad, "E-Learning Companies Making the Grade," CNET News.com, June 26, 2001 [http://www.news.cnet.com/news/0–1007–200–6386106.html].

6. [http://pages.ebay.com/community/aboutebay/foundation/index.html].

7. 1997 Cone/Roper Survey of 2,000 consumers [http://www.roper.com/resource/companyliterature/grgauge.pdf].

8. Bernadette Burke, "The Business of Philanthropy," *NUA Internet Surveys,* Apr, 19, 1999 [http://www.nua.ie/surveys/analysis/weekly_editorial/archives/1999/issue1no71.html].

9. Barna Research Group, "Annual Survey of America's Faith Shows No Significant Changes in Past Year," Webminister.com, 1999 [http://webminister.com/growth01/plan0021.htm].

10. Phyllis Tickle, *God Talk in America* (New York: Crossroad Publishing, 1997), p. 142.

11. Tickle, *God Talk in America,* p. 143.

12. Carlos Carrillo, "Barnes & Noble," *PC Magazine,* Nov.18, 1997 [http://www.zdnet.com/products/content/pcmg/1620/pcmg0087.html].

Chapter Three

1. Robert K. Greenleaf, *Servant Leadership* (Mahwah, N.J.: Paulist Press, 1983), pp. 37–38.

2. For further information on the "12 Principles of Civilization," visit www.mongoosetech.com/realcommunities/12PRIN.html. See also *Shared Knowledge and a Common Purpose: Using the 12 Principles of Civilization to Build Web Communities* (2000), available from www.realcommunities.com.

3. From the RealCommunities Web site (www.mongoose.com/realcommunities.com). The heading at the start of each discussion of a community principle in this chapter is from this site.

4. Cynthia Typaldos, personal interview, Sept. 14, 2001.

5. Robert M. MacIver, *A Textbook of Sociology* (New York: Farrar & Rinehart, 1937).

6. Amy Jo Kim, *Community Building on the Web* (Berkeley, Calif.: Peachpit Press, 2000), pp. xiii–xiv.

7. Brian Caulfield, "Talk Is Cheap—and Good for Sales Too," *Business 2.0*, Apr. 2001 [http://www.business2.com/articles/mag/0,1640,9571 l 2,FF.html].

Chapter Four

1. Black, "Lean on Me."

2. Sandeep Junnarkar, "Yahoo! Buys GeoCities," CNET News.com [http://technews.netscape.com/news/0–1005–200–337953.html].

3. Rosabeth Moss Kanter, *Evolve! Succeeding in the Digital Culture of Tomorrow* (Boston: Harvard Business School Press, 2001).

4. Larry Triplett, "My Organization," University of Washington Student Web [http://students.washington.edu/ltripple/207/myorg.htm].

5. Carrillo, "Barnes & Noble."

6. "Learn & Share Community," REI.com [http://www.rei.com/community/docs/index.html].

7. Donald Madsen, personal interview, Aug. 23, 2001.

8. Forbes.com, "Stock Focus: Timely Growth Companies" [http://www.forbes.com/2001/04/24/0424dsf.html].

9. "The History of The Motley Fool" [http://www.fool.com/Press/history.htm].

10. Jeff Tidwell, personal interview, June 13, 2001.

11. Jonathan Noel, "Ask Jeeves How Much He's Worth Now," IPO.com, July 1, 1999 [http://www.ipo.com/ipoinfo/news.asp?p=IPO&pg=143].

12. Jonathan Noel, "Dr. Koop Nets Nest Egg in IPO," IPO.com, June 9, 1999 [http://www.ipo.com/ipoinfo/printnews.asp?p=IPO&pg=135].

13. Geoff Williams, "Develop Your Own Cult Following. From

Underground Phenomenon to National Icon, Your Business Can Be a Leader in Its Own Right," *Entrepreneur's Start-Ups*, Mar. 2001 [http://www.entrepreneur.com/Your_Business/YB_SegArticle/0,4621,287125,00.html].

14. "People to Planet," Odwalla.com [http://www.odwalla.com/people/people.html].
15. Cross and Smith, *Customer Bonding*.
16. "Club Oracle," Oracle.com [http://www.oracle.com/cluboracle/index.html?content.html].
17. Monster.com [http://about.monster.com].
18. eLance.com [http://www.elance.com/c/static/main/displayhtml.pl?file=about.html].
19. Beerud Sheth, personal interview September 29, 2001.
20. "Leveraging the eXtended Enterprise," VerticalNet.com [http://www.verticalnet.com/aboutus].

Chapter Five

1. Lighthouse on the Web, "Virtual Community: An Idea out of Control" [http://www.shorewalker.com/hype/hype50.html].
2. Robert R. Schaller, "Moore's Law: Past, Present, and Future," [www.njtu.edu.cn/depart/xydzxx/ec/spectrum/moore/mlaw.html].
3. David P. Reed, "That Sneaky Exponential: Beyond Metcalf's Law to the Power of Community Building" [www.reed.com/papers/gfn/reedslaw.html]
4. Meg Wheatley and Myron Kellner Rogers, *Leadership and the New Science* (San Francisco: Berrett-Koehler, 1992), p. 123.
5. Kounalakis, Banks, and Daus, *Beyond Spin*.
6. Cross and Smith, *Customer Bonding*, p. 156.
7. Kanter, *Evolve!*, p. 38.
8. Hans Peter Brondmo, *The Eng@ged Customer* (New York: HarperCollins, 2000).
9. Hewlett-Packard, IT Resource Center Forums [http://forums.itrc.hp.com/cm/].

10. Jeff Siegle, personal interview, June 4, 2001.

11. Glen Van Lehn, personal interview, June 25, 2001.

12. Gil McWilliam, "Building Stronger Brands Through Online Communities," *MIT Sloan Management Review,* Spring 2000, p. 52.

13. J. A. Hitchcock, "Uncle Griff at eBay: A Colorful Character Doles Out Advice," *Link Up,* Mar. 2000 [http://www.infotoday.com/lu/mar00/luab3.htm].

Chapter Six

1. Palm.com [http://www.palmos.com/dev/programs/pdp/index.html].

2. Kanter, *Evolve!,* p. 38.

3. Yankelovich and Partners, "Getting to Know You" [http://www.yankelovich.com].

4. "Learn & Share," REI.com [http://www.rei.com/reihtml/LEARN_SHARE/index.jsp?stat=8032].

5. Heath Row, personal interview, June 5, 2001.

6. "Company of Friends," FastCompany.com, Nov. 3, 2001 [http://www.fastcompany.com/cof].

7. Megan Smith, personal interview, Aug. 30, 2001.

8. Margaret Spencer, personal interview, June 19, 2001.

9. Margaret Spencer, personal interview, June 19, 2001.

10. Michael Lowenstein, personal interview, Sept. 20, 2001.

Chapter Seven

1. George Anders, "Starbucks Brews a New Strategy," *Fast Company,* Aug. 2001, pp. 145, 146.

2. James Cothrel [www.participate.com/research/].

3. James Cothrel [www.participate.com/research/].

4. Arthur G. Armstrong and John Hagel III, "The Real Value of On-Line Communities," *Harvard Business Review,* May-June 1996, p. 135.

5. John Hagel III and Arthur G. Armstrong, *Net.gain* (Boston: Harvard Business School Press, 1997), pp. 58–59.
6. Forrester Research, "Making Net Shoppers Loyal," p. 13.
7. Michele Fitzpatrick, "Building Communities Online Is Building Business," *Chicago Tribune*, Sept. 28, 1999.
8. International Data Corporation, "1999 Worldwide Software Review and Forecast" [www.idc.com/getdoc.jhtml?containerid=20161].
9. "How Companies Sponsor, Listen in and Learn from Chat Rooms," Abstract, *Wharton's Technology Review* [http://know ledge.whartonupenn.edu/articles.cfm?catid=14&articleid=402].
10. AOL Affiliated Network, [http://affiliate.aol.com/affiliate/wel come.adp].
11. "Don't Count Your Chickens . . .—Incubators: Do They Produce Rotten or Golden Eggs?" *San Francisco Business Times*, Sept. 22, 2000.
12. Fara Warner, "Don't Shout, Listen," *Fast Company*, Aug. 2001, p. 136. [www.fastcompany.com/online/49/bestpractice.html]
13. Warner, "Don't Shout, Listen," p. 137.
14. Warner, "Don't Shout, Listen," p. 139.
15. Warner, "Don't Shout, Listen," p. 138.
16. Business Week Online, "Q&A with Hallmark's Tom Brailsford" [http://www.businessweek.com/magazine/content/01_28/b3740626.html].
17. Business Week Online, "Q&A."
18. Beerud Sheth, personal interview, Sept. 29, 2001.
19. Brian Caulfield, "Talk Is Cheap. And Good for Sales, Too," *Business 2.0* [http://www/business2.com/articles/mag/0,1640,9571,FF.html].
20. Caulfield, "Talk Is Cheap."
21. Michael Lowenstein, "Dot-Coms and the Casanova Complex," *Customer Loyalty Today*, May 2000.
22. Rafe Needleman, "Catch of the Day: Community Service," *Red Herring*, July 31, 2001 [http://www.redherring.com/story_redirect.asp?layout=story_generic&doc_id=RH640019864&channel=80000008].

23. Craig Newmark, personal interview, June 8, 2001.

24. FuckedCompany, [www.fuckedcompany.com/whatis/].

Chapter Eight

1. Charles Fishman, "But Wait, You Promised . . . ," *Fast Company*, Apr. 2001, p. 126. [www.fastcompany.com/online/45/customerservice.html]

2. Brett Lauter, personal interview, Sept. 11, 2001.

3. Megan Smith, personal interview, Aug. 30, 2001.

4 Kanter, *Evolve!*, p. 16.

5. Hagel and Armstrong, *Net.gain*, p. 33.

6. Hagel and Armstrong, *Net.gain*, pp. 159–164.

7. Hagel and Armstrong, *Net.gain*, p. 166.

8. Terry Marasco, personal interview, August 22, 2001.

9. Julie Landry, "Participate.com Hopes to Profit from Web Communities," *Red Herring*, Sept. 23, 1999 [http://www.redherring.com/index.asp?layout=story_imu&doc_id=1950011595&channel=40000004].

10. Landry, "Participate.com Hopes."

Chapter Nine

1. Esther Schindler, "Return on Interaction. Can You Build a Vibrant Online Community That Justifies Its Expense? Sure. The Experts Explain How," *Information Week*, July 2, 2001 [http://www.informationweek.com/story/IWK20010629S0030].

2. David Orenstein, "Hidden Treasure: How to Unearth Millions of Dollars in Market Intelligence Buried in Online Discussion Groups," *Business 2.0*, July 2001 [http://www.business2.com/articles/mag/0,1640,14841,FF.html].

3. Tom Weber, "E-World," *Wall Street Journal*, Sept. 24, 2001 [http://interactive.wsj.com/articles/SB1001280340257979520.html]

4. Ray Kurzweil and Michael Dertouzos, "Kurzweil vs. Dertouzos,"

MIT Technology Review, Jan.-Feb. 2001 [http://www.technology review.com/articles/dertouzoskurzweil0101.asp].

Afterword

1. Caulfield, "Talk Is Cheap."
2. Michael Lowenstein, "Viral Marketing on the Internet: The Often Overlooked CRM Potential of the Online Community" [http://www.crmguru.com/features/etc/mlowenstein.html].

Index

Expression, 85–86, 95. *See also* Community, building
EzBoard (ASP), 188

F

Fast Company, 36, 154; Company of Friends (COF), 154–155
Fees, 174–176. *See also* Value, creating
Fidelity, 105
Filene's Basement, 156
Florida, 136
FlyerTalk.com, 36–37
Fool.com, 85, 212
Forrester Research, 6
Frequency Marketing, Inc., 37
Friends and Family program (MCI), 26
Fritz, 232
FuckedCompany.com, 189, 190
Furlong, M., 64–65

G

Gap, 27; BabyGap, 27; Gap.com, 145; GapMaternity, 27
Gardner, D., 105
Gardner, T., 105
Gay.com, 144
GE Capital, 37
Geneology.com, 99
GeoCities, 78, 92, 98–99, 100, 232
"Getting To Know You" (Yankelovich and Partners), 151
God Talk in America (Tickle), 65
Godiva, 59
Gomez.com, 29
Google, 146
Gospel.com, 144
Governance, 79–80, 94. *See also* Community, building
Greenleaf, R. K., 75
Griffith, J., 133
Group discounts, 176. *See also* Value, creating
Group Forming Networks (GFNs), 117
Groups, 81, 94. *See also* Community, building
Growth: barriers to, 115–116; and expansion through communication, 120–128; and high-touch customer service, 130–131; and intrinsic collective size thresholds, 119–120; network effect on, 116–117

H

Habit, 149–150. *See also* Bonds, community
Hagel, J., 166–168, 196–198
Half.com, 96, 97
Hallmark, 183–184
Harry Potter, 232–234
Harvard Business Review, 166
Herman Miller, 59
Hewlett-Packard, 33, 56, 110–111, 133; Information Technology Resource Center (ITRC), 1, 93, 95, 111, 132, 133; Online Community, 133
High-touch service, 115–116, 130–131
History, 86–87, 95. *See also* Community, building
Holiday Inn, 93, 109–110, 180; Priority Club, 31, 180
Holocaust, 144
Home Depot, 153
Honesty, 188–190. *See also* Value, creating
Huizenga, H. W., 65
HungerSite, The, 64

I

IBM, 26, 93, 110–113, 126, 142, 218
Icenhower, G., 183
IDC, 56
IdeaLabs, 179
Identity, 77–78, 94. *See also* Community, building
iMac (Apple), 86
Improvingme.com, 61
Incubation, 84–85, 179–180. *See also* Value, creating
Industrial era, 10–11; economy, 11–12
Industrial Light and Magic (ILM), 31
Information Week, 221
Infrastructure, 82–83, 91, 96–98, 109–110, 121, 206–210
Instant Messenger (IM), 122
Instinctual needs, 46–49. *See also* Maslow's Hierarchy of Needs
Integration, seamless, 82–83, 91, 96–98
Intensity, 156–157. *See also* Bonds, community
Interaction, frequency of, 150–151. *See also* Bonds, community
Interactive voice response (IVR), 115, 130, 213

Tidwell, J., 105
Tiffany's, 58, 59, 61–62, 174
Tradition, 86–87. *See also* Community, building
Transcendence needs, 62–65
Trust, 83–84, 91, 95–98. *See also* Community, building
Typaldos & Associates, 64
Typaldos, C., 64, 76–77

U

Uncle Griff, 133–134, 185
United Airlines, 54–55
UNIX, 31–32, 49
Up the Loyalty Ladder (Raphel and Raphel), 26
Usenet, 31, 49, 76, 87, 92, 98–99, 146

V

Valuation metrics, 9–10
Value, creating: and advocacy, 176–177; and affiliation, 177–178; and competitive research, 181; and contributors to customer-community value, 169; creativity, honesty and, 188–190; and customer data, 170; from customer-communities, 161–191; and customer-to-customer commerce, 178–179; and effectiveness of customer-community efforts, 166–168; and enhanced efficiency, 171; and fees, 174–176; and group discounts and benefits, 176; and incubation companies, 179–180; and membership, 186–188; and monetizing community, 162–163; and offline events, 180–181; and pass-through revenue, 176–177; and peer-to-peer customer service, 184–185; and personalized experience, 170–171; and predictable purchasing patterns, 163–166; and proactive commerce, 161–162; and product development, 183–184; and product feedback, 182–183; and product testing, 181–182; and provision of customer access, 173–174; and selling customer data, 174; and selling market research, 174; and target marketing, 171–173
Van Lehn, G., 133
VerticalNet, 27, 93, 95, 111–113, 182, 183
Virtual community, 18–22, 76; and commerce, 52; early days of, 49–50, 98–99; evolving needs of, 70; principles for building, 87–89
Virtual Community, The (Rheingold), 18, 76
Virtual employees, 185. *See also* Value, creating
Voice, community, 28–29, 85–86, 135–136
Voice mail, 121
Volunteers, 100
Vulnerability, 156–157. *See also* Bonds, community

W

Wagner, R., 126
Wal-Mart, 153
Warner Bros., 232, 233
"We Won't Take a Backseat" (*Fast Company*), 36
Webber, A., 154
WebMD.com, 34
Wedding List, The, 155–156
Well, The, 49, 53, 76, 87, 92, 95, 98–99
Wheatley, M., 75
"Why Is the Americans with Disabilities Act Good for Our Country?" (Joyner), 55
Williams Sonoma, 59
Wine Club, 66–67
Wine.com, 54, 66, 66–67, 176, 194
Wingard Inc., 59
Wingard, K., 59
Women.com, 50, 99, 144, 174
WordPerfect, 6, 82–83
World Trade Center, 64, 144
Worlds Away, 53–54

Y

Yahoo!, 51, 60, 78, 87, 92, 98, 99–101, 143, 144, 154, 212, 232; My Yahoo!, 60, 78, 100, 168
Yankelovich and Partners, 151
Yanous!, 55

Z

Zing, 50, 99
Zippo Manufacturing Company, 93, 95, 107–109, 178, 178–179

The Authors

Fusing his eclectic background in engineering, visual arts, and management science, *Drew Banks* helps organizations leverage the networked knowledge economy. An active leadership consultant and author, he works with companies to architect organizational structures and operationalize Internet and intranet strategies that align the needs of customers and employees with business objectives.

For more than a dozen years prior to consulting, Banks led IS, communications, learning, and virtual community organizations within technology companies. He speaks regularly at professional forums on topics spanning the intranet-empowered workforce to the Internet-enabled business. He lives in San Francisco. You may contact him at dbanks@alum.mit.edu.

Kim Daus says her life's work is all about creating authentic connections. Whether designing communication or Web strategies that engage people's hearts, connecting customers in ways that empower, or creating new ways to learn that inspire peak performance, she is passionate about the convergence of community, business, media, and spirit.

A former newspaper and magazine publisher, Daus has also managed worldwide intranet operations and communication strategies, designed innovative learning architectures, and created virtual communities in various capacities with a variety of Fortune 500 companies in Silicon Valley.

She consults and speaks internationally and is currently pursuing a master's degree in theology and social ethics at Fuller Seminary. She makes her home in Sausalito, California. You may contact her at kim@daus.com.

The authors' previous book is *Beyond Spin: The Power of Strategic Corporate Journalism,*" coauthored with Markos Kounalakis (Jossey-Bass, 1999). Go to www.beyondspin.com for more information. For more information on *Customer.Community,* go to www.customer-community.com.